LOVE ME DO

LOVE ME DO

50 Great Beatles Moments

Paolo Hewitt

Quercus

CONTENTS

INTRODUCTION

Fascinating, endlessly fascinating. Other bands you discover, you get into, you hear all their music, check out their biographies, watch the documentaries, and then you move on. Not so with this bunch, this Liverpool band they call The Beatles. Even now, after months of research, writing about them, thinking about them, looking at them and hearing them, I wish to dig deeper – that is the hypnotic effect they exert. How so? Because not only was their music magical, not only was their story almost a fairytale, but their characters, in particular Lennon's, remain highly compelling.

John Lennon, like so many major artists, suffered from mood swings, which rendered him an unpredictable entity. One never knew quite where one was when in his orbit, and this character twist kept everyone on their toes, including the other Beatles. Lennon was a pain to be with – but fascinating to get near to.

Lennon died aged 40 but he was a man who lived three lifetimes, as did all the Beatles. The band crammed more into their 13 years together than other bands do in a lifetime. And because their constant change and improvement was played out in public, they created one of the great artistic stories of the 20th century. The more success they got the more daring they became. This band went from 'Love Me Do' to 'Tomorrow Never Knows' in just three years, an astonishing artistic leap.

That The Beatles were a band from Liverpool is important. The town they hailed from post-World War II was viewed as a city of crime and vice. Liverpool and its people were not civilized in the eyes of the nation; they were on the bottom rung. The Beatles changed that through their warm personalities, their cheeky humour and their innate sense of style.

Liverpool shaped The Beatles – it toughened them up. Their teenage years were spent in the shadow of Teddy Boy gangs whose viciousness was no laughing matter. People died at their hands. Many early Beatles gigs erupted into frightening mob violence, and this aggression coursed through Lennon. He spent many years with anger bubbling just beneath the surface and treated people with absolute contempt. If the boy had not been able to write songs he would have not have got away with the dreadful things he did. And yet Lennon was able to go from a man who thought nothing of hitting a woman to becoming a male feminist. Quite a leap, again.

But Liverpool was not all trouble and violence. The city also gave them Beatnik culture, which instilled in them ideas they would play with their whole careers. One of those was the need for individuality at all times. Take the name. At the time, most bands were named after their singer, for example Cliff Richard And The Shadows. This band had to do things differently. They intuitively recognized the importance of all four members (which is why any member could veto any idea at any time) and so christened themselves The Beatles, one of the first bands to use an all-encompassing moniker.

This name spoke of their bond, the gang-like mentality that they built up and which got them through Beatlemania relatively unscathed, and which – as this book shows – lasts to this day. The Beatles were a gang of four distinct characters who created their own family. As only one of them – George – had been given a childhood in which both his parents played a part, this is not all that surprising.

The Beatles loved and fought in equal measure like brothers and that just added to the charm of the whole thing. John, Paul, George and Ringo were, respectively, the bolshie one, the cute one, the quiet one and the happy one. They moved as one. When asked about the Maharishi once, George, replied, '*We* haven't decided yet.'

Of great importance to their story is the abolition in the late 1950s of national service. Lennon escaped the army by a few months, although the band's manager Brian Epstein did not. The threat of national service hung over all those born during or just after World War II, so its abolition brought huge relief to an entire generation. It allowed the band to look ahead to the future without anything to drag them back. Unlike their parents, the horrors of World War II exerted no grip on the band. As Ringo once noted, the war to him meant the excitement of bombed-out buildings to play in – and the more the merrier.

The impact of this band is hard to imagine today. In 1963 Beatlemania began in Britain and swept the world. It was as if four gods had descended to earth. On their 1964 Australian tour the band looked out of their window and saw nearly 300,000 people waiting to get a glimpse of them. Absolutely phenomenal. And that was just one incident in three of the craziest years they would ever know. That they survived three years of such utter madness is actually a thing to wonder at.

Here then are 50 moments in their career. Taken together these moments are a celebration of The Beatles, still undisputably the world's greatest rock band. Two of them are dead, the other two are approaching old age, but that doesn't matter. They are The Beatles, and nothing's ever going to change their world.

Paolo Hewitt
February 2012

JOHN
LENNON
meets Paul McCartney

DATE 6 July 1957, Woolton Village Fete, Liverpool

John Lennon sat in the shadow of St Peter's, and the heavens blessed him. Unbeknown to him, in a few hours he would meet Paul McCartney and so put in motion one of the 20th century's greatest stories. The date was 6 July 1957, evening time, temperature at about 15 degrees Celsius. All day, hundreds of people had been milling around Woolton Village Fete, the men in turned-up trousers with shirts, the women in flowery dresses, some of them backless and very daring.

It was in every way a typical village fete. The Liverpool police had put on a display of dog handling; there had been a fancy-dress parade. This year's Rose Queen had been named and crowned: step forward, please, Miss Sally White.

John Lennon – the genius, the wit, the bully, the beautiful poet, the angelic soul, the disturbed, capricious John Winston – was there. He wore a checked shirt and dark trousers. His hair was pushed upwards in public praise of rock'n'roll.

John had come to the fete to play some skiffle music with his band The Quarrymen. They had already done two shows that day, one on the back of a lorry and one in the church hall, where they were also scheduled for a final appearance at nine o'clock that evening. The band was now sitting in a circle talking, and Lennon was swigging beer.

John had history with St Peter's Church. He had first gone there aged six, sent by his Aunt Mimi and Uncle George. He lived with them because his parents had abandoned him. His father had gone to sea and his mother Julia, Mimi's sister, found herself in the arms of others. Julia settled with a man named Bobby Dykins, and they lived together, unmarried. It was 1946 and this was scandalous behaviour (although it does afford us a glimpse of the wonderfully defiant spirit that coursed through John's veins his whole life).

Mimi would have none of Julia's outrageous behaviour. She went to the authorities, signed papers and soon John was hers. But trauma would not leave him alone. A year later in Blackpool, with his mother looking on, John was asked by his father to decide which parent he wanted to live with. John was just six years old. John chose his father but then he felt his heart change and he ran after his departing mother. He did not see his dad again for 20 years. Nor did he see much of his mother. Of that, Mimi made sure.

At St Peter's, John discovered music and Jesus. He also met a gang of boys who carried names that would later embed themselves in his public history – Ivan Vaughan and Nigel Walley and, significantly, the gang's leader, Pete Shotton. Within a month, Pete was leader no more.

JOHN WORE A CHECKED SHIRT AND DARK TROUSERS. HIS HAIR WAS PUSHED UPWARDS IN PUBLIC PRAISE OF ROCK'N'ROLL

'Not only was he [Lennon] larger, stronger and more aggressive than the rest of us,' Shotton said later, 'he also seemed a lot wiser to the ways of the big bad world.' For example, John was astounded to learn that the boys had been giving money to the church collection. 'You idiots,' he sneered, 'you pocket the money and buy sweets with it.' The boys looked at Shotton. He had never told them that. From then until 1968, John would be the leader of a gang.

'Though I have yet to encounter a personality as strong and individualistic as John's,' Shotton sharply observed, 'he always had to have a partner. He could never abide the thought of getting stuck out on a limb all by himself.' In the gang, Shotton and Lennon became close and eventually got themselves excluded from church. No one was surprised.

Shotton remembered John as a cocky kid, who had little respect for authority and said what he liked, when he liked. There was only one worthy opponent in John's life – his Aunt Mimi, a strong disciplinarian, a sharp-tongued stubborn woman. Uncle George, her husband, was different. He played the soft dad alongside Mimi's stern mum.

Yet the relationship between John and Mimi cannot be cast in simple black and white terms. Both of them were complex characters and shared a great love of humour. And humour was often how John got himself out of trouble. It didn't matter what he had done, he could see the funny side of things – and get others to see it, too. Many recall Mimi severely chastising John for some misdemeanour and John reacting with a joke, and the next thing you knew, the two were howling with laughter and the case was closed.

Whatever their history, Lennon knew he owed Mimi. She was the one who put a roof over his head and put food on the table. No one else did. A child never forgets that, even as an adult. When he was rich and famous he bought Aunt Mimi a house, took her on tour and made sure she wanted for nothing.

As time passed, John's artistic impulses began to make themselves felt, to shape his slant on things. 'Life to him was a never-ending stage play,' Shotton revealed. 'He would discover something even in the most mundane event... whether as an active participant or simply an observer.' John thought differently, acted differently.

Under Lennon, the gang trespassed, vandalized, stole from shops and indulged in petty arson. At school, they let off alarm clocks in class, squirted black ink on to teachers' backs and rigged the blackboard to collapse. Within the gang, John was the comedian, the leader and the star. Note that last word. John now added a new weapon to his armoury, developing an acid tongue that he used to cut down all in his way. He got this from Mimi for she too had the same characteristic. It was a defence mechanism; attack before they attack you: that was the tactic.

In 1952 he and Shotton started at Quarry Bank School together. One day Lennon started mercilessly teasing his mate about a girl. Shotton reacted by ending the friendship on the spot. Lennon played it tough, but inwardly he was absolutely distraught. Days later he brought about a reconciliation, then told Shotton how shocked he had been by his belligerent actions. 'I knew you were in awe of me,' he told his friend, in one astounding remark. This knowledge of his power explains why Lennon would read newspapers and genuinely wonder why they had not featured him. The fools, couldn't they see his genius? The fact that he had not yet made a record or written a book seemed to have passed him by.

From an early age, John was drawn to books. The authors he admired growing up were Richmal Crompton (the *Just William* series), Edgar Allan Poe, James Thurber, Edward Lear, Kenneth Grahame, but, above all, Lewis Carroll. Carroll's strange dream-like worlds and fantastic characters had a huge impact on John's imagination and wonderfully prefigured the many LSD trips he would take in later life. Lennon was not just a bully, he was a dreamer too. It was a strange combination of conflicting traits – toughness tempered with sensitivity. And, according to Shotton, John himself nursed an ambition to write his own *Alice*.

At secondary school Lennon was disruptive because he hated authority, hated the discipline. He sneered at the swots who did their homework, and he became a feared figure of both pupils and teachers. In 1955 John was severely shaken when Uncle George passed away from a liver haemorrhage. It was a stunning blow to the young man. John loved George, who had always treated him if he was his own son. It had been George, after all, who taught him to read, to draw and to paint. And it was George who bought him his first

John and his mother Julia in happier days. Her defiant spirit would be passed on to her son although John's separation from her as a child and her early death would haunt him all his life.

mouth organ (it is fitting that John's first chart single, 'Love Me Do', was dominated by that instrument).

After George's death, John began moving away from Mimi and drawing closer to his mother who, he had discovered, was living not far from him. Pete Shotton recalled hanging out at Julia's house, where she organized sing-alongs and games and told them not to worry about a thing because everything was going to be all right. It was Julia who

taught John the banjo and it was Julia who bought him his first guitar – because by then, rock'n'roll had changed his life forever.

The first rock'n'roll record to spin John's head was Bill Haley's 'Rock Around The Clock'. But Bill was 30 years old, a little bit paunchy and not nearly sexy enough. Then, in January 1956, Elvis Presley's 'Heartbreak Hotel' hit the airwaves and from that moment on, John placed music at the very core of his being. Nothing would take its place until 1968. John loved everything about Elvis: his sneer, his swagger, his voice. He would adopt the very same attitude in The Beatles, certainly during the early years. He had never heard a record quite like 'Heartbreak Hotel' before – no-one had – and he was taken by its doomy bassline and echoey vocals. The sound of that record alone changed lives.

And then there was Lonnie Donegan's 'Rock Island Line', a folk song from the 1930s that Donegan performed in a skiffle fashion. Skiffle, like punk a generation later, was a limited musical style that would fade out quickly, but that encouraged hundreds of teenagers to form bands while it lasted. All you needed to play skiffle was a washboard and a banjo ...

And so John formed The Quarrymen, put his mate Pete Shotton in the band and started hustling for gigs – hence his presence at Woolton Village Fete. And one of the people watching The Quarrymen that day was Paul James McCartney.

Paul was exactly like John and yet nothing like John. He was a musician, a guitar player of substance and he had the same huge ambition, yet he carried none of Lennon's anger or deep-seated bitterness.

Paul's musical talent came from his grandfather via his father, Jim McCartney. A bit of a gambler, Jim McCartney taught himself some piano and then formed a band – The Masked Melody Makers. They wore masks on stage, but later dropped the gimmick and changed the name to The Jim Mac Band. The group played ragtime classics – such as 'My Pretty Little Poppy', 'The Birth Of The Blues' and Jim's personal favourite, 'Stairway To Paradise'. Jim also wrote his own song, 'Eloise'.

Jim met his wife Mary Mohin, a nurse, through his sister. On the night they first spoke, German bombers were flying over Liverpool so they retreated to an air-raid shelter, talked and fell in love. Mary was Catholic and Paul was her first child, born on 18 June 1942 in Walton Hospital. Mary gave up nursing to tend to him but later took up work as a health visitor.

IT WAS JULIA WHO TAUGHT JOHN THE BANJO AND IT WAS JULIA WHO BOUGHT HIM HIS FIRST GUITAR – BECAUSE BY THEN, ROCK'N'ROLL HAD CHANGED HIS LIFE FOREVER

During the war, on 7 January 1944, Paul's brother Michael arrived. It is his book *The Macs: Mike McCartney's Family Album* (1981) that provides us with the best picture of the young Paul. Mike recalls playing ships in the bath with Paul, sees the pair of them listening to *Dick Barton – Special Agent* on the radio. He remembers them playing conkers and marbles, collecting cigarette cards, dropping turnips on to train drivers' heads from a bridge. He recalls they were the first family to get a black-and-white TV in their road, and that they watched the Queen's coronation on it in 1953. There are memories of him and Paul stealing apples, joining the Scouts, breaking limbs and other adventures. But there are also significant reports of the young Paul wandering alone into the forest, shunning all company, trying to figure out his place in this world.

Something that is absent from Mike's trip down memory lane is his mother's utter determination to better the family. It is striking how many people who came into contact with Mary always remember her desire for the family to improve themselves. Wherever they were, for Mary it was never good enough: there was always another rung to climb, a better house and area to live in. This need to push forward and upward is something that McCartney would take with him into The Beatles.

Not surprisingly, Paul and Mike were good students – they both passed the 11-plus and sailed into The Liverpool Institute High School For Boys. Paul did well but then suddenly his world was turned upside down. His mother fell ill, was diagnosed with breast cancer and passed away within a very short period of time. It was October 1956 and the family was adrift. Paul's answer to his grief was to pick up a guitar and from that day onwards, he was a different man altogether. 'It was useless talking to him,' Mike McCartney recalled of this time. 'In fact I had better conversations with brick walls around this period. He even took it with him to the bogs ...'

THE GUITAR WAS McCARTNEY'S ROUTE TO BETTER PLACES. AS SOON AS HE STARTED PLAYING IT, THE WORLD WITH ALL ITS TRAGEDIES AND ILLS FELL AWAY AND HE WAS IN A KIND OF HEAVEN

Paul was highly sensitive to his father's position. He was able to see that his father was a man who had lost his wife and now had two boys to bring up on his own. Paul vowed not to cause Jim any unnecessary bother. Even when later Lennon would be urging him to tell his father to sod off, Paul resisted. If he wanted to rebel in any way, Paul would do it subtly and gradually. He had his trousers altered inch by inch, and his hair would be slowly massaged with Vaseline over time so as to acquire the necessary look without shocking his father.

Paul was drawn to the guitar. It was his route to better places. As soon as he started playing it, the world with all its tragedies and ills fell away and he was in a kind of heaven. And, of course, the better he was on the guitar, the better the places he could inhabit. John Lennon made the exact same discovery. When his mother Julia was killed in a road accident in July 1958, one of the first things John did was to fetch his guitar and sit on the front porch playing for hours and hours.

In later interviews both men attributed their closeness to the common loss of their mothers. But it was also down to the fact that music was the most important thing in the world to the pair of them. And there was another, all-important reason for their closeness – a deep and mutual admiration.

That admiration was present from their first encounter, at that fete in July 1957. As Paul watched, John forgot the words to a song and ad-libbed his way through. (At one point John spotted Mimi walking towards the stage and began singing, 'Here comes Mimi ...') McCartney fell for Lennon's ability to be so spontaneous. In later years Lennon's artistic courage would be passed on to the more timid Paul. In return, McCartney would give his songwriting partner the musical stability he needed.

That day, before the band set up for its final performance, Ivan introduced Paul to the gang and there were typical teenage grunts exchanged, nods of heads. Paul and John chatted, and at some point Paul picked up a guitar and went into Eddie Cochran's 'Twenty Flight Rock'. Much to everyone's surprise, he perfectly delivered every word of a song that contains three verses of six lines and four choruses of five lines. John instantly knew that Paul was not some fly-by-night boy. He had the feel for the song and was a man after his own dreams. John leaned over to Paul and demanded that he show him the chords. Paul smelled the beer on his breath, a moment he would remember forever.

And this is how it would now work between them. John would ad-lib, Paul would be word perfect; John would sneer, Paul would charm; John would attack, Paul would soothe. The one would balance out the other in absolute perfection.

Paul did not stay for the band's last show that night. He had his father's 55th birthday the next day to consider and so said goodbye. After he had gone, John drank more beer, performed the last show with the band and then, smart cookie that he was, he put the word out that he wanted Paul to join the band. Two weeks later, Paul McCartney was in The Quarrymen. He was now in Lennon's gang.

John Lennon meets
STU,
then
CYNTHIA

DATE	1957–8, Hope Street, Liverpool

joined a Franciscan order – her ambition being to teach in Africa). Charles Sutcliffe was a marine engineer whose work took him and his family to Liverpool.

Martha involved herself in local politics, canvassing for a local MP named Harold Wilson who would later play a minor part in The Beatles' story. Charles had different views and enjoyed arguing politics with his wife. Yet unlike his contemporaries in the male-dominated city of Liverpool, he never sought to control or dominate his wife. Stu's sister Pauline would later describe their father as, 'a modern man, a couple of decades before it became fashionable'.

The children grew up surrounded by books, painting and music and this artistic background paid off where Stu was concerned. At his school, Prescot Grammar, his teachers described Stu as, 'intense and studious, especially where art is concerned'. However, both he and Pauline were rocked by the break-up of their parents. Martha found herself bringing up the family on her own.

In 1956 Sutcliffe heard 'Heartbreak Hotel' and, like Lennon, his life did a back flip. He quickly became an Elvis fanatic. Pauline recalled her brother declaring that Elvis 'was the greatest thing that had hit the universe'. Stu began developing a look to go with his passions. Pauline noted that she often cut and lacquered Stu's hair, highlighting the sides and applying other feminine touches.

In 1956 Stu passed his exams and entered Liverpool College of Art a year before John. He soon made friends with Rod Murray and together the boys decided to look for their own digs close to college. They found a place on Canning Street, but after they moved in the landlady brought her own family to live there as well, so the boys headed home.

JOHN WAS ANIMATED, LOUD AND DOMINEERING; STU WAS INTENSE AND KNOWLEDGEABLE. IF JOHN EXERCISED HIS ACID TONGUE ON STU, HIS FRIEND WOULD FIGHT BACK

In his third year at college Stu moved out again, this time to 3 Gambier Terrace. At the same time Stu befriended John, and soon the boys were inseparable. Pauline recalled that, 'they dressed the same, walked the same, talked the same, yet never lost their individuality'. John was animated, loud and dominating; Stu was intense and knowledgeable – it was a good pairing. If John exercised his acid tongue on Stu, his friend would fight back verbally. And both shared a deep sense of being outsiders. It is noteworthy that this major relationship was formed not long after the tragic death of John's mother Julia, in the summer of 1958.

Pauline believes that John realized that there were gaps in his knowledge, gaps that someone like Stu could help fill. So, for example, John retained his distaste for anyone who buckled down in class, thinking them swots who obeyed authority. Yet after each class he would often go to Stu and ask him to explain and illustrate the day's subject.

LENNON AND SUTCLIFFE YEARNED FOR THE ARTISTIC LIFE. THEIR HEROES WERE SINGERS, WRITERS AND PAINTERS, MANY OF THEM DISSOLUTE OR DEBAUCHED CREATORS

John respected Stu enormously. He told Pauline her brother was a genius. Stu had already described John to his sister in those exact terms. Arthur Ballard, the only college lecturer who saw potential in John, saw Stu as John's mentor, a wise counsellor. In return, John gave Stu his humour. He once said of a Sutcliffe painting, 'it is too good for hanging'. Yet not everyone appreciated John. Jean Francis was a fellow student and she found his behaviour disturbing and alarming. She recalled the day Lennon told a very funny joke in front of his all classmates. Everyone laughed except John himself; he simply glared at them until their laughter reduced itself to an embarrassed uncomfortable silence. Then John walked out of the class.

Lennon and Sutcliffe yearned for the artistic life. Their heroes were singers, writers and painters, many of them dissolute or debauched creators. John warmed to the Italian painter Amedeo Modigliani who had once burnt his entire work to date because he said it had been made when he was a 'dirty bourgeois'. Modigliani afterwards dedicated his life to art, alcohol and hashish. (This process of reinvention is something Lennon would employ throughout his career.)

This was exactly the kind of artist that Lennon and Sutcliffe admired: someone who would challenge society, break artistic conventions and then die shockingly young due to huge alcohol or drug abuse. At college, Lennon would acquire bohemian ideas and principles that would firmly embed themselves in his artistic consciousness. At various points in his life he would bury these ideals but they would always resurface at some point.

Lennon and Sutcliffe were also huge fans of the BBC radio programme *The Goon Show*. Amid the stultifying conservatism of British radio in the 1950s, *The Goon Show* was a real anomaly. Featuring four performers – Spike Milligan, Peter Sellers, Harry Secombe and Michael Bentine – the show consisted of surreal stories and sketches, crazy sound effects and entertaining puns. All of the leading participants had served in the army during World War II and the craziness they had witnessed as soldiers was now channelled back into their radio work.

The show began in 1951 and by 1954 was a huge hit. Its influence was enormous – without *The Goon Show*, there would be no Monty Python. The Goons' humour also affected The Beatles. On stage, Lennon often employed Goon-like barks and whoops to puncture McCartney's pleasant announcements to the audience.

Lennon and Sutcliffe laughed themselves silly over *The Goon Show*. Humour, as well as art and a shared view of the world, made them the best of friends. Such good friends, in fact, that when they clashed over a woman, Lennon hit out at her rather than at Stu.

That woman was Cynthia Powell, a demure middle-class girl who entered Liverpool College of Art in 1957. Her father had passed away a year earlier and her brothers had left home. To enable her daughter to go to college her mother took in lodgers. Cynthia responded to her mother's sacrifices by becoming the model student, always on time, always completing the work demanded of her.

In her second year Cynthia moved on to graphics and it was in this class that John first introduced himself to her. At the time he was dressed as a Teddy Boy and moved around with his hands deep in his pockets. Cynthia was surprised to see him on the graphics course, as it involved painstakingly detailed work and Lennon did not look or act like a man with infinite reserves of patience. Cynthia later discovered that John had been moved there because no other teacher would take him.

AS SOON AS JOHN BEGAN PLAYING THE GUITAR CYNTHIA NOTED THE AUTOMATIC AND TRANSFORMATIVE EFFECT MUSIC HAD ON HIM

John spent much of his time teasing 'Cyn' about her accent and clothes, annoying the teacher, and drawing disfigured forms. At first, Cyn did not fancy him although she did later state, 'I had always been in awe of authority, and anxious to please and do well, but John was the opposite. He was aggressive, sarcastic and rebellious. He didn't seem to be afraid of anyone.'

John often brought a guitar into college and as soon as he began playing, Cynthia noted the automatic and transformative effect music had on him. 'As soon as he began to play I saw a different side to him. It was plain that he loved his music: his face softened and he lost his usual cynical expression.'

On their first date, John took Cyn to Stu's room at the Gambier Terrace flat and they made love. John was not a virgin (ex-girlfriend Barbara Baker had seen to that) but Cynthia was, and for John it must have felt like more proof of his power to make people bend to his will. After all, there were not many young men who could persuade a middle-class girl to make love at a time when doing so was not only viewed as morally deficient but also highly dangerous, as you could end up pregnant and be faced with having to choose between an illegal abortion or fronting up to outraged parents and authorities.

They were now a couple but Cynthia's happiness was soon restricted when she got up close to John's conflicted character. She was surprised by his jealous and possessive nature. Wherever he went, he demanded that she go with him. Lennon's mood changes and the inability to know what mood he was in were major problems.

'It was neither an easy nor a comfortable relationship,' she later confessed. 'There was an air of danger about John and he could terrify me ... Not only was he passionately jealous but also he could turn on me in an instant, belittling or berating me.'

In remorse, John could be highly romantic, writing Cynthia a succession of cards and love poems, declaring his love for her, recognizing his faults and swearing to try better. In fact such was the depth of their relationship, marriage already looked a possibility – and it was agreed then that Cynthia's mother and John's aunt should meet.

AS JOHN SPOKE OF THE FUTURE, CYNTHIA QUICKLY REALIZED THAT MUSIC WAS AT THE CENTRE OF HIS DREAMS

The meeting took place at Cynthia's house. It started pleasantly enough but soon ended in tears, with Mimi openly telling Cynthia's mother that her girl simply wasn't good enough for John. At this point, John bolted from the house. Cynthia found him outside, tears streaming down his cheeks. Mimi being so critical of his chosen girl had hurt and humiliated John, as did all her sharp comments about those he loved or admired.

One night at a dance John arrived late and was told that Stu and Cyn had danced together. The next day John followed Cyn into the college toilets and punched her full in the face. He then walked away without a word. Cynthia immediately ended the relationship. Three months passed. Cynthia saw other guys, John ignored her.

Then came the phone call, the begging for forgiveness, John swearing he would never strike her again – and he didn't. Reunited, John started opening up to Cynthia about his past. And as he spoke of the future, Cynthia quickly realized that music was at the centre of his dreams.

'By the time John and I got together, he talked, ate and breathed music,' Cynthia recalled. 'When he wasn't playing guitar he was writing lyrics or talking about the latest Lonnie Donegan, Buddy Holly or Chuck Berry record.' He was also rehearsing with The Quarrymen most lunchtimes, with his mate Paul McCartney and a new band member, a young lad named George Harrison. It was this endeavour, driven by his obsession for music, that would take Lennon out of college. He would leave as an angry bohemian Teddy Boy with artistic tendencies and become one of the greatest artists of his century. Unwittingly, art college had done its job.

Cynthia Lennon, the middle-class girl who John fell in love with at art college in 1958. They married four years later, on 23 August 1962, when she was pregnant with their son, Julian.

GEORGE HARRISON

joins The Quarrymen

DATE 6 February 1958, Wilson Hall, Garston, Liverpool

George stood out in The Beatles for one reason – he was the only member to be raised in a two-parent family. All the others had seen parents die or disappear from the family home. And that is why the idea of the gang exerted such a strong influence on them. In the gang one finds acceptance, honour and a shared vision of the world. Gangs replace then *become* family. The flip side – as we shall see – is that the gang can also be a very heartless monster.

George joined The Quarrymen in 1958 thanks to the prompting of his friend Paul McCartney. McCartney had befriended Harrison on the bus to their school, the Liverpool Institute for Boys, but had done so out of a sense of duty.

One morning George's mum had paid a penniless Paul's bus fare and he now felt obliged to acknowledge her son. It was hard for him to do so. George was eight months younger than Paul and at that age such a gap can mean a lot. Age was not their only difference. McCartney was a top-level student while Harrison was an anonymous pupil, a youth that teachers struggled to remember when The Beatles exploded into life, and the media came a-knocking for information.

Yet George had distinguished himself at school in one way. In early teenage years, clothes became George's passion, and he would often take his school uniform to a tailor to be altered to his own specific instructions. He also wore pink shirts around town (very daring for the time) and visited many Liverpool cobblers asking if they could make him shoes out of corduroy. He was laughed out of their shops but was proved right eventually.

IN EARLY TEENAGE YEARS, **CLOTHES BECAME GEORGE'S PASSION** AND HE WOULD OFTEN TAKE HIS SCHOOL UNIFORM IN TO THE TAILORS TO BE ALTERED TO HIS OWN SPECIFIC INSTRUCTIONS

Both boys owned guitars, and so it happened that music brought George and Paul together. It allowed them to overcome considerations of intelligence and age. Guitars made them equals, and their friendship grew out of exchanging musical knowledge. One night George cycled over to Paul's house to ask for advice on a challenging Django Reinhardt musical exercise. Paul was good at explaining theory but he was astounded by George's technical ability. As a fully fledged Quarryman, McCartney now set about easing Harrison into their ranks.

THE RECORD THAT CHANGED EVERYTHING FOR GEORGE WAS THE SAME RECORD THAT FLOORED JOHN – 'HEARTBREAK HOTEL'. INSPIRED AND DRIVEN, GEORGE LOOKED TO FORM A BAND

Paul liked George. For a start, he was quite a balanced young man. Born on 25 February 1943, Harrison grew up in working-class Liverpool, with two brothers and one sister. By his own account he had a happy childhood, protected and loved in equal measure by a large extended family. His first musical exposure was typical of a Liverpool upbringing at that time. George loved music hall, dance-band music, Bing Crosby, Josef Locke and Hoagy Carmichael. Later on there would be country artists such as Jimmie Rodgers, Hank Williams and Slim Whitman, and blues musician Big Bill Broonzy to astound him. Guitarwise, he became a devotee of Chet Atkins whose singular guitar lines George would ape in The Beatles.

As a youngster, he attended Dovedale Primary School before joining McCartney and many others at the Liverpool Institute. When he was 12 he went into hospital with a kidney complaint. While there he heard that a school friend was selling a guitar. Harrison secured the guitar but when he got it home, he foolishly unscrewed the neck and, unable to put it back together properly, put it in a cupboard and did not touch it for months. His brother Pete finally fixed it for him, and his father Harry put him on to a friend who agreed to give George free lessons every Thursday.

The record that changed everything for George was the same record that floored John – 'Heartbreak Hotel'. Inspired and driven, George looked to form a band. The success of Lonnie Donegan's 'Rock Island Line' was the spur to form The Rebels, a skiffle band that featured George, brother Pete and friend Arthur Kelly. They played one gig and then folded. So did the craze for skiffle. Many young Liverpudlians now turned to rock'n'roll to express themselves.

On 6 February 1958 at Wilson Hall in Garston, Liverpool, George went to see his mate Paul in The Quarrymen. It was the night Paul introduced him to John Lennon. George was instantly impressed by John's appearance, his long Teddy Boy sideburns and his worldly demeanour. Paul told John of George's prowess as a guitarist. John responded by saying that he admired the guitarist Eddie Clayton who was performing that night with his band, The Eddie Clayton Skiffle Group (a certain Ringo Starr was on drums). If George was anything like Eddie … George took out his guitar and played 'Raunchy' by Duane Eddy. John – as usual – gave nothing away. He did not tell the expectant George that he was in the band. But he did not tell him to go away either.

The key to John's indifference, as with Paul's earlier doubts about him, lay in George's age. Harrison was three years younger than Lennon. Worse, he looked it. When George took to visiting John at home, John cringed, although the ability of George's striking clothing to annoy Aunt Mimi went some way to assuaging John's acute discomfort. And John did admire George's guitar skills. Often on the bus home he would shout out for George to play 'Raunchy'. Harrison would take out his guitar with a grin and treat Lennon and any passengers to a performance.

For his part, George ignored John's discomfort. In fact, George would happily wait for John outside college and follow him and Cynthia down the street, hoping to be noticed. More often than not, the couple would include George in their plans for the evening, which usually meant a trip to the cinema. Hailing from a warm extended family background, this was normal behaviour for George.

John started to call George in when The Quarrymen guitarist Eric Griffiths could not make a gig. Harrison proved to be a good replacement for the much older man. Plus, he had won Lennon's attention in another fashion. One night at a party George had pulled one of the best-looking girls in John's college – that really impressed John.

ONE NIGHT AT A PARTY GEORGE HAD PULLED ONE OF THE BEST-LOOKING GIRLS IN JOHN'S COLLEGE – THAT REALLY IMPRESSED JOHN

Eventually, The Quarrymen band members started fading away, through indifference to the cause or perhaps through too much exposure to Lennon. They may not have subscribed to the gang mentality that was required of them. But John, Paul and George remained solid. All three now knew what they wanted from life. More than anything else, they wanted to be in a band and they wanted to be playing music.

John gets his picture in a

NATIONAL
NEWSPAPER

DATE July 1960, Gambier Terrace, Liverpool

In 1957 a young entrepreneur named Allan Williams raised £100 from his family and bought a property on Slater Street. Williams turned the premises into a club that he named The Jacaranda. Youth unemployment in Liverpool was high and the club offered a space where the young could while away the hours and make connections. It was through The Jacaranda that Williams met the band, and became The Beatles' first manager. He helped inspire the name that made them famous – and gave John his first national exposure.

Stu was now in the band but it was his painting skills rather than his musical talent that had secured him the position. In 1959 his work entitled *Summer Painting* had been selected for inclusion in the biennial John Moores exhibition at Liverpool's Walker Gallery. Moores himself had bought the work, handing the young painter the vast sum – back then – of £65. Sutcliffe went straight out and bought a Hofner President bass guitar from the Frank Hessy music shop. He began lessons but however hard he tried, it was apparent that painting not music was his true métier. Even so, Lennon insisted on his presence in the band.

John and Stu were the band's power base. They were the worldly ones, the art students, so much hipper and wiser than the others. Paul and George were the outsiders, the grammar school boys who could never infiltrate Lennon's relationship with Stu. Now that John had moved in with Stu at 3 Gambier Terrace that relationship had deepened further.

Free of Mimi, Lennon now had freedom to develop on all kinds of levels.

JOHN AND STU WERE THE WORLDLY ONES, THE ART STUDENTS, SO MUCH HIPPER AND WISER THAN THE OTHERS. PAUL AND GEORGE WERE THE OUTSIDERS, THE GRAMMAR SCHOOL BOYS

His artistic development expanded with the inspirational Stu by his side. Together the boys discovered Beatnik culture, the latest youth craze. If the sullen Teddy Boys sought freedom through rock'n'roll and loss of self in violence, the Beatniks looked to discover the true meaning of life through art and exploration.

IF THE SULLEN TEDDY BOYS SOUGHT FREEDOM THROUGH ROCK'N'ROLL AND LOSS OF SELF IN MINDLESS VIOLENCE, THE BEATNIKS LOOKED TO DISCOVER TRUE MEANING THROUGH ART AND EXPLORATION

Lennon was highly receptive to Beat culture. Although he would be forced to lay it aside during the early years of Beatlemania, it would later resurface in his solo career. Meanwhile the desire to innovate would be a defining characteristic of The Beatles throughout their career.

Take the change of name, instigated by Stu and John, with The Quarrymen now becoming The Beatles. Although much has been written about the actual genesis of this most famous of titles, one has to consider a much more salient point, which is the boys' refusal to go with

tradition and feature the singer in the title, such as Buddy Holly And The Crickets or Derry Wilkie And The Pressmen. The Beatles dispensed with that convention. Their name reflected their oneness, their togetherness, and placed music, attitude and dress under one banner.

When The Beatles broke into national consciousness, the teenage movement was given its first identity and focus. Their need to innovate laid them open to all kinds of artistic suggestions and explains how they ended up backing a Beat poet, named Royston Ellis, and a very well-endowed stripper, named Janice. Janice worked in one of Allan Williams' clubs, a strip joint named The Blue Angel. She always demanded a live band to back her as opposed to records, otherwise she refused to perform. Williams gave her The Beatles, who for a week played 'Begin The Beguine' and 'Summertime' as Janice gyrated on the floor, made eyes at George and caused tiny eruptions all around the room.

Royston Ellis met the band in the more sedate environment of The Jacaranda. 'My recollection,' Royston says, 'is that George approached me in The Jacaranda when I was standing by the jukebox and we spoke and we bonded immediately and he took me to 3 Gambier Terrace to stay and that's where I met Stuart, John, Paul ...'

Royston had written a new poem, and it was decided that the band would provide musical backing when Royston performed the work at The Jacaranda. The show went well, the band devising a 12-bar blues jam, which allowed Royston to talk over it. 'I planned to take the boys to London to back me in my performances of "Beat" poetry and when I asked John what name they were using he said: The Beetles. He explained that he chose that name because he liked the Volkswagen car, known as a Beetle. I told him that since he liked the Beats, played Beat music and I was a Beat poet, why not call themselves Beatles with an A. I did not know at the time that he had been considering that name as part of the term "Silver Beatles". A few days later I was quoted in the *Record Mirror* of London as saying I had found a group to back me and I was bringing them to London and their name was "The Beatles".'

Royston's memory is that Sutcliffe was the most Beat of The Beatles because he was the most passionate about art. He also recalled Lennon wrestling with himself over his future, debating whether to quit art college altogether and follow music. Royston told him to quit college as he had done himself to follow poetry. It was also Ellis who introduced the boys to amphetamines.

'I introduced the boys to chewing the Benzedrine strips inside a nose inhaler,' Ellis recalls. 'John has written about that and said I was the first person to introduce them to drugs. It was the drug of choice of London Rockers at the time.' Having ingested the drug, the group sat around talking until the morning light.

Royston adds, 'I was very taken with John's enthusiasm and we bonded very quickly. The result of one conversation was when we were talking about what we wanted to do and I said, "I want to be a paperback writer" ... That, of course, led to Paul and John eventually using the catchphrase ... in their hit, 'Paperback Writer'. I found John dynamic and interesting – Paul a bit inward looking.'

It was thanks to Allan Williams that Lennon made his first press appearance. Having helped the band out on several occasions, Williams now assumed the managerial role. In an effort to generate much-needed publicity, Williams got in touch with *The People* newspaper in London and sold them a yarn about decadent Liverpool Beatniks. The paper's editor bought his tale and sent a reporter and photographer to investigate. In July 1960 the newspaper ran an article entitled 'The Beatnik Horror'. It featured a photograph taken in the flat below Sutcliffe's, in which the 19-year-old Lennon was pictured lying on the floor. The man had done it – without creating a thing, the Beatnik John Lennon was in a national newspaper.

John Lennon, George Harrison, Paul McCartney and Pete Best in their famous all-leather look, which they developed in Hamburg.

THE BEATLES

go to Hamburg

DATE 16 August 1960, Grosse Freiheit, Hamburg

Oh what a joy it must have been to be a Beatle in the August of 1960, arriving in the happening city of Hamburg with music in your mind, youth on your side and dreams stretching out in front of you. Allan Williams was the man responsible. He organized the first German visit and by the time The Beatles had finished, they would be the premier band in Liverpool, brimming with the verve and confidence they needed to take on the world.

The catalyst was the steel band Williams had hired for The Jacaranda. They had jumped ship, been enticed to Hamburg by promoters offering them all kinds of opportunities in the St Pauli district, an area renowned for sex workers, gangsters and all kinds of ne'er-do-wells. At first Williams was annoyed at the band's disloyalty and then his business acumen kicked in. Perhaps, the St Pauli clubs would like some more Liverpool bands?

Williams made a tape up of four Liverpool outfits – The Silver Beatles, Cass And The Casanovas, The Spinners and Noel Walker's Stompers. Then he headed for Hamburg. On his second night in the city, Williams strolled past a club and heard a band playing a horrendous version of Little Richard's 'Tutti Frutti'. He ventured into the club, a joint called the Kaiserkeller and sought out the club owner, whose name was Bruno Koschmider.

Williams told Koschmider to forget the duffs on stage, he had a band that would rip the joint apart. Williams pulled out his tape and put it on the machine in Koschmider's office. Unfortunately for him, the tape was faulty. As the men struggled to hear the music, a fight suddenly broke out in the club. Koschmider excused himself, opened up his drawer, took out a

IT WAS A DEMANDING SCHEDULE BUT THE BEATLES DID NOT CARE. THEY WERE FULL OF YOUTHFUL EXUBERANCE, OBSESSED WITH MUSIC AND NOW PLACED RIGHT AT THE HEART OF THE ACTION

truncheon, walked out and waded into the fight, beating several men to a pulp in the process. Then he came back into the office, put the truncheon back in the drawer and carried on the conversation.

KINDRED SPIRITS ALWAYS RECOGNIZE EACH OTHER. THEY MIGHT HAVE DRESSED DIFFERENTLY TO THE BEATLES BUT THAT WAS THE POINT – THEY DRESSED DIFFERENTLY TO EVERYONE ELSE

After Williams left to go back to Liverpool, Koschmider was seriously intrigued by the idea of employing hot UK bands so in May 1960 he travelled to London to check out the capital's famous 2i's Coffee Bar, the hip joint where acts such as Tommy Steele And The Vipers had got big breaks. Meanwhile, Williams arrived in London with another of his bands, The Seniors, for a gig at the 2i's. Williams walked in and there was Koschmider. The men marvelled at the coincidence and then watched the band. They were good. So good that Koschmider booked them.

The Seniors landed in Hamburg in July 1960. They were seasoned performers, fit and powerful. They soon began making a name for themselves. When Williams wrote and told them he was now sending The Beatles over, The Seniors baulked at the idea. They had seen The Beatles in Liverpool and considered them a poor band. They advised Williams not to do it, saying that it would mess up the good thing he had going. Williams chose to ignore The Seniors and on 16 August The Beatles arrived in Hamburg to play at Koschmider's other club, The Indra. The band were shown their living quarters and had to blink – their 'bedroom' was essentially a small storeroom right next to the toilets in the Bambi Kino cinema.

The Indra itself was a strip bar on the skids. Crowd attendance was pitiful. Koschmider needed results and told the band they were to perform for four and a half hours each weekday night, and six hours on Saturday and Sunday nights. It was a demanding schedule but The Beatles did not care. They were full of youthful exuberance, obsessed with music and now placed right at the heart of the action. The beer flowed. Pills arrived. The call girls went off duty, many of them happy to teach the boys the ways of the world. George Harrison lost his virginity in his Hamburg bed. After he had finished, he heard a round of applause. John, Paul, Stu and Pete had been watching ...

They loved playing, their energy and drive quickly establishing a regular crowd. Koschmider was pleased. But there was one problem: an old lady lived above the club and the noise was unbearable. Koschmider was forced to relocate the band to his other club, the Kaiserkeller.

The club's old wooden stage was balanced precariously on beer crates. The living quarters were just as ropy. But the band was learning. On stage they had started to run out of songs. Rehearsing new material was out of the question so they started to extend the songs. Covers such as Ray Charles's 'What'd I Say' stretched out to 20 minutes or more. Meanwhile, customers sent up trays of drinks that the band would guzzle down, followed by the securing of a drug known as Preludin, an upper that enabled the band to stay awake until the early hours. The drug came in a tube and the gang knowingly started each night with the question, 'Anyone catching the tube tonight?'

Hamburg toughened up their playing skills and then as a further reward gave them Astrid Kirchherr, Jürgen Vollmer and Klaus Voormann, three German students who would prove crucial to their artistic development. The trio were European Beatniks, heavily into France's existentialist philosophy. They had a keen eye for style and therefore were of great interest to the Beatle gang. In one striking photo of the trio, Klaus wears a velvet top with a ruffle collar, pre-dating the New Romantic look by a good 20 years, Astrid wears a leather jacket and leather trousers, Jürgen ties his shirt together with a rose and his legs are also encased in leather.

Their hair – contrary to the Teddy Boy quiff sported by the band – pushes forwards not upwards and soon this cut would be adopted and made famous by the band. No one bar their contemporaries at college would be dressing in such a manner and so their clothing made them a target, especially in rough areas such as St Pauli.

Kindred spirits always recognize each other. They might have dressed differently to The Beatles but that was the point – they dressed differently to everyone else. The band were all smitten with Astrid but it was Stu she chose. Later on in his arms, Astrid revealed to him her dreams of becoming a photographer. So Stu insisted she shoot them and a date was arranged, Astrid pointing her camera at the band in a nearby fairground one grey day. Her stark and evocative pictures are now some of the most iconic shots of the band in existence. The band look mean and moody and refuse to smile. Astrid captured their insolence beautifully. Unlike the prevailing wisdom of the day, the band did not try and win the viewer's admiration.

It is worth noting that drummer Pete Best shows up in only a few of the pictures. On stage he was a Beatle; off it he had no interest in the band for there were other pursuits on offer to him. It was a fatal mistake. Best was organized, competent, useful for booking gigs, for arranging the life of the band, but once a certain Brian Epstein assumed those responsibilities, Pete's value was halved and that left him exposed. Soon the gang would turn on him. And Lennon was still the leader of that gang, no doubt about it. 'He dominated the boys. In fact, he spread his rather baleful and disturbing presence wherever he went,' Williams later wrote.

Lennon spiralled out of control in Hamburg. He dropped countless pills and drank to massive excess. Drink and drugs took away his pain, but heightened the anger that raged in his brain. Williams sometimes saw Lennon so drunk before a gig that he could hardly believe the man would be able to stand let alone walk on stage, play and sing. But he did, Lennon made it up there and sang and then he would taunt the Germans with Sieg Heils and call them 'fucking Nazis'.

Drunkenness and chaos reigned supreme, but what the others – especially McCartney – thought remains unreported. (When the band hit the big time, they kept quiet about their Hamburg adventures. Pills and call girls are not exactly the image to woo a young girl's heart.)

Still, Hamburg brought other treats. The Beatles made their first records here. On 15 October 1960 at Hamburg's Akustik Studio, they cut three songs with Lou Walters of The Hurricanes, another Liverpool band making their way in the Hamburg clubs. 'Summertime', 'Fever' and 'September Song' were the songs committed to tape. What is so special about this date is that Pete Best did not attend the session, Lou bought his own drummer

along and his name was Ringo Starr. Fitting that their first recording should feature John, Paul, George and Ringo. Four copies were made of the session and all four copies have since disappeared.

> **LENNON SPIRALLED OUT OF CONTROL. HE DROPPED COUNTLESS PILLS AND DRANK TO MASSIVE EXCESS. DRINK AND DRUGS TOOK AWAY HIS PAIN, BUT HEIGHTENED THE ANGER THAT RAGED IN HIS BRAIN**

The second session was with a singer named Tony Sheridan who The Beatles looked up to, especially George Harrison. Sheridan was a promising English musician whose talent had allowed him to back Gene Vincent on UK tours, hold down residencies at prestigious spots like the 2i's and create something of a cult following in Britain. He was once managed by the famous Larry Parnes but his stubborn refusal to take advice and his rebel spirit (if he got bored playing certain songs he would start adding his own chords thus throwing his backing band into disarray) rendered him unfit for success.

Just as his fortune seemed to be running out, his band were approached by a German promoter. Sheridan ended up in Hamburg, a city he loved because he could be himself there and not have to worry about agents or managers. Sheridan was a success, got himself signed by Polydor Records and then along came The Beatles and, after watching him play, made clear their admiration. Sheridan replied in part by asking them to back him on his album. Over a two-day period The Beatles and Sheridan cut a number of songs, including the single 'My Bonnie'. Why that song, who knows? Maybe being a contrary sort, Sheridan thought that in a city swamped by rock'n'roll the way forward was to speed up a famous Scottish folk song. (It served its purpose, as this was the recording that helped bring Brian Epstein into the gang.)

Unwittingly, it would be Sheridan who would bring the band's first Hamburg sojourn to a close. Koschmider had forbidden the band to even enter rival clubs let alone perform there. But one night the band got on stage with Sheridan at a club named The Top Ten, and the news went straight back to Koschmider. He plotted revenge. The next day, he reported Harrison to the police for being underage. Harrison was arrested and then deported.

Peter Eckhorn of The Top Ten offered the remaining band members a residency at his club with much better accommodation. The band accepted. As a leaving present for Koschmider, Paul and Pete set fire to a condom in their room. Koschmider saw red and summoned the authorities, accusing the pair of arson. The band was swiftly deported. Except for Stu – love had got the better of him and he decided to quit the band, go to art college and stay with Astrid. McCartney now moved to bass.

The Beatles returned to Hamburg four more times. On their third visit tragedy awaited them. On 11 April 1962 they landed at Hamburg airport to be greeted by Astrid. Where was Stu they asked? The bass player had been in Liverpool the previous December and worried many with his pallor. Yet on his return to Germany Stu's long letters to John had continued and so the worry had turned to vapour.

Astrid told them Stu had died the day before. He had fallen into a coma and been rushed to hospital. He had a clot on his brain. John in particular was devastated. Pete Best claims he broke down at the airport and cried, the only time the drummer ever saw tears on Lennon's face.

McCartney in later years better understood the exact nature of the band's dynamics. He and Stu had not got on well. 'We all competed for John's friendship,' he recalled. 'And Stuart being his mate from art school had a lot of his time and we were jealous of that.' McCartney also revealed that one night the band made a pact that if one of them should die he would return and let the others know what awaited them. It was a teenage act but it made one thing clear: being in this gang meant as much in death as in life.

THE
BEATLES
PLAYED
HERE
292
TIMES

The CAVERN
PRESENTS
SWINGING
LUNCHTIME
SESSIONS
NOON to 2.15PM
MONDAYS TO
FRIDAYS

VERN

IS
WHERE IT ALL
BEGAN!
THE
Cavern

AT THE CAVERN
A STAR
SPANGLED
WEEKEND

SPENCER DAVIS

WILSON PICKETT

THE CAV ERN

FIX

The Beatles perform at

THE CAVERN

DATE 9 February 1961, Mathew Street, Liverpool

As a band whose need to innovate bordered on the insatiable, the relationship The Beatles developed with The Cavern Club on Mathew Street in Liverpool was absolutely crucial. Many firsts were established there. To begin with, no band had ever bonded itself so closely to a club. By the end of their relationship, The Beatles and The Cavern (and by extension, Liverpool) were inextricably linked.

The first wave of Beatles fans grew and developed at The Cavern. Their audience was loyal and mainly female. The fans' devotion proved bountiful, allowing the band not only to imagine national success but also giving them the impetus to try out new ideas. The collarless jacket they would make famous got its first UK preview at The Cavern and so did many original Lennon and McCartney songs, including 'Love Me Do' and 'When I'm Sixty-Four'.

The club itself had its roots in Paris. Founding owner Alan Sytner holidayed in France as a schoolboy and fell in love with Paris. When he came to buy the premises, he recalled the Parisian jazz club Le Caveau de la Huchette and named his basement club The Cavern in its honour.

The club opened for business on Wednesday 16 January 1957 and featured three jazz bands and a skiffle outfit. Queues stretched around the corner and for its first years of existence The Cavern featured only jazz and blues artists with some skiffle bands allowed on to the stage. The Quarrymen played there one night and against express orders Lennon led the band into various rock'n'roll numbers, a musical style Sytner had imposed a club ban on. Lennon did not give a toss. Be Bop A Lula, I'll play what I want ...

When he returned with The Beatles in February 1961, times had changed. Ray McFall was now in charge, rock'n'roll bands were in the ascendancy and Lennon was the leather-jacketed blue-jeaned kid

LENNON WOULD LEAN AGAINST THE PIANO, EAT SANDWICHES, TELL DIRTY JOKES, CHEW GUM, SMOKE, SWIG COCA-COLA AND ENGAGE IN HEAVY BANTER WITH HIS FANS

leading the hottest band in town. The band played evening and lunchtime sessions, the latter attracting hundreds of young office workers who worked in the club's catchment area.

The band played on a stage that their fans eagerly crowded around. In their denim and leather they looked completely different from every other band around. Everyone else wore suits or jackets and ties on stage. Not The Beatles. In fact, Ray McFall had to be persuaded to let them play in jeans, a clothing item he had banned from the club.

TO BALANCE OUT LENNON'S AGGRESSION AND CRUEL WIT, McCARTNEY WOULD PLAY GOOD COP. WHERE JOHN SCOWLED, PAUL WOULD SMILE. WHERE JOHN GRIMACED, PAUL GRINNED

At The Cavern, the girls and the boys fell in love with the band, their looks, their musical power. Drummer Pete Best was the girls' favourite. A quiet, moody-looking boy, Best's obvious shyness simply increased the female interest in him. McCartney would later dub him, 'mean, moody and magnificent'. Best would recall

coming home to find girls waiting for him in the front garden. Best's attitude was not one of arrogance or superiority – he viewed their devotion as positive for the band.

Lennon was, as you would expect, a bolshie, outrageous character. He would lie on the floor playing guitar. He would insult the audience and pick his nose on stage. He would lean against the piano, eat sandwiches, tell dirty jokes, chew gum, smoke, swig Coca-Cola and engage in heavy banter with his fans. He really did not give a damn and so made a case for viewing The Beatles as the country's first ever punk outfit. Often, he would change songs for his own amusement. Singing Buddy Holly's 'Oh Boy', Lennon would shout, 'all my life, I've been waiting, tonight there will be no masturbating'.

To balance out Lennon's aggression and cruel wit, McCartney would play good cop. Where John would scowl, Paul would smile. Where John grimaced, Paul grinned. Paul's impulses were hewn from the showbiz virus that had infected him from an early age. His instinct always led him to please the crowd, not provoke them. Once when the electricity failed, Paul sat down at the piano and led the crowd through a selection of Ray Charles songs until the power was restored.

Paul's viewpoint was simple: like Roman crowds watching gladiators, the audience held your destiny in their hands. Why antagonize them? This desire to please would feed into his songwriting and account for the high levels of sentimentality apparent in a few of his creations. Lennon's viewpoint was that the crowd had come to watch the band and therefore the band could do what the hell they liked. Lennon's arrogance and McCartney's pacifism formed the yin and yang of The Beatles, which served them beautifully to the very end. 'Only John Lennon did the swearing,' one Cavern regular recalled. 'They had the audience in the palms of their hands.' A musician wilfully swearing on stage – another first for The Beatles.

The Beatles' set list was mainly covers. Although Paul and John had been writing together for years now, accumulating some 100 songs, very few of them were played live. Most of them did not stand up to scrutiny against the likes of 'What'd I Say', 'Hippy Hippy Shake', 'C'mon Everybody', 'Twenty Flight Rock', 'Lucille', 'Hallelujah I Love Her So', 'Some Other Guy', 'New Orleans', 'Will You Love Me Tomorrow', 'Red Sails In The Sunset' and 'Money'.

The band also veered away from rock'n'roll to cover songs such as 'Besame Mucho' or 'Over The Rainbow' from *The Wizard of Oz*. The band's attitude towards covers was simple – at all times outdo the original. Certainly in the case of 'Over The Rainbow', many Cavern regulars felt The Beatles' version would have made an excellent single.

Playing frequent sessions at The Cavern created high levels of creativity within their ranks. In 1961 The Twist dance craze hit Britain. An Italian-American named Peppy visited The Cavern to demonstrate the dance. The Beatles watched him then retired to their dressing room. When they took to the stage they announced they had just written a new song, 'The Pinwheel Twist', and played it. That was why they were the town's numero uno band. Their rivals simply could not match their imagination.

LENNON'S ARROGANCE AND McCARTNEY'S PACIFISM FORMED THE YIN AND YANG OF THE BEATLES, WHICH SERVED THEM BEAUTIFULLY TO THE VERY END

The Beatles played their first Cavern show in leather jackets and jeans and were paid £10 for their efforts. Two years later, after appearing 291 times, the band played their last Cavern show in August 1963. They did so in mohair suits and the fee they were paid was £300 – that is how far they had come in such a short space of time. The man who took the money on behalf of the band that night first saw The Beatles at The Cavern on 9 November 1961. His name was Brian Epstein and he was now a key member of the gang.

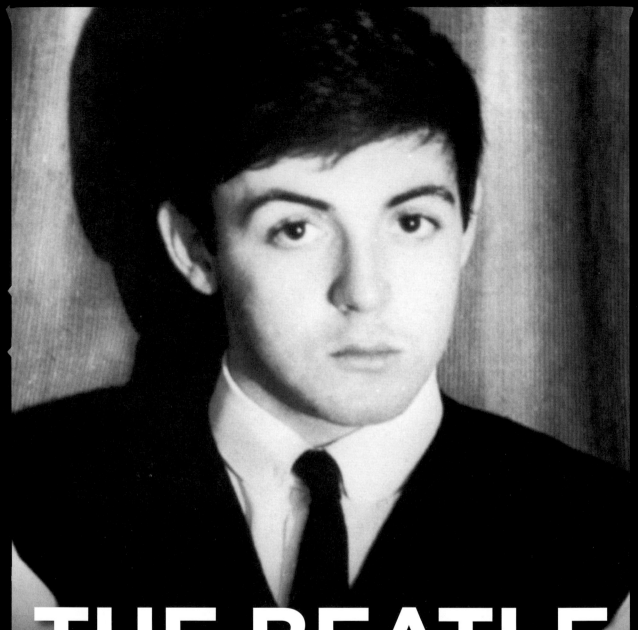

THE BEATLE
HAIRCUT
is born

DATE October 1961, Montparnasse, Paris

It was a huge amount of money at the time – £100 – but it was John's 21st and his aunt truly loved him so she made the gift. John was overjoyed with this financial windfall. Mimi of course counselled caution, advised him to put it in the bank, but John had a much better idea. He was going to pay for him and Paul to go on holiday in Spain. To save money they were going to hitchhike.

McCartney loved the idea, of course, got to planning the trip straight away. He suggested they wear bowler hats while hitchhiking. At the time, the bowler hat was the ultimate symbol of mainstream success. Prime ministers and prominent businessmen wore them to big offices in big cities. McCartney reasoned that two young ruffians wearing such apparel might well intrigue drivers to pull over out of sheer curiosity. And he wasn't wrong.

'We still had our leather jackets and drainpipes ... in case we met a girl,' Paul recalled. 'But for the lifts we put the bowlers on. Two guys in bowler hats – a lorry would stop ... This and the train is how we got to Paris.'

They were so exhausted after reaching the French capital that the boys decided to stay put. Furthermore their old friend from Hamburg, Jürgen Vollmer, was in town and by hooking up with him they could access Paris. This change of plan would prove to be a fortuitous twist of fate. They found Jürgen at his hotel on the Left Bank. The young German was overjoyed to see his friends from Hamburg and took charge of their stay.

As they walked around the capital the boys could not help noticing how their French counterparts were dressed. 'We saw guys walking round in short leather jackets and very wide pantaloons. Talk

DURING THIS TRIP JOHN AND PAUL SPENT MOST OF THEIR MONEY ON CLOTHING ... BUT THE MOST IMPORTANT THING THE BOYS DID IN PARIS WAS TO LET JÜRGEN CUT THEIR HAIR

about fashion!' remembered Paul. 'This was going to kill them when we got back. This was totally happening. They were tight to the knee and then they flared out.'

John and Paul each bought a pair of these trousers and spent the day with Jürgen, strolling around Montmartre, trying out their new look. Much as they wanted to fit in, they just did not feel comfortable. After years of wearing

THE BEATLE CUT WAS BASICALLY A SCHOOLBOY CUT BUT OVERGROWN. THE CUT BROKE WITH TRADITION BECAUSE IT WAS DIFFERENT TO THE USUAL 'SHORT BACK AND SIDES'

tight-fitting jeans, this was a flare too far. According to Neil Aspinall, the band's road manager, writing in *Fab 208* a few years later, during this trip John and Paul spent most of their money on clothing. Paul even bought himself a plastic police cape, which he treasured for years. But the most important thing the boys did in Paris was to let Jürgen cut their hair.

In Hamburg, Jürgen, Klaus and Astrid had worn their hair pushed forward over the forehead. It was a radical cut for the time. Certainly, it marked you out on the street and made you something of a target for the bully boys. The Beatles at the time proudly wore quiffs. One night George Harrison did wear his hair brushed forward on stage but got so many threatening looks from onlookers that he quickly reverted to a quiff. In Paris, different rules applied. The boys consented to have their hair cut like Jürgen's and in doing so set in motion the birth of the Beatle haircut, which would dramatically enter national consciousness in 1963.

The Beatle cut was basically a schoolboy cut but overgrown. It was considered long because of its thickness rather than its length. The cut broke with tradition because it was so different to the 'short back and sides' worn by so many. What is interesting about their style is that they never once referred to it. The world went mad for the cut but they had no agenda apart from the fact that they thought it looked fab.

On their way home the two boys stopped off in London and went sightseeing in Covent Garden. There they came across a shop named Anello & Davide. Founded in 1922, the shop supplied bespoke dance shoes to theatres. John and Paul were entranced by the shop's window display, especially a Chelsea-style boot placed at the back that caught their eye. With holiday money still in their pockets, John and Paul went in and ordered a couple of pairs, but with a proviso – they wanted

Paul's violin-like Hofner bass was part of his style; John's sharp-edged Rickenbacker was part of his. Paul's left-handedness meant they appeared as mirror images of each other when on stage.

a Cuban heel added to the design. Pete Best remembered John arriving back in Liverpool and declaring of these shoes, '"I fell in love with them and just had to get some. So did Paul" – and so did we all after they swaggered back to Merseyside.'

The Beatles resumed their live engagements wearing clothing that instantly marked them out from the crowd. 'We were, to put it mildly, different,' McCartney recalled. Later, the band adopted collarless jackets, which then became known as Beatle jackets. Yet as soon as another band started wearing them The Beatles dropped the item and moved on to another style.

The principles of innovation that they applied to their music would also be applied to their clothes all the way through their career. Their ability to move forward was driven by their open mindedness. They were the generation that looked towards places such as America, India and France for inspiration. Their hair might have been falling over their eyes but they could see the future better than anyone else.

The Beatles meet

BRIAN EPSTEIN

DATE 9 November 1961, The Cavern, Liverpool

At the start of the 1960s, British society was sharply divided by class. The public schools produced the future government, the run-down secondary schools gave up the next generation of factory workers. The day Brian Epstein ventured into The Cavern, the gap between upper, middle and working class was highly acute and this is why his meeting and subsequent love for The Beatles is so significant.

Here was an urbane, upper-middle-class, man who adored wearing expensive clothing, going to the theatre and listening to classical music, stepping into a club where young working-class boys and girls danced with abandon to raucous rock'n'roll. The worlds of The Cavern and Brian Epstein were so far removed it was ridiculous but the common denominator was, of course, The Beatles.

The reason that Brian Epstein came to The Cavern in the first place is simple. Brian needed to be in a gang. He just didn't know it at the time. Epstein's sexuality made him an outsider. Homosexuality was illegal at the time and so Brian was at risk of imprisonment at all times. The Beatles were outsiders, too, and this formed a bond that brought band and manager together.

Brian Samuel Epstein, born 19 September 1934, was raised in an affluent Jewish family headed by Harry and Queenie Epstein. The family's wealth emanated from a large furniture store and several other shops selling household goods and musical instruments.

Brian was placed in many prestigious schools. He responded by getting expelled from many of them. While at public school, Epstein wrote a letter to his father expressing his wish to become a dress designer. Harry instantly quashed the idea and ordered his son home. Within a year he was working for the family business.

EPSTEIN'S SEXUALITY MADE HIM AN OUTSIDER. THE BEATLES WERE OUTSIDERS, TOO, AND THIS FORMED A BOND THAT BROUGHT THEM TOGETHER

And then national service came a-calling. Epstein was initially stationed at Aldershot but somehow managed to wangle himself a posting in London. Returning home one Friday night, a soldier at the gate mistakenly saluted Epstein. Such was the quality of Epstein's clothing, the soldier naturally assumed he was a ranking officer. Such incidents led to his quiet removal from service. Epstein

EPSTEIN FELT TRAPPED – BY SOCIETY AND BY FAMILY. HE MIGHT HAVE ALL THE RICHES IN THE WORLD BUT HE HAD NO FREEDOM

returned to Liverpool and after squiring a few Jewish girls around town, confessed his sexuality to his parents. It was a brave move although his mother had suspected it for years. So had some of the Jewish girls he knew – their nickname for him was 'the immaculate deception'.

The family continued to expand its business empire. They now opened up a music store on Great Charlotte Street, which they called NEMS (North End Music Stores) and later relocated to Whitechapel Street. Although Epstein would now distinguish himself as manager of the family shops, the fact remained that he was hemmed in on all sides. His sexuality was illegal, the circles he moved in were highly conservative and his career had been mapped out for him. He would enter the family business and stay there until retirement. Epstein felt trapped – by society and by family. He might have all the riches in the world but he had no freedom. Furthermore, the nature of his sexuality was a real problem. Epstein liked rough sex. Perhaps as an indicator of his self-esteem, he liked to be dominated and humiliated. This penchant would at times impact on his later career.

As he awaited nirvana, a young man named Raymond Jones walked into his shop and ordered a record by a band called The Beatles – their recording of 'My Bonnie' with Tony Sheridan. Epstein phoned Polydor Records who informed him that the single was an import. Epstein tracked the single down but by now his curiosity had been aroused. Who was this Liverpool band he had never heard of?

In a way, Epstein already knew the answer to that question. In 1961 one of Lennon's friends from art college, Bill Harry, had started *Mersey Beat*, a newspaper dedicated to covering the hundreds of Liverpool bands. The Beatles had been featured on the paper's front cover, posing in their all-leather gear, an image that would instantly intrigue any gay man in 1961. That issue was stocked in Epstein's shop, a shop the band and their fans used on a regular basis. Subliminally at least, Brian Epstein knew who The Beatles were.

When he and assistant Alistair Taylor ventured into The Cavern, their presence made public by the club DJ Bob Wooler's announcement, Epstein went and stood at the back of the club and waited. What he saw was not what he expected. The Beatles broke every showbiz rule there was. They were rude, arrogant, louche and scruffy. Yet to Epstein they had something incredible about them, something indefinable.

The essence Epstein was feeling was freedom – the elixir of the new decade. Epstein hailed from a claustrophobic world full of conventions. The Beatles had built a world without any rules. In fact, so taken was Epstein by their humour and freshness he would soon be dressing like them and listening to the same music.

Epstein went backstage, saw his chance and duly grabbed it. One month and one day later, Epstein and The Beatles joined forces. Epstein fitted the band's notion of a manager perfectly. He was well spoken, rich (he had his own car, wore handmade suits) and therefore able to deal with the top levels of record companies.

Epstein was savvy enough to know that for the band to fulfil their destiny, wholesale changes had to be made. No more eating, drinking, swearing and smoking on stage. And no more leather suits, otherwise no promoter outside Liverpool would consider booking them.

In consultation it was decided they switch to a uniform of mohair suits. Many were shocked that Lennon went along with this proposition – but that is because few knew just how ambitious he was at this stage. Lennon craved money, sex and acclaim. Furthermore, if The Beatles failed he would be left in a precarious position. Outside of music, what future was there for him apart from the factory line?

When he was told 'ditch the leather and more doors will open up to you', Lennon discarded the lot saying he did not love the material that much anyway. In later years he would pinpoint this moment as proof that the band had sold out, but Paul didn't recall having to drag any Beatle to the tailors kicking and screaming.

EPSTEIN WAS SAVVY ENOUGH TO KNOW THAT FOR THE BAND TO FULFIL THEIR DESTINY, WHOLESALE CHANGES HAD TO BE MADE

Naturally, the band told Epstein they would have a say in the suits they wore. The last thing The Beatles would do is look like any other band around. And this is how the relationship between Brian Epstein and the band developed. Epstein would show them the way and the band would walk it in their own unique style. In other words he could help guide the gang – but he could never be their leader. The Beatles would soon make that abundantly clear.

The band in their bespoke mohair suits, made in Liverpool by tailors Beno Dorn. Pete Best (second from left) would soon be replaced, however, causing much controversy.

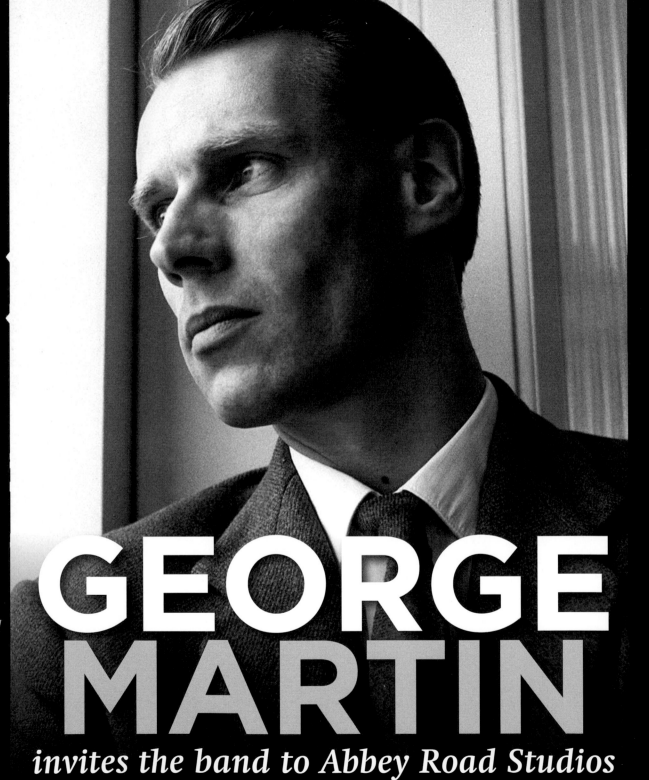

GEORGE MARTIN

invites the band to Abbey Road Studios

DATE 6 June 1962, St John's Wood, North London

Four days after returning from Hamburg, The Beatles entered Abbey Road, the studio that – like The Cavern before – would serve to define them. Originally a Georgian townhouse, the Gramophone Company (later to become EMI Records) bought the premises in 1929 and opened it as a studio in 1931. One of its earliest clients was the great British composer, Sir Edward Elgar. The Beatles were there because a month earlier Lady Luck had turned her spotlight on them.

On 8 May 1962, Brian Epstein walked into the HMV department store on Oxford Street and asked to see Bob Boast. (Epstein had met Boast a year before on a retail-management course in Germany and the two men had become friendly.) He played Boast the demo tape that he had been playing to record companies with no success whatsoever. Boast listened to the tape and suggested that Brian have it transferred on to disc, using their facilities on the first floor.

Boast then introduced Epstein to Jim Foy who began the tape-to-disc transfer process. As the music played, Foy told Epstein he liked the songs. The manager replied that some of them were original compositions. At that time it was unusual for bands to produce their own material so Foy asked Epstein if he had a publisher.

Above them were the offices of Ardmore and Beechwood, an EMI music-publishing company run by Syd Coleman.

Foy fetched Coleman who then listened to the material. Epstein told Coleman he was flattered by his interest but his priority was a recording deal. Coleman then returned to his office

THE BAND ARRIVED LATE AFTERNOON IN THEIR WHITE VAN. THEY WORE BLACK LEATHER COATS AND SUITS AND SUCH WAS THEIR INDIVIDUAL STYLE PEOPLE NOTICED THEM STRAIGHT AWAY

A public sign for the road the band made famous. To this day, tourists from all over the world descend on Abbey Road to look at the studio and walk on its famous zebra crossing.

with Epstein in tow and phoned a man named George Martin, the head of A&R at the EMI subsidiary label, Parlophone Records. Martin was working with singer Matt Monro at Abbey Road when Coleman called so Epstein made the journey from London W1 to London NW8. There he met the producer and arranged a second meeting for the following day.

At that second visit, Martin listened to Epstein's tape and declared there to be something of interest in the music but he would need to see the band in the flesh. An evening date was set – 6 June 1962. The band rehearsed for two days at The Cavern and then on the 6th made the trip to London. While they were en route, Martin assigned Ron Richards to take the session. Richards was Martin's rock'n'roll producer and his assistant was Norman Smith. The band arrived late afternoon in their white van. They wore black leather coats and

suits and such was their individual style people noticed them straight away.

The band set up their equipment. Instantly, Smith saw it would be unsuitable for the night's purposes. Under his supervision, wires were soldered, speakers added. The session could now begin. The band played four songs, 'Besame Mucho' and three of their own, 'Love Me Do', 'P.S. I Love You' and 'Ask Me Why'.

It was 'Love Me Do' that caught Smith's attention and made him send tape operator Chris Neal off to bring Martin up to the studio. Neal returned with Martin, who watched the band perform and then sat down with them. He explained that it was essential they know about recording technique, how things worked, how the process happened. The band maintained an air of studied indifference. One observer recalled Lennon lolling on a speaker and Harrison lying on the floor.

Martin finally said, 'Look, I have laid into you for some time now and you haven't responded. Is there anything you don't like?'

'Yes, your tie,' Harrison replied. For the next quarter of an hour the band kept Martin and Smith in a state of hysterics. By the end of it Smith would report that he had tears streaming down his face, such was the quality of the band's quick wit. Humour gave the band freshness and

THE BAND RECALLED MEETING GEORGE MARTIN AND NOTED RIGHT AWAY HIS POSH ACCENT. BUT ONCE THEY HAD CRACKED THE ICE ALL DIFFERENCES FELL AWAY

a joie de vivre that was contagious and allowed them to jump all kinds of barriers. Martin is a case in point. The band recalled meeting him and noted right away his posh accent. However, once they had cracked the ice and employed humour, all differences fell away.

Like Epstein, you would not initially place Martin with four young Scousers who had no interest in their country's past or its traditions. Martin hailed from leafy north London, had attended a prestigious grammar school, found work as a quantity surveyor before joining the RAF and rising to the position of commissioned officer.

Yet Martin was also a man obsessed with music – from the age of six his childhood desire had been to 'become the next Rachmaninov'. He also had a great liking for humour of all kinds. In the 1950s he produced an album with The Goons and once the band heard this they stepped much closer towards him. The band and producer bonded therefore over music and humour, two of the band's finest and strongest qualities. These two elements dissolved all class divisions on that day in June and George Martin would now prove to be perfect for the band's recording career. His desire to create and innovate may have emanated from the world of classical music but it was the same desire that shot through The Beatles.

The band left Abbey Road that night full of joyful anticipation. They knew they had made a significant step forward in their quest for success. Martin, for his part, told Smith soon after that he would sign the band. 'What have I got to lose?' he told the engineer. There was only one problem with The Beatles as far as the producer was concerned. And that was the drummer.

RINGO STARR

joins the band as drummer

DATE 16 August 1962, Brian Epstein's Office, Liverpool

Pete Best went into Brian Epstein's office expecting the usual conversation about gigs and venues, for within the band he was the one you spoke to about such matters. Ten minutes later Best was no longer a Beatle. Epstein had told the drummer bluntly, 'The lads don't want you in the group any more.' Best felt the world give way beneath him. Surely Epstein had it wrong? He had put everything he had into the band and they were ejecting him just as success beckoned?

But Epstein was not fooling around. He informed a shocked Best that the band had already lined up Ringo Starr as his replacement. There was no going back.

This incident has inspired as much attention as any other in Beatle history. What were the real reasons behind Best's dismissal? Many people suspected that Best's position as the most desirable Beatle had tipped the scales. They assumed that Lennon and McCartney were insanely jealous of the attention the fans gave the reticent drummer. Others put the blame George Martin's way.

After the 6 June session at Abbey Road, Martin had told Epstein that Best, 'was not a very good drummer and we need one to bind this group together'. Martin later said that he had been the unwitting catalyst in Best's removal, 'I didn't realize that The Beatles were thinking of getting rid of Pete anyway.'

Why were the band heading towards this decision? Paul McCartney is a good place to start. His drive to better the band often led him to challenge other band members on a musical level. There are several reports of Paul at band rehearsals sitting at the drum kit instructing Pete how to play certain songs. Publicly, there had been no complaints about Best's drumming in the two years he had been

MANY SUSPECTED THAT BEST'S POSITION AS THE MOST DESIRABLE BEATLE HAD TIPPED THE SCALES. THEY ASSUMED THAT LENNON AND McCARTNEY WERE INSANELY JEALOUS

with the band. And given The Beatles' set list of straight-to-the-beat rock'n'roll songs, the demands put on Best were pretty straightforward.

McCartney addressed the issue in Barry Miles' biography *Many Years From Now* (1997). He pointed to the drumming on the Ray Charles record 'What'd I Say'. 'We used to love it. One of the big clinching factors about Ringo as the drummer in the band was that he could really play that so well.'

BEST NEVER FITTED IN WITH THE GANG. A SHY MAN, HE RARELY HUNG OUT WITH THE BAND, SHARED THEIR JOKES OR THEIR ETHOS

It is also worth noting that McCartney was about to or had just written 'When I'm Sixty-Four', a highly sophisticated song for someone so young. It is possible that Paul already knew the music he was creating would prove too difficult for Pete.

Best's drumming skills, his looks and his attitude provoked different responses at all times. But one fact remains – Best never quite fitted in with the gang. A shy man, he rarely hung out with the band, shared their jokes or their ethos. Early interviewers of the band said that Best often sat apart from the others and you were lucky to get a grunt out of him. What Best did not realize was that if you show indifference to the gang, eventually the gang will turn on you. 'He was a harmless guy but not quick,' Lennon later said. 'All of us had quick minds but he never picked up on that.'

The best drummer in Liverpool – the only man who soloed at that time – was Johnny Hutchinson from the band The Big Three. They too were under Epstein's management but never really followed his instructions. Perhaps if they had done then national success would have been theirs. Prior to Best's sacking, Epstein had approached 'Hutch', as he was known, about the possibility of joining the band. Hutch turned him down. As far as he was concerned his band were far superior to The Beatles, plus he and Lennon would never have got on.

The man The Beatles chose was perfect for the job. A drummer of great repute and a man given to slips of the tongue on a regular basis, Ringo Starr was approached by the band two days before Best's sacking. He was well known to them, having played with them out in Hamburg and at The Cavern. George Harrison in particular had taken to a liking to Ringo and hustled John and Paul for his inclusion.

What then of the new boy the band had chosen, the boy born Richard Starkey on 7 July 1940? Out of all four Beatles, Ringo hailed from the poorest background.

He was raised in the area of Dingle, the product of a one-parent family. His father had divorced his mother when he was three. Like most of the other Beatles his childhood was scarred by a missing parent.

At three years of age, Ringo moved to Admiral Grove and attended St Silas School. Afterwards it was on to Dingle Vale Secondary Modern. 'Sometimes those days come back to me with great clearness,' he would tell Billy Shepherd (aka Peter Jones) for the first authorized Beatles book, *The True Story of The Beatles* (1964). 'I can remember being given dinner money by my mum. I'd buy a few pennyworth of chips and a hunk of bread and then save the rest for the fairground or the pictures.'

At age seven, he developed an inflamed peritoneum, and spent a month in hospital. This set the tenor of much of his childhood: illness would dog him from now until teenage years. At 13 Ringo went to London where he contracted pleurisy. He had another lengthy soul-sapping stay in hospital and when he emerged, his school days were over.

Ringo began an apprenticeship in an engineering firm. He also fell for the skiffle craze. When he was 18 and a half, his mother and stepfather gave him a present – a drum kit. 'Why did they think I'd like drumming?' he once pondered. 'Because I suppose I'd always been a noisy lad.'

He was also an amusing lad, unintentionally so, for Ringo was someone who spoke before his brain had clicked in. He often called his stepfather his 'stepladder' and would later conjure up phrases such as 'eight days a week', which would enter Beatle folklore. It was this endearing characteristic that Lennon, with his fondness for wordplay, loved.

Ringo entered the music world by forming a band called The Eddie Clayton Skiffle Group. He then sat in with other bands including Rory Storm And The Hurricanes, and The Texans. Rory Storm was in fact Alan Caldwell, and his sister was dating one George Harrison. In 1959 Ringo joined the band on a regular basis and spent three years playing with them. During that time he acquired his nickname and a reputation as a fine drummer.

In October 1960 the band landed a gig in Hamburg and it was here that Ringo met the men that would change his life. When Pete frequently failed to show up for gigs, the band asked Ringo to sit in instead, and every time he did the other band members felt it all coming together.

George would later remark, 'Although Pete had not been with us all that long ... when you're young it's not a nice thing to be kicked out of a band and there's no nice way of doing it.' In an interview conducted months after the band's break-up, Lennon would remark that, 'You have to be a bastard to make it. That's a fact. And The Beatles are the biggest bastards on Earth.'

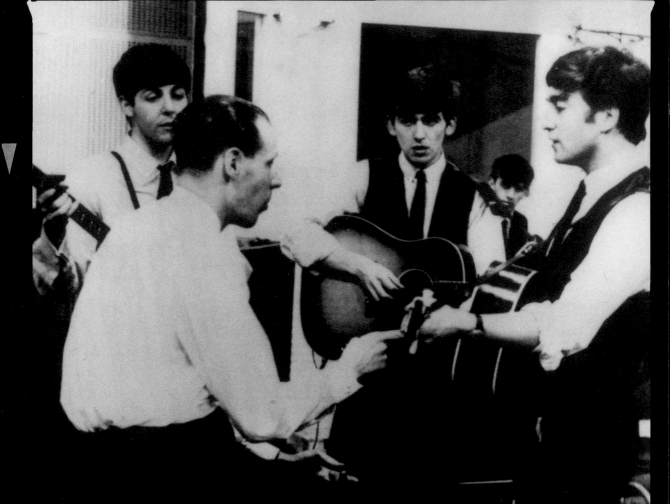

The Beatles record

LOVE
ME DO

DATE September 1962, Abbey Road Studios, London

In the 1960s, record companies were tight with their money and tight with their time. They allotted their bands and producers just three hours to record a single and a B-side, which would be mixed by the end of play. On its release the band would earn a single penny in royalties for every copy sold.

At Abbey Road Studios, EMI records had devised a strict schedule, cutting the day up into three defined sessions: ten till one, two till five and seven till ten. Bands were expected to show up on time having rehearsed the necessary material. The only activity they would indulge in would be work and they would at all times remain obedient and polite. Enter The Beatles. Their gradual chipping away at Abbey Road protocol would change the way all bands worked in the future – another first for The Fabs.

At their first Abbey Road date on 6 June 1962, The Beatles recorded four songs between six and eight o'clock. On their return to Abbey Road they spent three hours rehearsing their material, broke for food and then began the recording session at seven, ending at ten.

George Martin already had the band's first single in mind. He had sent up to Liverpool a song he felt should be the band's debut release, a sure-fire hit named 'How Do You Do It?', written by Mitch Murray. This was normal practice. Bands rarely wrote their own material; instead producers and music publishers would get together and offer each other songs they had been given by jobbing songwriters.

Unsurprisingly the band hated the song. It was whiney and white sounding and as far away from their vision of themselves as rhythm-and-blues-based Rockers as a song could be. At the evening recording session the band laid their cards on the table. They wanted to perform their own material and no one else's. George Martin smiled and told them that only once they had written a song as good as 'How Do You Do It?' would he countenance the suggestion. The Beatles remained adamant. They were there to break the mould.

Dutifully the band recorded the song, but they put a lot more effort into their second recording of the night, 'Love Me Do'. Lennon later revealed that McCartney had written the song as a teenager, well before they had begun their songwriting partnership. Lennon's contribution was his harmonica, inspired by the Bruce

Channel hit, 'Hey! Baby'. Where previously harmonicas had been used for rhythmic purposes, in the hands of Lennon the instrument now became a melodic asset. This bouncy but somewhat flat song now had a unique sound.

At the end of the session, George Martin was not happy with either recording. He asked the band to return in a week's time. When they did, one of them had a shock and that man was Ringo. Dissatisfied with his drumming on 'Love Me Do', Martin had brought in session man Andy White to play drums. According to Ron Rogers who was there, Ringo took the move with great ease and grace. Inwardly, he was highly distraught. He sensed a Pete Best situation developing around him. The problem had arisen in the last session when the drummer found himself having to play drums and maracas at the same time.

Ringo was left to shake the maracas on the B-side, 'P.S. I Love You', another McCartney song, written in the style of The Shirelles in Hamburg. Ten takes of this song plus a further 18 of 'Love Me Do' were completed by the band. They also played a new composition to Martin, a Lennon song entitled 'Please Please Me', which they had initially earmarked as the B-side.

'We had been going over it a few times,' Lennon would later reveal, 'and when we came to the question of the flipside, we intended using "Please Please

Me" ... We were getting very tired and we just couldn't seem to get it right.'

The problem with the song was its tempo. Lennon, who had written the song with Roy Orbison in mind, had delivered

> **AT THE END OF THE SESSION, GEORGE MARTIN WAS NOT HAPPY WITH EITHER RECORDING. HE ASKED THE BAND TO RETURN IN A WEEK'S TIME. WHEN THEY DID, ONE OF THEM HAD A SHOCK AND THAT MAN WAS RINGO.**

it to the band as a slow bluesy number. At a later session, Martin would tell the band to speed it up and in doing so would secure the band a huge chart hit. The work the band had put in now paid off. Martin mixed 'Love Me Do' and 'P.S. I Love You' and days later contacted the band with the news that those two songs, their very own, would make up their debut single. 'How Do You Do It?' would go to another band. The boys were ecstatic.

On 5 October the single was released and began a curious chart journey. Normally singles enter the charts, move upwards to their highest point and then fall. 'Love Me Do' followed a completely different trajectory. It came in at 49, hit 46,

Despite his drumming being rejected on 'Love Me Do', Ringo's no-frills style proved perfect for the band as it developed musically. And his slips of the tongue were a great source of lyrics.

41 and 32 then it slipped to 37. This would normally signal the end of its run. But the next week it went up to 29, 23 and 21 before again slipping to 26. From there it climbed to 19, dropped again to 22, before reaching 17, its highest point.

It was rumoured that Epstein had bought 10,000 copies via his NEMS store and hyped the single into the charts. Others argued that the band's huge following in the North West accounted for all the sales. Whatever the truth, the single's success gave the band a real boost. It thrilled them to hear it on the radio and delighted them that their wage packets from live work now increased. But most importantly of all, 'Love Me Do' opened up the door to television and radio for the band. And from there the phenomenon known as Beatlemania was born.

BEATLEMANIA

sweeps Britain

DATE | 13 October 1963, The London Palladium

Beatlemania started in 1963 between the end of the Profumo affair and the murder of JFK. It was created by The Beatles' willingness to take on a schedule so punishing most bands would have quit in exhaustion. Not these boys. Hardened by their experiences in Hamburg and Liverpool, the band completed three UK tours, their first foreign tour, numerous radio and TV appearances, several print interviews and recorded two albums. By the end of the year, The Beatles had instigated the phenomenon known as Beatlemania and performed before royalty.

The journey into the consciousness of Buckingham Palace began on 19 January 1963 when the band appeared on the prestigious TV show *Thank Your Lucky Stars*. At about six o'clock that Saturday night, millions of teenagers saw The Beatles perform their bright and catchy song, 'Please Please Me'. From then on the band was engulfed in an unrelenting schedule of gigs, more gigs, recording sessions and countless media appearances.

In terms of recording, the band's most memorable session took place on 11 February. On this day the band recorded ten songs, four of them originals ('I Saw Her Standing There', 'Misery', 'Do You Want To Know A Secret?', 'There's A Place') and six covers ('Anna', 'Chains', 'Boys', 'A Taste Of Honey', 'Baby It's You' and 'Twist And Shout'). The latter was recorded at ten at night. Lennon's throat, ravaged by the day's exertions, squeezed out a raw vocal that would echo down the years. The next day the band played two gigs, one in Sheffield, one in Oldham.

GIRLS SCREAMED UNCONTROLLABLY, RUSHED THE STAGE, FAINTED, FOUGHT BOUNCERS AND EACH OTHER INSIDE THE VENUE, AND FOUGHT POLICEMEN OUTSIDE

Amid all this playing and recording, the band did not refuse one media request; they could not afford to be choosy. In 1963 British television consisted of two channels – the BBC and ITV – and they spared little time for pop music. Meanwhile radio rarely played pop music and the newspapers seldom wrote about it. Compared with today's vast media outpouring, exposure was highly limited. For the word to be spread far and wide the band had to breach these walls and they did so with a charm and freshness that all found highly contagious.

McCARTNEY WAS SO SAVVY WITH THE PRESS THAT AFTER HIS FIRST TV INTERVIEW HIS BROTHER MIKE ASKED WHY HE SOUNDED LIKE HE WAS PUTTING ON HIS LIVERPOOL ACCENT

McCartney was the leader in this field. The band wisely let him do most of the talking. They knew his natural charm and warm approach would win over many friends in the press. McCartney was so savvy with the press that after his first TV interview his brother Mike asked why he sounded like he was putting on his Liverpool accent, not talking in it. McCartney replied, 'I know that, you know that but they don't know that.' McCartney saw that a full Scouse accent had the potential to repel the nation. Liverpool was regarded by many as a rough city, full of unsavoury types. If The Beatles were going to be successful they would have to tone down their links with the city and that included their accents. Indeed it was in this year that the band decamped to London.

Their Cavern fans were distraught. When, in February, Cavern DJ Bob Wooler announced that the band were in the top ten with 'Please Please Me', the crowd went silent, as if at a wake. It was then they began saying goodbye to the band they loved with such a passion. The Beatles now belonged to the whole country.

Their biggest television break came when they were invited to headline Val Parnell's show *Sunday Night At The London Palladium* on 13 October. Prior to the show's start scores of Beatles fans mobbed the entrance to the theatre, screaming for the band. On hand were several journalists and photographers. It was they who coined the term 'Beatlemania', which was splashed all over the next day's papers. The show was watched by 15 million people.

As for live work, the band undertook three UK tours. On two of them they started off as support, to Helen Shapiro and Roy Orbison respectively, and by the end of both of jaunts they were the headliners. It was now that Brian Epstein started informing promoters that the band would only play theatres. The ballrooms and clubs they had been booked into were not equipped to withstand the crowd's frenzied reaction to the band, a response that placed the four of them in acute physical danger. Girls screamed uncontrollably, rushed the stage, fainted, fought each other, fought the bouncers inside the venue, fought the policemen outside.

IT HAD BEEN AN AMAZING YEAR AND IT WAS GOING TO GET EVEN BETTER. FOR BEATLEMANIA WAS ABOUT TO GO WORLDWIDE

By the end of the year the band that had performed gruelling seven-hour sets in Hamburg were now playing half-hour concerts, if that, to a barrage of female screams. This would be the nature of their concerts for the next three years.

Remarkably, the demands on the band seemed only to heighten their creativity. They scored their first number one with 'From Me To You' and then broke through all the barriers with the brilliant, 'She Loves You'. The freshness and loudness of the record transfixed the nation. 'She Loves You' turned The Beatles into a national obsession. And that included the Royal Family.

On Monday 4 November the band performed four songs before HRH The Queen Mother and Princess Margaret at The Prince of Wales Theatre in the West End of London. They played their first number one, 'From Me To You', 'She Loves You', 'Till There Was You' and 'Twist And Shout'. Introducing the latter song, Lennon addressed the audience: 'Could the people in the cheaper seats clap your hands? And the rest of you, if you'll just rattle your jewellery.' It was a brilliant quote, a sly dig at class prejudice wrapped up in warm, knowing humour. Even the royals giggled. Once again, The Beatles had used music and humour to vault seemingly impregnable class divisions.

Brian Epstein also laughed but he did so with great relief. When he had asked Lennon backstage what he was going to say to the royalty present, Lennon snapped, 'I'll tell them to rattle their fucking jewellery.' It is mark of the man's open and belligerent character that Epstein fully believed he would make such a statement and in doing so bring the fantastic dream they were in to an abrupt end.

The band finished the year with a two-week Christmas show at Finsbury Park, London, in which they played music, dressed up in costumes and took part in comedy sketches. A hundred thousand tickets were snapped up within three weeks. It had been an amazing year but it was going to get even better. For Beatlemania was about to go worldwide.

Beatlemania focused on the two main songwriters, Paul and John, but all four Beatles had their worshippers and devotees.

MARSHA
ALBERT

writes a letter to her local DJ

DATE December 1963, Washington D.C.

In December 1963, a 15-year-old American teenager named Marsha Albert wrote a letter to a man named Carroll James. James was a big shot around town. He was a DJ in Washington, D.C. shouting it out for a station named WWDC, and Marsha desperately wanted him to play a record by an unknown band called The Beatles. The song was called 'I Want To Hold Your Hand'.

Marsha had first seen the band on television. In November, CBS News and *The Jack Parr Show* had filmed the band live in Britain and screened the footage back in the States. Parr showed the material not because he believed he had unearthed a worldwide phenomenon. He screened it because he thought it was 'funny'. This would be the general reaction of America to The Beatles for the next month or so. Funny. Wacky.

Marsha was different from Parr. She was absolutely entranced by the band, so much so that she decided to spread the word. Carroll James was her first target. 'I wrote that I thought they would be really popular here,' she later recalled, 'and if he [James] could get one of their records, that would really be great.'

How right she was and credit to James for he went out that week and secured an import copy of the track. He then invited Albert into the studio to announce it before he played it. 'Carroll James called me up the day he got the record and said, "If you can get down here by five o'clock, we'll let you introduce it",' Albert recalled. She made the trip and at five o'clock that afternoon leaned into the microphone and announced The Beatles on air for the very first time in the continent that in just two months' time – incredibly – would belong to them. She said, 'Ladies and gentlemen, for the first time on the air in the United States, here are The Beatles singing "I Want To Hold Your Hand".'

AT THE SONG'S END, CARROLL ASKED HIS LISTENERS TO PHONE IN WITH THEIR OPINIONS. THE RESPONSE WAS BEYOND ANY EXPECTATIONS. HUNDREDS HIT THE PHONES

At the song's end Carroll asked his listeners to phone in with their opinions. The response was beyond any expectations. Hundreds hit the phones, most of them expressing their favour. The station manger was not stupid and the record was quickly put into heavy rotation. It was the first break The Beatles had enjoyed in America even though at this point they had no idea what was going on. All they knew was that up to this point America had been treating them very poorly.

BEATLE WIGS WERE MADE AND SENT TO RECORD SHOPS. DISTRIBUTORS WERE URGED TO WEAR THEM. MEANWHILE, STICKERS PROCLAIMING 'THE BEATLES ARE COMING' SUDDENLY APPEARED ALL OVER NEW YORK

The American label's view of them was symptomatic of the country's apathy with regard to The Beatles. Capitol records, the American branch of EMI, had refused point blank to release the band's first few singles, opting instead to license the songs to smaller labels. 'Please Please Me' and 'From Me To You' went to Vee Jay Records in Chicago while 'She Loves You' ended up on the Swan label. (For R&B enthusiasts such as The Beatles, there was kudos in this arrangement – Vee Jay had released records by John Lee Hooker and Jimmy Reed; Swan had Eddie Bo.)

Epstein knew that if they were to make any serious inroads into the American market this state of affairs would have to change. He would have to win Capitol over. He decided to use his trump card – Beatlemania. In November a determined Epstein flew to the States and met with Bob Precht, a producer on *The Ed Sullivan Show*, one of the highest-rating shows on American TV. They met in a New York and Precht quickly voiced the current thinking on Epstein's beloved 'boys'. They were a novelty act, right, so kind of interesting ...

Epstein adjusted his tie and set to work on Precht. *The Ed Sullivan Show's* representative in London had first alerted his bosses to Beatlemania. Epstein gave Precht an even more detailed picture of the hysteria that had gripped Britain. Precht listened. By the end of that meeting The Beatles had been promised three headlining slots on the show to take place over consecutive weeks. Three slots, not one. Those who argue that Epstein was never up to managing The Beatles properly, that he was inept and naive, should study this incident.

When Epstein told Capitol Records of his coup, they sat up and started to change their thinking. Meetings were held, decisions in the band's favour now made. Capitol agreed to a January release of

'I Want To Hold Your Hand' and promised to put US$50,000 into a marketing campaign. Beatle wigs were made and sent to record shops. Distributors were urged to wear them. Meanwhile, stickers proclaiming 'The Beatles Are Coming' suddenly appeared all over New York.

ON BOXING DAY 1963 CAPITOL RECORDS RELEASED 'I WANT TO HOLD YOUR HAND'. ASTONISHINGLY, IT SOLD A QUARTER OF A MILLION COPIES IN ITS FIRST THREE DAYS

On Boxing Day 1963 Capitol Records released 'I Want To Hold Your Hand'. Astonishingly, it sold a quarter of a million copies in its first three days. The demand was so great that Capitol contracted the job of printing more copies to rival companies. By mid-January 1964 the song was shooting up the charts and on 1 February, six days before their arrival in a country they had not played one note in, The Beatles had their first US number one. Meanwhile Vee Jay and Swan started pushing their Beatles singles. 'I Want To Hold Your Hand', which would sell over five million copies, was replaced at the top by 'She Loves You'. Only Elvis before them had managed to knock himself of the top spot with one of his own songs.

Lennon was astonished. 'No one has a hit in America,' he told friends. The band was in Paris at the time, starting a two-week residency at the Olympia Theatre. It had not been the best of times. An early Paris gig was ruined by equipment problems and their audience, which interestingly seemed to contain more boys than girls, were far less vociferous than their UK counterparts. (In fact, on their return to Britain, to show their relief to be home, George Harrison stepped off the plane in London waving a Union Jack flag.)

Any pains Paris caused The Beatles were quickly dissolved when they returned to their hotel to discover that America had just adopted them wholesale. Later on in their hotel room, a photographer suggested that the band stage a pillow fight for the cameras. 'That is the most stupid thing I have ever heard,' Lennon snapped at him. A minute later he picked up a pillow and threw it at Paul, as capricious as ever.

As for Marsha she got to meet the band on 11 February when Carroll James brought her along to his interview with them. 'Hello Marsha,' Paul said. 'Good old Marsha,' John shouted and then George pleasantly called her, 'Marsha Mellow'. Perhaps the most pertinent comment came from Ringo. He simply said, 'Thank you, Marsha.'

The Beatles perform to
70 MILLION
Americans

DATE 9 February 1964, 53rd Street, New York

Pandemonium, it was absolute pandemonium. Pandemonium at the airport, pandemonium at the press conference, pandemonium at the hotel and then later on at the gig – complete craziness. The Beatles arrived at JFK Airport on 7 February 1964 and so loud were the screams that fired out from the waiting fans, onlookers reported that they literally drowned out the noise of the landing plane.

Thousands of young Americans, a fair number of them boys, screamed and yearned and waved banners welcoming the band to their country. The Beatles emerged to a sight that was now de rigueur for them at airports, the sight of the young baying for their approval and attention. The band waved and smiled and smiled and waved and smiled again, and did so until they found themselves inside a room facing their very first US press conference.

The knives had already been drawn. The journalists arrayed in front of them were not Beatles fans in the slightest. They were hardened and cynical and having experienced the Capitol Records campaign, heard the music and viewed pictures of the four long-haired musicians, they believed The Beatles were all hype, a bubble they were eager to burst. Only things didn't go quite as they planned. The Beatles were now a seasoned media machine. They knew the drill by heart, knew that smart one-liners and jokey asides would always play to the gallery. The Americans were totally unprepared for such banter. The people they interviewed at such events – musicians, film stars and so on – always went through the motions. Glad to be here, lovely to see you, hello to my fans, blah-di-blah, yawn, yawn, yawn.

The Beatles – as you would expect of course – were something else completely.

THE JOURNALISTS ARRAYED IN FRONT OF THEM WERE NOT BEATLES FANS IN THE SLIGHTEST. THEY WERE HARDENED AND CYNICAL. THEY BELIEVED THE BEATLES WERE ALL HYPE, A BUBBLE THEY WERE EAGER TO BURST

The Beatles and Ed Sullivan take a break from rehearsals for the show. The band got on well with Sullivan who would introduce them at their groundbreaking Shea Stadium concert in 1965.

'What do you think of Beethoven?' *Ringo*: 'Great. Especially his poems.'

'A psychiatrist recently said you're nothing but a bunch of British Elvis Presleys.' *John*: 'He must be blind.'

'In Detroit Michigan, they're handing out car stickers saying, "Stamp Out The Beatles".' *Paul*: 'Yeah? Well first of all we're bringing out a "Stamp Out Detroit Campaign".' Much laughter – only the others knew that Paul had used the exact same joke during their last British TV interview, conducted just after the sojourn in France.

From the press conference, with a documentary film crew headed by the Maysles brothers in tow, The Beatles were herded into big car that swept them to The Plaza Hotel. Awaiting them was a very nervous staff. The Plaza was an upper-class establishment that had prided itself for years on its wealthy clientele and its discreet, polite aura. The hotel had accepted the booking believing The Beatles to be businessmen. When they realized their mistake, so panicked were they that one of their executives went on the radio and offered the band to any hotel that wanted them. There were no takers.

The band settled into their suite and watched the TV coverage of themselves (except for George, who felt 'flu-like and so took to his bed). With the remaining Beatles were numerous photographers and anxious hotel staff. One cameraman asked John to lie on the bed so he could photograph his Beatle boots. 'Oh no, please don't do that at The Plaza,' cried an employee. 'It's all right,' said John, 'we'll buy the bed.' Arrogance was now starting to surface.

Meanwhile downstairs the violinist in the foyer refused to play Beatles songs. It was not the proper instrument for such music, he explained with disdain. Outside the hotel, hundreds of young girls waited and waited, screaming every time they saw a shadow cross a window, all the time singing, 'Yeah, yeah, yeah ...' At one point in their vigil, they mobbed a policeman because he had touched a Beatle. Many thought the world had started to go crazy.

The next day, after visiting Central Park, the band (minus George) asked if they could see Harlem. No doubt they would have been shown the Apollo Theatre where so many of their musical heroes had performed. In fact, the band displayed top Mod instincts and spent a lot of their time in New York ringing up radio stations and asking them to play their favourite Motown and R&B songs.

THE PLAZA HAD ACCEPTED THE BOOKING BELIEVING THE BEATLES TO BE BUSINESSMEN. WHEN THEY REALIZED THEIR MISTAKE, ONE OF THEIR EXECUTIVES WENT ON THE RADIO AND OFFERED THE BAND TO ANY HOTEL THAT WANTED THEM. THERE WERE NO TAKERS

After Harlem, work began and they rehearsed for *The Ed Sullivan Show* at the CBS studio on 53rd Street, Neil Aspinall standing in for George. George appeared later on and after rehearsals, the band went and ate, preparing themselves for the big day. That night three Beatles watched television and Paul slunk off to The Playboy Club. The next night he took his mates there. By then they had another first under their belts. An estimated 73 million people had watched the band perform five songs: 'All My Loving', 'Till There Was You', 'She Loves You' in the show's first half, and 'I Saw Her Standing There' and 'I Want To Hold Your Hand' in the second.

Seventy-three million people had been interested in a band that had not played a note of music in their country, a band that two months before had been complete unknowns and whose look and style was anathema to many. Quite incredible. From now on The Beatles had America in their hands. No wonder they would now feel so powerful, so invincible.

SEVENTY-THREE MILLION PEOPLE HAD BEEN INTERESTED IN A BAND THAT HAD NOT PLAYED A NOTE OF MUSIC IN THEIR COUNTRY, THAT TWO MONTHS BEFORE HAD BEEN COMPLETE UNKNOWNS

The next day the band awoke to good and bad reviews for their TV work. *The Daily News* said that Presley was 'but a lukewarm dandelion compared to the 100 per cent elixir served by The Beatles'. *The New York Herald* disagreed: '75 per cent publicity, 20 per cent haircut, and 5 per cent lilting lament', was its analysis.

That day the band met several journalists. Again, they showcased their sharp minds and their witty comebacks.

'What is a bigger threat to your careers – the H Bomb or the dandruff?' *Ringo*: 'The H Bomb – we have already got dandruff.'

'Do you have a leading lady for your film?' *George*: 'We are trying to get the Queen. She sells.'

On Tuesday 11 February The Beatles played their debut American concert at the Washington Coliseum. The band was forced to play on a revolving stage. After every number the band turned 180 degrees. Over 8,000 fans screamed and cried and wailed. They threw sweets on the stage and their minds in the air. Again, one word: pandemonium.

After the show the band attended a party thrown in their honour at the British Embassy. The night was a complete disaster. The band was treated abysmally by people who really should have known better. One lady guest approached Lennon and said, 'Look, sign this for my daughter! Can't think why she likes you! Must be out of her mind.' And that was not a one-off. Lennon later – and rightly – snarled, 'These people are worse than the fans. These people have no bloody manners.' Not long after he said those words, a guest went up to Ringo from behind and cut off a lock of his hair. As they left the Ambassador apologized for his guests' behaviour. 'Which one are you again?' one of the band asked.

Back in New York the band played two shows at the prestigious Carnegie Hall – again there was utter chaos. It was promoted by Sid Bernstein and several stars showed up, but could not access tickets. The Governor of New York's wife arrived at the last minute with her daughter, demanded both entry and Beatles merchandise. Again, Lennon raged at the impertinence on display.

The band played two half-hour shows and the next day flew to Miami to rehearse for their second appearance on *The Ed Sullivan Show*. While there, a publicity stunt was devised and they were taken to meet the up-and-coming boxer Muhammad Ali, then known as Cassius Clay. Clay was training to fight Sonny Liston and had no idea who these four skinny Brits were. Still, he figured if all the cameras were there, something was going on, so he joked around with The Beatles – whoever they were – then stripped down to his shorts, put on his gloves and pretended to take all four on for the pressmen. As they walked out of the gym, Lennon said quietly, 'but he'll never beat Liston,' a commonly held view that Clay smashed to bits on 25 February that year.

On Sunday 16 February the band played six songs live from the Deauville Hotel in Miami for *The Ed Sullivan Show*. They were all Beatles originals – 'She Loves You', 'This Boy', 'All My Loving', 'I Saw Her Standing There', 'From Me To You' and 'I Want To Hold Your Hand'. Estimates of the watching TV audience were again around 70 million.

The band stayed in Miami and swam and sunbathed, chased the girls and fell totally in love with super-modern America.

Compared with Britain with its tight laws, grey buildings and stuck-up authorities, America was colourful and fun and everything a young Beatle could hope for.

COMPARED WITH BRITAIN WITH ITS TIGHT LAWS, GREY BUILDINGS AND STUCK-UP AUTHORITIES, AMERICA WAS COLOURFUL AND FUN, EVERYTHING A YOUNG BEATLE COULD HOPE FOR

Ringo summed up their feelings in the *The Beatles Anthology* book (2000). He recalled how the band had got used to big crowds and to landing at airports where thousands of screaming fans awaited them – but America operated on a much larger scale and the fans proved far more enthusiastic than anything they had experienced previously. For The Beatles who had to constantly fend off questions about their talent and how long they would stay at the top, America's congratulations meant a hell of a lot. Ringo recalled the ride from the airport, especially the fans who lined the route. 'They were all outside and there's barriers and horses and cops all over the place … with the four of us sitting in the car giggling. I'll speak for everybody – we couldn't believe it!'

The band's first American live gig took place at the Washington Coliseum on 11 February 1964 and was marked by absolute chaos.

The Beatles make their debut film

A HARD
DAY'S NIGHT

DATE March–April 1964, UK

Yet another first – The Beatles' debut feature film *A Hard Day's Night* was the first film ever to go into profit before it had even been released. That was the kind of power the band was now operating on, a power never before bestowed on four musicians. They were a sensation, a phenomenon that no one could get a grip on. Whatever they wanted they were given. Whatever they touched turned into magic. Wherever they went, the whole world went with them.

Every day, multitudes of fans, media and police fought around them, pushing and shoving and shouting, and at the centre of it all, always the smiling, laughing, joking Beatles. 'Beatlemania was beyond comprehension,' Lennon would later reflect and he was spot on.

The first film the band was offered came from London. The film was called *The Yellow Teddy Bears*. The plot revolved around a girls' school – where yellow teddy-bear badges were worn to denote promiscuity – and a well-meaning teacher. The band was initially interested. Cinema was something they had grown up with, an avenue they were very keen to follow. It gave them options. As Lennon would later tell biographer, Ray Coleman, 'At least cinema allows you to grow up.'

Once the deal was put on the table, however, the band grimaced. The producers wanted the band to turn up in a couple of scenes and perform some songs, which they would take the copyright on. The Beatles walked away. They felt strongly that although a record might last a month, a film lived forever. Ever conscious of their image, the band agreed that the film they signed up to would have to be something very special to warrant their involvement.

Enter *The Goon Show*. In 1959 Peter Sellers was looking for a way to transfer *The Goon Show* from radio to TV. He needed

CINEMA WAS SOMETHING THEY HAD GROWN UP WITH, AN AVENUE THEY WERE VERY KEEN TO FOLLOW. IT GAVE THEM OPTIONS

a director who understood surrealist humour and visuals. One night he watched *The Dick Lester Show*, an ad-libbed show (featuring among others the Liverpool writer Alun Owen) that sought to replicate Goon-like humour on television. Sellers contacted the show's director, a 23-year-old man named Dick Lester.

Using the 16mm movie camera Sellers had just acquired, plus a field in

The band's first film premiere for *A Hard Day's Night*, which took place at the Pavilion Theatre in London on 6 July 1964.

north London and a cast including Spike Milligan and Graham Stark, they made an 11-minute film they named *The Running, Jumping And Standing Still Film* (1960). Lester not only directed it but also wrote the music. The footage was for private use but was seen by a TV critic who insisted they enter the piece in the Edinburgh Festival. This they did and the film was eventually given a British cinematic release.

Lester was then employed to direct a film called *It's Trad, Dad!* (1962). The film – a musical comedy – had been rushed into production to cash in on the trad-jazz trend that was pervading the UK pop charts. Musicians employed in the film included Chubby Checker, Helen Shapiro, Gene Vincent, Chris Barber and Acker Bilk.

The Beatles saw both of Lester's films but it was the *Running* piece that really caught their attention. 'We discussed this [a film idea] with Brian on a number of occasions and he asked if we had any ideas of our own,' Paul McCartney recalled. 'The only person we could think of was whoever had made the *Running Standing* film because that was brilliant.'

Lester was a child prodigy, capable of reading and writing up to 250 words by the time he was two. He entered university at age 15 and graduated with a degree in clinical psychology. He went into music and TV, singing in a vocal band and working as a floor manager for CBS.

He moved to London and landed the job directing ATV's jazz show *Downbeat*. He also befriended the writer Alun Owen who featured in *The Dick Lester Show*.

It was Owen he turned to for a script, but only after Johnny Speight, later creator of the classic TV series *Till Death Us Do Part*, had turned him down. Owen, who described himself as 'a Bohemian with working-class roots', was perfect; he was from Liverpool and his last big TV hit, *No Trams To Lime Street* (1959), had been set in his home town.

THEY STRONGLY FELT THAT A FILM LIVED FOREVER. EVER CONSCIOUS OF THEIR IMAGE, THE BAND AGREED THAT THE FILM THEY SIGNED UP TO WOULD HAVE TO BE SOMETHING VERY SPECIAL

The band had seen the play and asked Owen to join them on tour, to observe their characters and capture their unique language. This Owen did although he only stayed a short while with the band. In fact he wrote the script in about a month, a very short time for such an endeavour.

Filming had now been set for March, hence the urgency. Meanwhile the band went into the studio on George's 21st birthday and over four days recorded seven songs plus a cover of Little Richard's 'Long Tall Sally'. This was a band that thrived on pressure, pressure that came unrelentingly from all angles. Yet despite this weight of huge expectation, Lennon and McCartney's songwriting improved immeasurably.

One only has to hear John's 'If I Fell' and 'You Can't Do That' and Paul's 'And I Love Her' and 'Things We Said Today' to see the progression. That such creativity should be reached amid the chaos of Beatlemania is quite astonishing. Success, they both later said, was spurring them on to greater things. When Dick Lester informed Lennon and McCartney that the film was to be named after one of Ringo's slips of the tongue (after working day and night in the studio once, Ringo remarked it had been a hard day's night) he asked them to write a song around that title.

Lester figured the task would take the men a week at least. The next day the pair handed over the song, 'A Hard Day's Night'. And it was superb. It was this ability to work so brilliantly under huge pressure that sustained the band's position as number one for so many years.

Filming started on 2 March and ended on 24 April. In the first set of days, filming took place on a train to the West Country. Other locations included Twickenham Film Studios and the Scala Theatre in London. The film was an attempt to capture the band experiencing the phenomenon of Beatlemania while displaying their individual characters.

It was a cinematic trend that began with the Neo-Realist movement in Italy and was realized in Britain later on by directors such as Karel Reisz (*Saturday Night And Sunday Morning*, 1960) and Lindsay Anderson (*This Sporting Life*, 1963). The

> TO BEGIN A FILM IN MARCH AND HAVE IT READY FOR TRANSMISSION BY JULY IS AN INCREDIBLE FEAT – BUT NOT PECULIAR IN BEATLE LAND WHERE MAGICAL EVENTS SEEM TO HAPPEN AS A MATTER OF COURSE

Beatles were keen to tread a similar artistic path. They were sharply aware that pop music films up until that point had been highly risible productions and they wanted no part in following that tradition. Their artistic self-respect, another quality that served to sustain their success, would not allow it. Lennon would later state, 'Never mind all our pals, how could we have faced each other if we had allowed ourselves to be involved in that kind of movie?'

Lester and the band worked well together. The director was sensitive to the band's vision and was keen to incorporate their natural spontaneity as comedians wherever possible. Accordingly the band ad-libbed in many scenes although the need to shoot from different angles did serve to rob a lot of the immediacy. 'The director knew we couldn't act,' Lennon later said. 'So he had to try and catch us almost off-guard, only you can't do that in a film, you've got to repeat things over and over. But he did his best. The minutes that are natural stand out like a sore thumb.'

For Ringo, filming was a gas. 'It was incredible for me, the idea that we were making a movie. I loved the movies as a kid. I used to go hell of a lot ... It was a great fantasy land for me.' At one point American executives asked Lester to wipe The Beatles voices and replace them with the voices of American actors. The outraged Lester told them where to get off. So did The Beatles.

As the filming drew to a close, the soundtrack was now prepared. United Artists, who would release the album in the US, printed up half a million copies of the LP. On Thursday 25 June they handed over a copy to a prominent New York radio station to preview. Such was the audience's positive reaction to this batch of new Beatles songs, by Monday advance orders had soared to a million copies. Incredibly, a week later they stood at two million. Cinemas in America, Britain and Europe meanwhile ordered over 1,700 prints. The public was yet to see the film but already it was in profit.

The film was edited and put together at breakneck speed. To begin a film in March and have it ready for transmission by July is an incredible feat – but not peculiar in Beatle Land where magical events seem to happen as a matter of course. The band attended two major film premieres to promote it, one on 6 July in London and one on 10 July in their home town of Liverpool.

The band were deeply nervous about going home. Since their move from Liverpool, nasty whispers and rumours had followed them to London – how everyone hated them, how they were traitors, Judases who should have stayed at The Cavern. Knowing Liverpudlians, the band expected in tiny part some public anger to be directed their way as soon as they hit home soil.

No such thing. The nervous Beatles, who landed at Speke Airport (today known as Liverpool John Lennon Airport) then clambered into the obligatory huge limousines, were completely astounded to be greeted by 200,000 cheering Scousers. It was the best homecoming ever. 'After this, nothing matters,' Harrison enthused as he looked out over the sea of people. 'This is the ultimate.'

The band run down a Notting Hill alleyway while filming *A Hard Day's Night*. Britain had not yet fully recovered from the ravages of World War II and the band's exuberance often contrasted with their dilapilated surroundings.

The Beatles meet

BOB DYLAN

DATE 28 August 1964, The Delmonico Hotel, New York

It was not just the fans who wanted to get as close as possible to the creators of Beatlemania. The rich and famous were just as eager to rub shoulders with these long-haired magicians from Liverpool. Lennon raged against most of them. He had no interest whatsoever in meeting middle-aged crooners, the Hollywood film establishment or the super wealthy. In normal circumstances, such people would not give him a moment's attention; why should he now be pally with them just because he was in The Beatles?

Lennon particularly detested those who pulled rank to get near him. While true fans were left waiting hours in awful conditions just to get a glimpse of their heroes, the band were forced to smile and pose with the children of the privileged. 'It was always the chief's daughter or the Lord Mayor's daughter; all the most obnoxious kids, because they had the most obnoxious parents,' Lennon recalled. 'We had these people thrust on us and were forced to see them all the time. Those were the most humiliating experiences.'

Lennon was only interested in meeting either those who had heavily impacted on his consciousness – Elvis was number one on that list, followed by the likes of Ray Charles and several Motown and R&B acts – or the very hip, and Bob Dylan fitted that category perfectly.

Although Paul McCartney had heard bits of Dylan, it was not until the band went to Paris that he and the others really engaged with Dylan's work. At a radio interview, a kindly French DJ slipped them a copy of the album *The Freewheelin' Bob Dylan*. 'I think that was the first time I ever heard Dylan at all.' Lennon later recalled.

ALTHOUGH DYLAN'S BEATNIK CROWD CYNICALLY VIEWED THE BAND AS 'BUBBLEGUM', DYLAN WENT THE OPPOSITE WAY. HE CALLED THEIR CHORD CHANGES 'OUTRAGEOUS'

'We were doing a radio thing there and the guy had the record in the studio ... we took it back to the hotel. And for the rest of our three weeks in Paris we didn't stop playing it. We all went potty on Dylan.'

BUDDING ADDICT THAT HE WAS, RINGO SMOKED THE JOINT ALL BY HIMSELF. HE HAD NO IDEA OF THE ETIQUETTE THAT THE JOINT SHOULD BE PASSED ROUND

The man who arranged the meeting was writer Al Aronowitz. His piece covering The Beatles' arrival in America for the *Saturday Evening Post* was liked by the band for its perceptive and serious approach. Al had also visited Liverpool and spent time with John. He enthused to him about the power of marijuana. 'To me,' Al would later write, 'marijuana was a wonder drug ... As Aldous Huxley had taught me, pot opened The Doors of Perception.'

At the time Aronowitz was hanging out a lot with Dylan so was able to bring the two parties together. For his part, Dylan was a fan of the band. On tour earlier that year he had heard The Beatles on the radio and was immediately taken by their clever musicality. Although Dylan's Beatnik crowd cynically viewed the band as 'bubblegum', Dylan went the opposite way. He called their chord changes 'outrageous'.

When he arrived at their suite, the band – with Brian Epstein and Mal Evans also present – welcomed him and asked what he wanted to drink. Dylan asked for wine. Mal Evans was sent out to procure some. As they waited, the band told Dylan they had speed pills if he wanted some. Dylan suggested they have a smoke instead. At first, the band was puzzled and then realization dawned. Sheepishly, they looked around the room until Epstein confessed they had never smoked marijuana before. This was not quite true. After a gig in Southport, the band had tried the drug and then spent the night twisting the night away, wondering when it was going to work. The next day they forgot all about it. At that point they were strict whisky-and-pills men.

When told they were not smokers, Dylan looked puzzled. 'But what about your song?' he asked, 'The one about getting high?' More confusion and then understanding. Dylan had misheard the line, 'I can't hide' in their song, 'I Want To Hold Your Hand'. John explained this then added that if Bob wanted to roll a joint it was fine by him.

It was a dangerous undertaking. Smoking marijuana could land you a hefty prison sentence. The world stood outside their hotel room, including many policemen. To that end, wet towels were placed at the foot of doors and the party moved into a second room, away from the corridor. Dylan rolled the first joint and passed it to Lennon who instantly passed it to Ringo, 'his royal taster', which tells us a lot about the hierarchy at work.

Budding addict that he was – Starr would join Alcoholics Anonymous in later life – Ringo smoked the joint all by himself. He had no idea of the etiquette that the joint should be passed round. More joints were rolled and the drug quickly got to work. As with many first-time smokers, The Beatles got a case of the giggles. Epstein kept saying he was as high as a ceiling, the others roared with laughter. Dylan kept answering the room phone and shouting, 'This is Beatlemania!' much to the band's enjoyment. The party went on into the early hours and then Dylan split.

Both parties would maintain a healthy respect for each other. Dylan never saw the band as a threat to his progress. Both were playing to different audiences. Certainly, Dylan's fans were older, far hipper, far more socially aware than those of The Fabs. For The Beatles the effect of Dylan and dope on them was enormous. They soon became heavy marijuana smokers, starting their day off with a joint and carrying on until oblivion. They made their second film, *Help!*, while high most of the time. Marijuana helped kill the boredom they were starting to feel.

Artistically, the biggest effect was on Lennon. He now began to use Dylan's music as a springboard for some of his own compositions. The most obvious song in this respect was 'You've Got To Hide Your Love Away' and later 'Norwegian Wood', both compositions with distinct Dylan-esque melodies. Dylan himself responded with his song '4th Time Around' on the *Blonde On Blonde* album.

THE EFFECT OF DYLAN AND DOPE ON THEM WAS ENORMOUS. THEY SOON BECAME HEAVY MARIJUANA SMOKERS, STARTING THEIR DAY OFF WITH A JOINT

Dylan's lyrical talents and his persona also proved inspirational to Lennon. Dylan hailed from America's folk traditions and did not write to order in the way John and Paul did on occasions. Rather, he used words to express political and personal views. This approach rubbed off on John. He now started veering away from the boy-meets-girl approach that had brought him so much success and began creating more introspective songs such as 'Baby's In Black', 'Help!' and 'In My Life'. Naturally, Lennon admitted to the Dylan influence but could not help adding, 'But I am sure he took a lot from us!'

John and George experiment with

LSD

DATE April 1965, Strathearn Place, London

They sipped at their coffee and suddenly the room expanded. Cynthia Lennon peered and realized that George Harrison and his girlfriend Pattie Boyd were now specks on the horizon. Incredible. A minute ago they were sitting right in front of her. She took a deep breath and wondered what the hell was going on. Meanwhile, John, who was sitting beside her, seemed absolutely lost, and the dentist's girlfriend Cindy started shouting 'The Bismarck is sinking!' LSD had just entered Beatle Land and everything would be changed forever.

The man responsible was a man of teeth. John Riley was a dentist who operated out of Harley Street and had many high-profile clients, including George Harrison. Riley was in his mid-30s, a charismatic man, hip to the trip with a glamorous girlfriend, Cindy Bury. Riley and George had bonded and become good friends. George invited Riley out to the Bahamas when the band were filming their second film, *Help!*

In April 1965 a dinner date was arranged and George and John along with partners, Cynthia and Pattie, showed up at his flat on Strathearn Place. The conversation that night centered on the arrival in London of a super-drug named LSD (acid). For Harrison this was the first time he had heard of the drug. That state of ignorance would not last long. After dinner, Riley slipped LSD into their coffees.

As the drug worked its strange hallucinatory powers, the two Beatles and their wives suddenly felt the urge to get out of the house. Riley tried to stop them. He confessed to putting the drug in their drinks. His actions were misunderstood. The girls became convinced that he wanted an orgy to take place. This heightened their sense of panic and they rushed out to George's nearby car and drove off to The Pickwick Club where the trio Paddy,

GEORGE NOW STARTED TO FEEL THE BENEFITS OF THE DRUG. HE WANTED TO TELL THE WORLD HE LOVED EVERYTHING AND EVERYONE IN IT

Klaus & Gibson was performing. Then they moved on to The Ad Lib Club. To access the club customers had to get into a lift and ride up four floors. As they ascended a red light came on and all four instantly thought the lift had caught fire. They stumbled into The Ad Lib screaming.

Somehow they managed to settle themselves at a table. A fellow pop star (unnamed) sat next to Lennon. 'Mind if I sit here?,' he asked the Chief Beatle. 'Only if you don't talk to me,' Lennon growled. Then the dentist appeared. He had followed them to the club. He sat down and instantly turned into a pig.

George now started to feel the benefits of the drug. 'I felt in love,' he recalled. 'Not with anything or anybody in particular, but with everything. Everything was perfect, in a perfect light, and I had an overwhelming desire to go round the club telling everybody how much I loved them – people I had never seen before.' This was some experience for a man believed to be the band's drollest character. George carried little of John's charisma, Paul's optimism or Ringo's likeable persona. But now he wanted to tell the world he loved everything and everyone in it.

The four left the club, got into George's car and drove at about ten miles per hour back to George's Surrey residence. Cynthia climbed into bed, still tripping and very fearful she would never regain her sanity. George and Pattie left John downstairs drawing on bits of paper, convinced that George's house was a submarine and it was his job as captain to guide the party through rough waters (even in this distorted state, John saw himself as the leader). The colour of the submarine, incidentally, was yellow.

LSD CAST ASIDE ALL PREJUDICE. FOR THE SHARP-TONGUED, DOMINEERING LENNON, THIS WAS A REVELATION. LSD PUT LENNON ON A COMPLETELY NEW PATH

Four months would pass before John and George took the drug again, during their 1965 American tour at a huge Hollywood house that had been rented for them. Ringo ingested it as well. Paul didn't. He was far too concerned about the long-term effects of the drug. Marijuana he loved; LSD was something else. He would let the others travel into the unknown. Paul often likened his relationship to John to two men standing on the edge of a cliff. John would always throw himself off and then report back to Paul on his experience. So it was with LSD.

The band The Byrds were there and so was the actor, Peter Fonda. As a child Fonda had experienced serious illness.

Twice his heart had given out, only for it to be revived. As everyone tripped, Fonda kept approaching Lennon, telling him, 'I know what it is like to be dead.' Lennon, who was revelling in the sun, the scene and the models in front of him, kept moving away, only for Fonda to follow him and repeat, 'I know what it is like to be dead.' John would use that line for his composition 'She Said She Said' on the band's *Revolver* album, a work that, in its use of sounds and images, reflected the band's consumption of the drug.

LSD TOOK THE BAND AWAY FROM THE SCREAMING GIRLS AND INTO THE HEART OF LONDON'S UNDERGROUND CULTURE

Yet this was not the band's first LSD-inspired song. That honour goes to a Lennon song, called 'The Word', placed on the band's sixth album, *Rubber Soul*. Although at the time it was assumed to be a love song, it was no such thing. Many advocates of LSD experienced deep ecstatic emotions. George wanting to say 'I love you' to everyone in The Ad Lib Club the first time he took LSD is typical of its effect. LSD cast aside all prejudice, and for the sharp-tongued, domineering Lennon, this was a revelation. LSD put Lennon on a

completely new path. 'The Word' therefore celebrated the deep feelings of love that he was experiencing.

For three years John took LSD on a regular basis and it helped shape his songwriting. LSD took The Beatles out of Beatlemania and turned them into a completely different band. It changed their music, their outlook, their lives, their clothes. LSD coupled with their uncontrollable impulse to move forward artistically took the band away from the screaming girls and into the heart of London's underground culture. Soon the band's mission was to spread the word ...

The first song John wrote after his first LSD experience was 'Help!'. After LSD, he rarely wrote the kind of love songs that had brought him a huge fortune, opting instead either to examine himself and his past – such as 'In My Life' and 'Nowhere Man' – or to return to his Beatnik impulses and begin writing in a much more fragmented way where the images did all the work – such as 'Strawberry Fields Forever' and 'I Am The Walrus'. It was a remarkable transformation.

The Beatles did something no other band had done: they managed to reinvent themselves and maintain their position as the world's number-one band. And as for McCartney his experiences on acid led The Beatles somewhere rather unexpected.

The Beatles play their
BIGGEST EVER
CONCERT

DATE 15 August 1965, Shea Stadium, New York

WE LUV YOU BEATLES

'**N**ow ladies and gentlemen, honoured by their country, decorated by their Queen, they love being in America ... here are The Beatles.' Thus Ed Sullivan introduced the band at their landmark Shea Stadium show. Over 55,000 people attended and a staggering US$304,000 was taken in ticket sales. It still remains one of the largest concerts ever staged, an audacious undertaking that solidified the band's all-conquering status and began their eventual downfall.

The stadium was home to New York's baseball and football teams, the Mets and the Jets, and had never been used for a concert before. No football stadium had – another first for the band. The Beatles' promoter in America, Sid Bernstein, knew that the band could fill such a giant space. When he approached Epstein with the idea, The Beatles' manager said he would need a deposit of at least US$50,000. Bernstein did not have that kind of money but he did have nous. He placed an advert in a New York newspaper in January 1965 asking for ticket money up-front. By doing so, he hoped to raise the deposit. Instead, when he went to open his mail a month later US$100,000 was waiting for him, double the amount required. He set to work immediately.

The support acts that night included Brenda Holloway And The King Curtis Band, and NEMS artists Sounds Incorporated. The band never got to see either act. Instead, they clambered into a helicopter and were taken to a location near the stadium. Then an armoured Wells Fargo Bank truck full of policemen took them to the stadium. Along the way, the police in attendance kindly gave the band their badges. These the band pinned on to

VOX HAD ESPECIALLY DESIGNED 100-WATT AMPLIFIERS FOR THE BAND TO PLAY SUCH VENUES BUT THEY PROVED INEFFECTIVE. EVERYTHING WAS JUST NOISE AND MAYHEM

their quasi-military beige collarless jackets before rushing on to the stage.

The stage itself was set hundreds of yards away from the fans. This was the furthest the band had ever been from their audience. Ringo later said, '... it was the first time we had played to thousands and thousands of people, and we were the first band to do it, but it was totally against what we had set out to achieve which was to entertain, right there, up close.'

LENNON WAS THE FIRST TO GO. ON THE SONG 'I'M DOWN' HE STARTED PLAYING THE ORGAN WITH HIS ELBOWS, JERRY LEE LEWIS STYLE. HIS FACE CONTORTED MANICALLY

In the dressing room the band had been assaulted by nerves but on stage the butterflies inside seemed to evaporate, especially when their leader started clowning around. John's jokey actions gave the band the licence they needed to relax and enjoy themselves rather than take the show so seriously.

The band opened up with 'Twist and Shout', not only a nod to their rock'n'roll roots, but a song they had made their own to the point that most people thought they had written it. Then it was into 'She's

A Woman', 'I Feel Fine', 'Dizzy Miss Lizzy' and 'Ticket To Ride'. The band now put the spotlight on George and the guitarist sang his composition 'Everybody's Trying To Be My Baby'. After a frantic 'Can't Buy Me Love' and 'Baby's In Black', the spotlight then fell on Ringo who sang the Buck Owens song 'Act Naturally'. The band headed for the finishing line with 'A Hard Day's Night', 'Help!' and 'I'm Down'.

As the band played, the screams, shouts and pleas of 55,000 teenagers rushed at them, the intensity never relenting. Adult onlookers – policemen, roadies, staff – had to place their hands over their ears to deal with it. VOX had especially designed 100-watt amplifiers for the band to play such venues but they proved ineffective. Everything was just noise and mayhem. Meanwhile, fans regularly breached the fence set up between them and tried to get to the band. They never did. The distance was too far, the police too quick.

Lennon was the first to go. On the song 'I'm Down' he started playing the organ with his elbows, Jerry Lee Lewis style. His face contorted manically, sweat poured off him. John screamed obscenities at the crowd. They just screamed back louder. Paul did his normal clean-up job, jovially talking to the fans, who did not hear a word he said. George and Ringo stood there and let it all wash over them. The band played 12 songs and America screamed its approval.

'It was the biggest live show anybody's ever done, they told us,' Lennon recalled. '... up there with the mike, you don't try to work out what it all means, you forget who you are. Once you plug in and the noise starts, you're just a group playing anywhere again ...'

This quote allows us great insight into why the band so willingly undertook such heavy touring schedules. On stage they lost Beatlemania and became musicians. 'I always feel safe on stage,' Lennon later said. 'Even when they break through I just feel as though I am all right when I'm plugged in.' However it was off stage that the madness became dangerous.

George Martin their producer recalled once, 'Wherever they went there were hordes of people trying to get hold of them ... The only peace they got ... was in the hotel room, watching television and hearing the screams outside ... A hell of a life really.'

Shea Stadium contained many firsts but what no one knew at the time was that the band had reached the pinnacle of their success. They would never again play to so many people at one concert and they would never again fill such an arena. Beatlemania would start to wane. They did return the following year to play the stadium again but they were four very different individuals to the men who played that night. Their unstoppable creativity and fascination with drugs would push the band in a completely new

direction. Within two years the screaming would stop – it moved on to The Monkees, America's answer to The Beatles – and the fans would now become the avatars of the new hippy movement.

SHEA STADIUM CONTAINED MANY FIRSTS BUT WHAT NO ONE KNEW AT THE TIME WAS THAT **THE BAND HAD REACHED THE PINNACLE OF THEIR SUCCESS**

On a more prosaic level, concerts such as Shea were a nightmare, and did no one any favours. The fans paid good money to sit in seats and squint at their heroes who were apparently playing music somewhere far in the distance. Meanwhile, the band who wanted to be bigger than Elvis could not hear themselves play. They began looking back to their Cavern days when they could play rock'n'roll all night long to an audience who would lap up every note, and then everybody went home happy. Not any more they didn't.

The Beatles meet
ELVIS PRESLEY

DATE 27 August 1965, Hollywood, Los Angeles

They say that you never forget your first love. For The Beatles that meant one man and one man alone – Elvis Aaron Presley. Presley meant the world to them because he had literally changed their lives. Without Elvis, there would be no Beatles and this remains a fact.

Before he exploded into their orbit, The Beatles were restless and discontent boys who lived in an unfocused, pre-teenage world, and listened to all kinds of styles – music hall, blues, jazz, and country and western. All these influences would eventually feed back into their own compositions and brilliantly separate them from the every other band. But then Elvis arrived from out of nowhere and nothing was ever the same again.

Elvis's music was unlike anything they had heard before. It was raucous, raw and rough and above all it was sexy. Suddenly, the teenagers had a focus, a symbol they could use to bring down forever the unremittingly hostile grey post-war world they had grown up in. And this is what The Beatles did, they changed that world forever. Thanks to Elvis.

For Lennon in particular, Elvis was the special one. Elvis gave John something he had never experienced before – direction. When Lennon saw Elvis large on a cinema screen, the teenage confusion that had been gripping John's brain for years magically cleared. He would become a rock'n'roller. Simple as that. For giving him that knowledge, he would forever be in debt to the man they called The King of Rock'n'Roll.

When The Beatles went global all kinds of stars eagerly queued up to meet them. Most did so out of a worrying curiosity, wanting to know who these cheeky long-haired boys were. The Beatles shook some of their hands but blanked many of the others. As they did so, they all knew that the only one they really needed to meet was Elvis. Even if he had slid downwards since the halcyon days, the

SUDDENLY, THE BEATLES FOUND THEMSELVES EXPERIENCING AN EMOTION THAT HAD NOT TROUBLED THEM FOR YEARS – FAN WORSHIP. THEIR SELF-ESTEEM AND POWER VANISHED

band still held him in the highest esteem. He was Elvis and that was enough.

It took three days of planning with messages going back and forth between both camps about times and places, with secrecy a top priority. However, once the arrangement was made someone clearly blabbed, because when The Beatles arrived at Elvis's Hollywood home, hundreds of fans were waiting for them. The band swept into the driveway to be met by Elvis's people, all of whom (including Priscilla, Elvis's wife) were excited to meet them. Elvis himself was indifferent. Four skinny boys from little ol' Britain taking his crown? He didn't think so...

SOME INSTRUMENTS APPEARED. ELVIS PICKED UP A BASS, JOHN, PAUL AND GEORGE TOOK GUITARS AND RINGO IMPROVISED, USING THE SIDE OF HIS CHAIR TO BEAT OUT A RHYTHM

He greeted them in the hallway. He was wearing a red shirt, black trousers and a black waistcoat. Suddenly, The Beatles found themselves experiencing an emotion that had not troubled them for years – fan worship. Their self-esteem and sense of power vanished, and left them looking up to the man who meant so much to all of them.

John Lennon later said, 'This was the guy we had all idolized for years – from way back when we were just starting out in Liverpool. He was a legend in his own lifetime, and it's never easy meeting a legend in his own lifetime.'

The party moved into the huge sitting room. As befitted the band's hierarchy, John and Paul sat either side of Elvis, while Ringo and George sat on the floor. The Beatles now found themselves completely tongue-tied. They literally did not know what to say to the man who had changed their lives. So they just stared at him and grinned. Eventually Elvis said, 'If you're just going to sit there and stare at me, I'm going to bed.' That eased the tension.

Then some instruments appeared. Elvis picked up a bass, John, Paul and George took guitars and Ringo improvised, using the side of his chair to beat out a rhythm. They played a range of songs from Cilla Black to Presley to The Beatles to The Shadows with Paul switching to piano for the latter. They played for around an hour and then put the instruments away.

Talk turned to their experiences of fame. Lennon pointed out that the four Beatles could watch each other's backs, while Elvis had to face the fire on his own. Some reports also suggest that Lennon, unable to bite his tongue, criticized Elvis for abandoning raw rock'n'roll in order to make movies and records that meant little to him. Elvis responded: 'Well, I might just get around to cutting a few sides and knocking you off the top.' Laughter, slightly uneasy laughter, filled the room. There was more talk about cars and planes, George smoked a spliff with an Elvis employee out in the garden, and Ringo played a game of pool. Brian Epstein and Colonel Tom Parker played roulette.

IN HIS INTERVIEW WITH NIXON, ELVIS ATTACKED THE BEATLES. THEY WERE DRUG TAKERS AND A TERRIBLE EXAMPLE TO AMERICAN YOUTH

The meeting ended, Elvis saying he had work the next day. The band then suggested Elvis meet them the next night at their hotel. Elvis said he would see what he could do. He showed the party to the door. They said goodbye and knowing that Elvis was a big Peter Sellers fan, Lennon shouted in his best Sellers voice, 'Tanks for ze music, Elvis – and long live ze King!'

The next day an Elvis employee turned up at The Beatles' hotel to tell them Elvis would not be coming. Lennon sent Elvis a message back. It read, 'If it hadn't been for you I'd be nothing.' When he received it Elvis just smiled. Although in public The Beatles always kept to the party line – it

was a great night, Elvis was fab and so on – privately they were disappointed.

There was a strange twist to this meeting, which was discovered many years later when FBI files revealed that Presley had made an unauthorized visit to President Nixon in December 1970 to deliver a letter. Elvis's written request was that the president make him an FBI agent, which would allow him to spy for the government. He delivered his letter at 6:30 a.m. then went back to his hotel to wait. The White House, fearful of bad publicity if they ignored such a musical hero, invited him over to take coffee with the President.

In his interview with Nixon, Elvis attacked The Beatles. They were drug takers and a terrible example to American youth, he said, a focus for anti-American activity. Elvis's work as a performer put him in the perfect position to keep an eye on subversive types within the showbiz industry and then report any wrongdoing to the authorities. Nixon listened to his ideas and then to keep him happy and send him on his way, he handed Presley what he desired the most – an FBI badge.

Presley returned home full of joy. He was an FBI agent, and a friend and companion of Richard Milhous Nixon. But he never did get round to recording the songs that would put The Beatles in their place and he never did realize that at the time of his meeting with Nixon, The Beatles had already split up.

THE
QUEEN
awards the band MBEs

DATE 26 October 1965, Buckingham Palace, London

Although in later years Lennon would often claim that The Beatles sold out on the day they threw away their leather outfits and put on their mohair suits, this assertion is somewhat unfair. But if they ever did commit such a crime against their own generation, then surely it was on the day they travelled to Buckingham Palace to be awarded the MBE (Member of the British Empire) by the Queen.

On any level this was a remarkable event – the Royal Family acknowledging four working-class Scousers who had proved themselves to be cheeky, irreverent subjects? Quite amazing. That they were also four Scousers who were highly promiscuous and regular drug takers was no doubt kept from royal eyes.

Ringo and Paul asserted they were all highly impressed when Brian Epstein first broke the news to them. 'We all thought it was really thrilling,' was Ringo's memory. Then, said Paul, a certain cynicism started to creep in. When told what it actually meant – that they got £40 a year and free entrance into St Paul's Whispering Gallery – some of the excitement began to diminish.

For his part, John said he wanted no part in the event although Cynthia recalled things differently. At no time did he object to the award, she stated. In fact he was thrilled because it would impress Aunt Mimi no end. Lennon said otherwise. He claimed – as did others around him – that the letter he received, formally asking him if he would accept the award, was thrown into a heap of fan mail and only the intervention of Epstein and others persuaded him to change his mind. No doubt it would have been made clear to him that if news of his snubbing the Queen became public – as it inevitably would – the damage to the band would be colossal. The Beatles might have been a huge act but the Queen was royalty and in Britain you don't mess around with royalty. The press would have torn him and the band apart. Was it worth it?

The irony of the situation would not have escaped Lennon's quick mind. As the band became more successful, the more they became trapped. Pop music was meant to bestow freedom on its most favoured sons; instead it entwined them in a never-ending set of unpalatable situations that they could not control or escape from. Furthermore, how ironic that the man who should talk Lennon into accepting the award, Brian Epstein, was himself snubbed by the Palace. In the national consciousness Epstein was as much a Beatle as anyone else, and yet he did not receive an invite to the ceremony. It was surmised by observers that his religion and sexual preference told against him. George decently held out a hand to him, declaring that the award actually stood for Mr Brian Epstein. Princess Margaret, one of the more liberal members of the family, also used that line to display her support for Brian.

HOW IRONIC THAT THE MAN WHO SHOULD TALK LENNON INTO ACCEPTING THE AWARD, BRIAN EPSTEIN, WAS HIMSELF SNUBBED BY THE PALACE

Lennon's reticence was countered by his ability to lay aside prejudice so as to absorb the situation. On an artistic level, Lennon the songwriter was always hungry for a new experience. Talking to the Queen certainly fitted that bill. 'Although we don't believe in the Royal Family,' he said, 'you can't help being impressed when you're in the Palace when you know, you're standing in front of the Queen. It was like in a dream.'

Lennon then said that the band were giggling like crazy because they had smoked a joint in the toilets. Peter Brown, who worked for NEMS Records, took the story further in his book, *The Love You Make, An Insider's Story Of The Beatles* (1984), claiming that Lennon had rolled a joint for the 16-year-old Prince Charles who he knew to be a Beatles fan. Lennon wanted to turn him on.

George Harrison quickly snuffed this story out. They did go to the toilet and there they smoked cigarettes, not spliffs. 'We never smoked marijuana at the investiture,' he said. Then he added, 'Years later I'm sure John was thinking back and remembering, oh yes we went in the toilet and smoked and it turned into a reefer ... But we never did.'

When the band met the Queen, she asked Ringo if he had started the band. Ringo said he was the last to join. She enquired how long the band had been together and instantly Paul and Ringo sang the lyrics are from an old music hall song called 'My Old Dutch', written by Albert Chevalier. Here we had two Scousers singing a cockney song to the Queen. Only in Beatle Land do such events occur – it is no wonder Lennon recalled it as 'a dream'.

And no wonder also in stuffy Britain that several soldiers sent their medals back in protest at four long-haired pop musicians from Liverpool being given the same accord as them. Lennon was brilliantly cutting about the matter. 'They got theirs for killing people. We got ours for not killing people.' He also found himself feeling sorry for Elizabeth.

As Lennon told biographer Hunter Davies in his book *The Beatles: The Authorized Biography* (1968), 'I really think the Queen believes in it all. She must. I don't believe in John Lennon, Beatle, being any different from anyone else, because I know he's not. I'm just a feller. But I'm sure the Queen thinks she's different.'

In a later *Newsfront* TV interview with Mitchell Krause he added, 'Imagine being brought up like that for 2,000 years! It must be pretty freaky. They must have a hard time trying to be human beings ... you feel sorry for people like that, because it's like us – but only worse.'

Having accepted their awards – with Buckingham Palace surrounded by screaming Beatles fans – the band swept away in a limousine to continue the great Beatle dream. But over the years the award nagged at Lennon. The others were fine about it, displayed a cheeky light touch to the affair. Two years later when they were photographed for their iconic *Sgt. Pepper's Lonely Hearts Club Band* album sleeve, Paul and George both pinned their medals to the chests of their hired uniforms.

Lennon meanwhile had given his medal to his Aunt Mimi, knowing full well that as a fully paid-up admirer of all things royal, it would mean the world to her. But he could not leave it alone. Where the others happily went along with it, Lennon's heart was different – it had to be squared off against his conscience for him to accept and move forward. Finally, in November 1969, he took the medal off Mimi's mantelpiece and sent it back to the Palace with a note saying he was returning it in protest against Britain's involvement in Africa and Vietnam, and because his new single was slipping down the charts.

IN 1969, JOHN TOOK THE MEDAL OFF MIMI'S MANTELPIECE AND SENT IT BACK TO THE PALACE WITH A NOTE SAYING HE WAS RETURNING IT IN PROTEST

'It was hypocritical of me to accept it,' he said later, 'but I'm glad, really, that I did – because it meant that four years later I could use it to make it a gesture.' He was 29 years old when he made that move and so very different from the man who met his enemy and felt sympathy for her on that day in October 1965.

The music of
LENNON
AND McCARTNEY
becomes a TV show

DATE 17 December 1965, Granada TV Studios, Manchester

In 1965 Johnnie Hamp, like the rest of the country, was fascinated, intrigued and compelled by the phenomenon known as Beatlemania. And like the rest of the world he was a big fan of the band. Hamp had just acquired the position of head of light entertainment at Granada Television and knew that the band were swamped with offers. For anything to get their nod, it would have to be stylish, imaginative and in keeping with the band's high standards.

That was when the idea of a show, introduced by John and Paul but dedicated to other artists singing their songs, was conceived. Hamp threw it the band's way. Television rarely honoured pop in such a manner, and the boys quickly signalled their approval.

Asked if they had any suggestions for artists themselves, the band requested Ella Fitzgerald. Her version of 'Can't Buy Me Love' had given the band an unexpected presence in the jazz world. Unfortunately, the singer was not available. Those who were included film composer Henry Mancini, duo Peter and Gordon, Dick Rivers (a French Rocker who sang 'Things We Said Today' in French), Esther Phillips, Lulu, Peter Sellers, Cilla Black, Billy J. Kramer and Marianne Faithfull.

The show highlighted the duo's great songwriting versatility – 'She Loves You', 'A Hard Day's Night' and 'We Can Work It Out' representing their ability to craft highly catchy singles; 'Yesterday', especially, displaying a mature, deeper side. The show was made at a time when LSD was yet to feature strongly in John's songwriting. The following April they would start recording the *Revolver* album, a work that would take them into a whole new field of artistic excellence. This show then in many ways marked the end of phase one of their writing, John's particularly.

There is only one account of the two men writing songs pre-LSD and that occurs in Michael Braun's book, *Love Me Do* (1964). He was allowed to sit in on the pair as they wrote the song, 'One And One Is Two' for singer Billy J. Kramer. As the session started, Paul was at the piano and John was on the guitar. Paul had the first lines written and sang them to John.

George stuck his head round the door and advised removing one of the repeated lines, John agreed and started considering other words that would fit the song. John then took over piano and Paul switched to guitar. They taped the finished song three times before Paul recorded a message for the publisher Dick James. Meanwhile, John was overheard saying, 'Billy J. is finished when he gets this song.'

Lennon and McCartney's initial ambition in life was to match the artistic excellence of the songwriting partnership Gerry Goffin and Carole King, whose songs they adored. When they began their partnership their way forward was to craft songs in a calculated fashion. There was never a thought of producing songs that expressed their own personal feelings.

John later said that he kept all his personal musings for his books, *In His Own Write* (1964) and *A Spaniard In The Works* (1965) but even they were clouded by wordplay. That is why in their early songs they directly addressed their fans – 'Love Me Do', 'She Loves You', 'From Me To You', 'All My Loving'. In doing so, they wrote songs that every one of their fans thought was written personally to them and them alone. 'I'd have a separate songwriting John Lennon who wrote songs for the meat market,' he later confessed, 'and I don't consider the lyrics to have any depth at all, they were just a joke.'

The men's antennae were sharp and attentive and picked up on all kinds of influences. Lennon's 'Please Please Me' was inspired by the 1932 Bing Crosby song 'Please' in which the singer swooped and swapped between the words, 'please' and 'pleas'. John's song 'Run For Your Life' was inspired by a line in the Elvis Presley song, 'Baby, Let's Play House'. Naturally, other musicians inspired them. John was forever trying to emulate one of his heroes Smokey Robinson, and the band were always trying to write an authentic Motown song.

UNLIKE JOHN, PAUL SOMETIMES STRUGGLED WITH WORDS BUT MADE UP FOR IT WITH HIS WONDROUS MELODIC GIFTS

John's songwriting changed after he heard Bob Dylan and he started to adopt a more personal style. His songs, 'You've Got To Hide Your Love Away', 'Help!' and 'I'm A Loser' all signposted this new direction, and his song 'Nowhere Man' has the distinction of being the first Beatles song not to deal with love.

Two media people also played their part in Lennon's development. The writer Maureen Cleave asked him why his songs never carried words with more than two syllables. He replied by writing 'Help!' and deliberately inserting words such as 'independence' and 'appreciate'. The other influence was the TV presenter Kenneth Allsop. He had been impressed by John's book, *In His Own Write*, and asked the Beatle why he explored his deeper feelings in print, but not in his songs. Lennon took the criticism on board and responded with 'I'm A Loser', a startling admission for a smiling Beatle at the top of his game. This strain of songwriting found its apotheosis with 'In My Life', which with its beautiful melody and wistful, restrained vocals, brilliantly evoked John's past, his friends, his family, his Liverpool.

McCartney was always more straight-forward. His early songs stuck to the tricks of the trade and if he did move outside the boundaries, it was normally as a reaction to John. When John wrote 'I'm A Loser', Paul retorted with 'I'm Down'; when John wrote 'In My Life', Paul penned a song called 'Penny Lane', which looked at his past in Liverpool.

Unlike John, Paul sometimes struggled with words but made up for it with his wondrous melodic gifts. This is the man who woke up with the melody for 'Yesterday' in his head, convinced it belonged to someone else, so familiar was its nature. That song alone, covered by thousands of artists, would guarantee anyone a place at the top table. When one then discovers that his song 'Michelle' was written as a teenager and played as a joke at Beatnik parties in Liverpool, one's admiration can only grow.

Musically, The Beatles were born in a fortuitous time and place. Liverpool is a music town. When growing up, there were hundreds of venues dedicated to live music of every sort. Music spilled out of pubs and clubs as much as the drunks. All four Beatles absorbed this music and were deeply influenced by it. This meant that they sucked in country and western, jazz, blues, early R&B and swing. McCartney was also attentive to the music his father played in the family home. Jim McCartney adored the standards of the 1930s and 40s and his son would often employ such devices and sounds in his own work. John was the same: 'Honey Pie' and 'Goodnight' from *The Beatles* double album (*The White Album*) are just two examples.

The perverse nature of youth-culture music (I'm a Rocker so I won't listen to soul; I'm a Mod so I won't listen to Elvis) bypassed The Beatles. They loved music of all kinds and all natures, and by aligning their talent with the music of the past that they had unconsciously soaked up, they were able to forge their own unique style and sound.

The Music Of Lennon And McCartney was transmitted on 17 December 1965. Few could have predicted that the two men who introduced the acts then played their new single, 'We Can Work It Out', were just about to take their music to yet another level with *Revolver*, the album many consider their best – and therefore the best album ever made.

John says The Beatles are

BIGGER
THAN JESUS

DATE 4 March 1966, Weybridge, Surrey

In early 1966 the *Evening Standard* secured exclusive interviews with all the band, plus Brian Epstein. The writer they selected for the job was Maureen Cleave, a personal friend of Lennon's, a relationship that can be divined by her perceptive description of the Beatle as imperious, unpredictable, charming and quick-witted.

As part of the profile, Cleave mentioned Lennon's book collection. She told her readers that Lennon was a voracious buyer of books and had created a room specially for their keeping. In that room, she spotted leather-bound editions of Leo Tolstoy, Oscar Wilde, plus works by the poets Swift and Tennyson, and the writers Huxley and Orwell. She also noted with great interest Lennon's collection of *Just William* books, his favourite childhood reads. There were also oddities. Cleave referred to *Forty-One Years In India* by Field Marshall Lord Roberts and *Curiosities Of Natural History* by Francis T. Buckland standing on his shelves.

One book that Lennon had recently read and that Cleave did not mention was Hugh Schonfield's *The Passover Plot: New Light On The History Of Jesus* (1965). Schonfield's thesis was that Jesus was not the Son of God but a man of royal blood who had come to rescue his Jewish people from Roman oppression. He planned to fake his death on the cross and then be found alive in his tomb three days later, thus giving him God-like power over the masses.

The problem was that a Roman soldier stabbed him and he bled to death on the cross. Schonfield also argued that the 12 disciples were of 'limited intelligence', country bumpkins compared with the sophisticates living in Jerusalem.

It was on this subject that Lennon let loose the quote that would cause him untold aggravation and heavily impact on his career. 'Christianity will go,' he said. 'It will vanish and shrink. I needn't argue about that; I'm right and I will be proved

THE BAND WAS STRETCHING OUT, GROWING UP, AND THESE INTERVIEWS WERE INTENDED TO PREPARE THE WAY. INSTEAD, LENNON'S COMMENTS PLUNGED THE BAND INTO THE BIGGEST CONTROVERSY OF THEIR LIVES

right. We're more popular than Jesus now; I don't know which will go first, rock'n'roll or Christianity.'

When the article was published on 4 March 1966, the newspaper did not highlight Lennon's opinion on Christianity at all nor did his statement send shockwaves around the country. Britain's relationship to organized religion was – and is – tepid. Religion tends to be bound up in civic matters. Remembrance Day, for example, in no way carries the weight that it enjoys in the Mediterranean

DJS ASKED LISTENERS FOR THEIR VIEWS ON THE MATTER. NATURALLY 99 PER CENT OF THEM FELT THAT LENNON HAD WILDLY OVERSTEPPED THE MARK

or indeed America's Bible Belt. Moreover, the thoughts of pop stars were not exactly awaited with bated breath. As the eminent Beatle writer Steve Turner points out, 'The opinions of pop stars on anything other than pop music were not taken terribly seriously in the Britain of 1966.'

This was a particular bugbear of musicians – the refusal of the world to let them grow up – hence the thinking behind the *Evening Standard* articles, which was to present The Beatles as assured intelligent young men growing away from their mop-top image. Unknown to many, the music they were now creating – inspired in part by LSD and marijuana – was many miles away from the bright simplicity of their earlier work. The band was stretching out, growing up, and these interviews were intended to prepare the way. Instead, Lennon's comments plunged the band into the biggest controversy of their lives. And unwittingly their organization was to blame.

The day after Cleave's article appeared, Tony Barrow, The Beatles' then press officer, called up an American teen magazine called *Datebook* and offered them rights to the profiles. It was important that America knew of the changes going on in The Beatles camp and *Datebook* was a perfect vehicle to carry the message. Created in 1965, *Datebook* was a teen magazine that approached its subjects with intelligence, giving young people what they wanted but in a thought-provoking way. Recent subjects had included Mary Quant and the effects of a new wonder drug called LSD.

The editor was Art Unger. He knew full well the financial value of The Beatles. He had already produced a one-off publication called *All About The Beatles* and watched it sell nearly a million copies. The band had seen the magazine, liked it, and had given him access on tour.

Having secured the rights to Cleave's profiles, Unger cut the first two paragraphs from the Lennon piece and then he pulled out the most provocative quote. The piece ran with the headline, 'I don't know which will go first, rock'n'roll or Christianity.' He did the same with the McCartney profile in which the Beatle had condemned American racism in the sharpest terms. Unger was smart, knew that to gain real publicity for the magazine he only had to send the magazine south.

Doug Layton and Tommy Charles were two DJs operating out of Birmingham, Alabama. Right in the heart of America's Bible Belt. It is here that Christianity in all its various guises has its strongest appeal, with many viewing this part of America as 'fundamentalist' in its approach to religion. *The Layton And Charles Show* was Radio WAQY's main morning show. When the magazine reached them in the last week of July, Layton disregarded McCartney's stance on racism and instead live on air asked Charles, 'Did you hear what John Lennon has said?' Tommy replied that he had not heard a thing. Layton filled him in. 'He said The Beatles are bigger than Jesus.'

Instantly Charles reacted, 'Oh! That does it for me. I am not going to play The Beatles any more,' and so began the bushfire that would engulf the band.

The DJs then asked listeners for their views on the matter. Naturally, 99 per cent of them felt that Lennon had wildly overstepped the mark and needed chastising. Charles had the perfect punishment for the band. On 19 August the band was due to play in Memphis. On that day all those outraged by Lennon's comments would build a bonfire of Beatles material – albums, badges, books and so on – and set fire to it.

ON 19 AUGUST THE BAND WAS DUE TO PLAY IN MEMPHIS. ON THAT DAY ALL THOSE OUTRAGED BY LENNON'S COMMENTS WOULD **BUILD A BONFIRE OF BEATLES MATERIAL – ALBUMS, BADGES, BOOKS AND SO ON – AND SET FIRE TO IT**

At this point the affair was still a local matter and therefore containable. Unfortunately for The Beatles that state of affairs would not last for long. Driving into work Al Benn, who was the Bureau Manager for the UPI news service, heard *The Layton And Charles Show*. That morning he filed a report that went direct to New York. The story was picked up nationally. By early August all of America was aware of Lennon's comments. Dozens of radio stations banned The Beatles from their playlists, although as Turner points out many of them did not play the band's music and were just cashing in on the publicity.

In the UK Brian Epstein and the band were starting to get seriously worried. On 5 August, the day *The New York Times* carried the story on its front page, Epstein issued a press statement saying that Lennon's quote had been taken out of context. 'He did not mean to boast about The Beatles' fame,' Epstein stated. 'He meant to point out that The Beatles' effect appeared to be a more immediate one, certainly on the younger generation.' The statement did little to stop the wave of vicious anti-Beatles sentiment firing across America. Senators came out against the band, religious teachers condemned Lennon in the strongest

possible terms and bonfires built out of Beatles records burned brightly.

On 11 August The Beatles flew into America. Lennon in particular was nervous. According to his wife Cynthia when he left for the tour he was frightened and downcast. He had never meant to provoke so much anger and hatred for stating what he saw was the truth. The first thing they did was hold two press conferences, one for the national media, and one for the media that would be following them on tour.

SENATORS CAME OUT AGAINST THE BAND, RELIGIOUS TEACHERS CONDEMNED LENNON IN THE STRONGEST POSSIBLE TERMS AND BONFIRES BUILT OUT OF BEATLES RECORDS BURNED BRIGHTLY

Before appearing in front of the cameras, Lennon took advice from Epstein and Tony Barrow. He was caught in the middle. Part of him, the arrogant all-powerful Lennon, was loath to apologize. The other part, the intelligent musician, knew he – and therefore The Beatles – was swimming in very dangerous waters.

At the conference held at their Chicago hotel, he explained himself thus, 'I'm not saying that we're better, or greater, or comparing us with Jesus Christ as a person or God as a thing or whatever it is, you know. I just said what I said and it was wrong, or was taken wrong. And now it's all this.' But the one thing he did not say was sorry. At the second conference he managed to utter the words all America were waiting to hear. Told that Tommy Charles was demanding an apology, Lennon said, 'He can have it, you know. I apologize to him if he's upset and he really means it, you know, I'm sorry. I'm sorry I said it for the mess it's made. But I never meant it as a lousy or anti-religious thing, or anything. You know, and I can't say any more than that. There's nothing else to say really, you know – no more words. But if an apology is – if he wants one, you know, he can have it. I apologize to him.'

Suddenly the mood changed. Some journalists stated their sympathy for the band, informing them that the Bible Belt were 'quite notorious for their Christian attitude'. Soon, the whole thing was forgotten. But amid the fierce questioning, there was another question of greater pertinence. 'Is this an attempt to raise your flagging popularity?' a journalist asked.

The band depart for America in August 1966. Only they knew that this was the last ever tour. After this they would break new ground by becoming a studio-only band for the next three years.

The Beatles record
REVOLVER

DATE 6 April 1966, Abbey Road Studios, London

The Beatles were not the only ones dropping acid and watching the world explode into a kaleidoscope of colours. Bob Dylan was a fellow traveller, using all kinds of chemicals to turn him away from folk music and towards creating a hurricane of sound and words that belonged totally to him. His landmark double album *Blonde On Blonde*, released in 1966, opened with the single 'Rainy Day Women # 12 & 35', its chorus urging everyone to go and get stoned.

No need for elucidation there. Most of Dylan's album fitted in perfectly with the emerging drug culture. His lengthy songs, elliptical imagery, use of instruments (a brass band on the opening track, for example) and his world-weary vocals brilliantly reflected the drug experience.

That was New York. Over in Los Angeles, Brian Wilson of The Beach Boys was busy trying to replicate the sounds he heard while tripping the light fantastic. Wilson likened his trip to 'a religious experience'. This was not unusual. Most trippers truly believed you could get close to God just by taking acid. In between trips, Wilson heard The Beatles album *Rubber Soul* and flipped. For him, The Fabs had created the first ever album. Up until this point, albums tended to carry a band's hit singles and a few filler tracks. The Beatles had been edging away from that formula

for some time now, as the *Help!* album suggested. Wilson's response was to send The Beach Boys out on tour, and write, produce and arrange one of the great albums of all time – *Pet Sounds*.

In 1966, two weeks after *Pet Sounds* belated release in the UK, *Revolver* appeared and sent Wilson back to the drawing board, this time to work on his famous album *Smile*. McCartney loved *Pet Sounds* and you can see why. Wilson's talent to conjure melodies, to create great waves of joy from harmonies and striking instrumentation, created a style that was totally unique. McCartney now set out to outdo *Pet Sounds*. He was certainly building up a formidable artistic armoury with which to do so.

Of late, McCartney had moved out of girlfriend Jane Asher's house on Wimpole Street, bought his own house in St Johns Wood, London, and gone out to expose himself to as many different influences as possible. Living with Asher had already shown McCartney the joys of traditional art forms, such as classical music and the theatre, and this had been reflected in some of his most famous songs, including 'Yesterday' and 'Eleanor Rigby'.

CYNTHIA NOW HAD A GHOST FOR A HUSBAND. HALF THE TIME HE WAS IN ANOTHER WORLD, FOR THE OTHER HALF HE WAS COMING DOWN BADLY AND SCREAMED TO BE LEFT ALONE

But Paul wanted more. He wanted to get hip with London's alternative scene. To do so, he called on his friend, Barry Miles. Miles was the proprietor of London's first alternative bookshop called The Indica (after *Cannabis indica*) and co-founder of the underground newspaper *The International Times*. He now gave McCartney access to the alternative scene.

'I don't think he would say I was a major influence, but he met interesting people through me,' Miles recalled. 'I would take [Allen] Ginsberg or [William S.] Burroughs over to his house. He was very systematic in his exploration of the London scene ... He had his antennae out.' McCartney's interest in the weird and the wonderful does seem incongruous given his talent for writing highly commercial tunes that cross all divides. But Paul was always open to suggestion. He instinctively knew that his talent could only prosper no matter what he discovered. In fact, when he started exploring the works of challenging artists such as Karlheinz Stockhausen and Luciano Berio, he said that he thought such people weird. Later on, he thought that people who didn't like the cutting edge were weird. It should be stressed, though, that McCartney did not like everything that was put him in front of him. He later admitted he liked only one Stockhausen record, the rest was a little 'too fruity'.

The effect of being exposed to a multitude of ideas expressed itself when McCartney began creating his own avant-garde sound collages using a Brenell tape recorder at home, preceding Lennon and Ono's *Two Virgins* experiment by at least two years. His most famous work was entitled 'Carnival Of Light' and was recorded in January 1967. The genesis of the track came from designer David Vaughan who painted a psychedelic design on one of Paul's pianos. Vaughan delivered the piano to McCartney's Cavendish Avenue address, and asked if he would contribute a musical piece for the upcoming 'Million Volt Light And Sound Rave', an event held at London's Roundhouse Theatre in early 1967. To

Vaughan's surprise McCartney agreed to make a musical contribution. 'Carnival Of Light' was a 13-minute unreleased collage of, according to Beatles historian Mark Lewisohn, 'distorted, hypnotic drum and organ sounds, a distorted lead guitar, the sound of a church organ, various effects (water gargling was one) and, perhaps most intimidating of all, John Lennon and McCartney screaming dementedly and bawling aloud random phrases like "Are you all right?" and "Barcelona!"'

His mate John, meanwhile, was content to let Paul do the exploring and report back to him. He was happy tripping out in Weybridge, much to his wife Cynthia's angst. Reluctant to ingest the drug after 'the dental experience' as George called it, Cynthia now had a ghost for a husband. Half the time he was in another world, for the other half he was coming down badly and screamed to be left alone. Cynthia and their son Julian walked on eggshells when John was around.

LSD served to open up a gap in the band as well. Paul's wariness of its long-term effects meant that for the first time The Beatles were not moving as one. McCartney did eventually take the drug but only four or five times. In contrast, Lennon remarked that he had taken thousands of trips in an attempt to kill off his ego, an undertaking endorsed by the writer and LSD evangelist Timothy Leary.

Miles remembered McCartney bringing Lennon into his shop Indica to buy books, including Timothy Leary's book *The Psychedelic Experience*. The first song to be recorded for *Revolver* was Lennon's 'Tomorrow Never Knows', which basically drew on whole chunks of Leary's writing and then set it to the most radical Beatles music yet.

LSD SERVED TO OPEN UP A GAP IN THE BAND AS WELL. PAUL'S WARINESS OF ITS LONG-TERM EFFECTS MEANT THAT FOR THE FIRST TIME THE BEATLES WERE NOT MOVING AS ONE

And what then of Harrison? By the time the band were making *Revolver*, Harrison had mastered the sitar well enough to create a whole song around the instrument called 'Love You To'. Harrison had discovered the Asian Music Circle, an organization that promoted Indian arts. He spent three months visiting them in Finchley, London, and being taught various techniques.

John, Paul and Ringo were also impressed by Indian music and used some of its techniques in their own compositions. When Lennon played them 'Tomorrow Never Knows' on his guitar, he used just one chord and sang his song over that droning sound. The fractured rhythms of songs such as 'Rain' also expose a knowledge of the workings of Indian-style music.

The sense of experimentation surrounding the band extended itself to George Martin and his engineer Geoff Emerick. When the writer of 'Tomorrow Never Knows' told his sound people that he wanted his song to sound like a thousand monks chanting on a hill and then walked away, what did one do?

'The group encouraged us to break the rules,' recalled Emerick. 'It was implanted when we started *Revolver* that every instrument should sound unlike itself: a piano shouldn't sound like a piano, a guitar shouldn't sound like a guitar. There were lots of things I wanted to try ...'

Although Lennon gets the credit for 'Tomorrow Never Knows' it was really McCartney's involvement that turned it into a classic. 'Paul in particular used the make his own loops at home and walk into the studio with bags full of little reels saying "Listen to this!" The seagull-like noise on 'Tomorrow Never Knows' is really a distorted guitar,' said Emerick. (Other loops used on the track included the sounds of a wine glass and a speeded-up guitar.) 'We did a live mix of all the loops,' Martin revealed. 'All over the studios we had people spooling them onto machines with pencils while Geoff did the balancing. There were many other hands controlling the panning.'

Where *Revolver* succeeds is by meeting McCartney's determination that the band forged ahead sonically. The songs adopted many musical coats: early funk in 'Taxman'; sublime love songs in 'Here, There And Everywhere' and 'For No One'; Indian influenced in 'Love You To'; acid influenced in 'She Said, She Said' and 'Tomorrow Never Knows'; a children's song, 'Yellow Submarine'; and sheer joyful pop in 'Good Day Sunshine' and 'Got To Get You Into My Life'.

ALTHOUGH LENNON GETS THE CREDIT FOR 'TOMORROW NEVER KNOWS' IT WAS REALLY McCARTNEY'S INVOLVEMENT THAT TURNED IT INTO A CLASSIC

The cover design was handed over to their old Hamburg friend, Klaus Voormann, now working as a graphic designer. He was given bundles of Beatles pictures cut out of the papers by John, Paul and Pete Shotton the night before. Using the memory of their old days together, Klaus took the band's hair as his starting point and created a highly distinctive album cover that portrayed all kinds of images pouring out of the band's heads.

The cover for what many consider their finest album, *Revolver*. It was designed by Klaus Voormann, who they had befriended in Hamburg days. He later revealed that he had used the fuss surrounding their haircuts as his starting point.

'I had a few strange ones where John was pulling a face, or Paul was laughing, but in general, the photos show their sweet side,' Klaus recalled. 'There was one picture where Paul was sitting on a toilet. I think that photo was taken in Hamburg.'

Klaus took the design to George Martin's office and set up the artwork on the filing cabinet. The band, Brian Epstein, George Martin and his secretary were present for the unveiling. Apart from George Martin objecting to the shot of Paul on the toilet, everybody loved it. Brian Epstein was even moved to tears, saying, 'Klaus, this is exactly what we needed. I was worried that this whole thing might not work, but I know now that this is the cover. This LP will work — thank you.'

McCartney may have been pleased with the album cover but that was nothing compared with his excitement about the music inside. On its release he said, 'Unlike our previous LPs, this one is intended to show our versatility rather than a haphazard collection of songs. We use trumpets, violins and cellos to achieve new effects ... We don't intend to go back and revive ideas of 20 years ago.'

It is often said that *Revolver* is *Rubber Soul* Part Two but it might be better to view it as *Sgt. Pepper* Number One. Undoubtedly it has so much endeavour behind it that whether one is a hippy or a banker, a monk or a model, the music dives straight into your heart. The original title was *Abracadabra*. Magic might have been a better word.

The Beatles go to the
FAR EAST

DATE July 1966, Japan and The Philippines

They flew into Japan and headfirst into controversy. Such was their popularity, their promoter had been forced to book them into the Budokan Theatre, a spacious venue viewed as a highly spiritual place. The traditionalists were outraged that The Beatles were even being allowed into the building, let alone performing there. In response, they had started a vicious campaign against the band. One of their stunts was to send George a letter while he was touring in Germany with the message, 'You won't live past next month'.

When they landed in Tokyo, armed police surrounded them from the moment they left the plane and did not leave their sides. The band was hurried into expectant limousines. The cars moved off. As thousands of fans screamed as the band rushed by, others held up banners saying 'Beatles Go Home'. They arrived at the Tokyo Hilton, which was now guarded by more armed police. There, the chief of police informed them they were not to leave the hotel under any circumstances except to go to the gig.

At the press conference, John and Paul addressed the subject, and their attitudes neatly summed up the men's differences. A journalist asked, 'Some Japanese say that your performances will violate the Budokan, which is devoted to traditional Japanese martial arts, and that you set a bad example for Japanese youth by leading them astray from traditional Japanese values. What do you think of all that?'

Paul replied, 'The thing is that if somebody from Japan, if a dancing troupe from Japan goes to Britain, nobody tries to say in Britain that they are violating the traditional laws, you know, or that they're trying to spoil anything. All we're doing is coming here and singing because we've been asked.'

AS THOUSANDS OF FANS SCREAMED AS THE BAND RUSHED BY, OTHERS HELD UP BANNERS SAYING 'BEATLES GO HOME'

John's view was far more succinct. He sourly responded, 'It's better to watch singing than wrestling, anyway.' Once again, Paul had to intervene, to cut off any potential trouble the gang leader's loose tongue might drop them in. 'We're not trying to violate anything, you know … We're just as traditional, anyway.'

AN INVITATION FROM IMELDA MARCOS HAD BEEN RECEIVED, AND A TELEGRAM HAD BEEN SENT POLITELY DECLINING IT. THE MARCOS REGIME SIMPLY IGNORED THIS

The shows passed without incident and the relieved band flew on to the Philippines, to the country whose behaviour towards them would be so provocative that it would herald the end of their touring days. From the moment they arrived the band were treated with hostility. Normal procedure was that the band's plane would land at the furthest end of the airfield. The band would disembark, dive into waiting cars and be driven to their hotel. Epstein would then deal with passport control and immigration. This procedure allowed the band not only to avoid screaming fans but also to carry their precious marijuana.

Only, in Manila, the arrangements proved different. A number of armed men surrounded the band as they left the plane, told them to leave their bags on the ground and then ushered them all into a car, which sped off at high speed.

Neil Aspinall hastily grabbed their bags, flung them in the back of another limo and ordered the driver to take him to where The Beatles were. Meanwhile the band were at Manila harbour being herded onto a boat. 'For the first time ever,' George recalled, 'we were cut off from Neil, Mal and Brian Epstein. There was not one of them around, and not only that, but we had a whole row of cops with guns lining the deck …' Aspinall and then Epstein arrived after about an hour, the band were taken back to shore, handed their luggage and taken to their hotel where they fell into a fitful sleep.

In the morning, some of The Beatles' entourage were awoken by loud banging on the door. The band was expected to go to the Malacañan Palace for a party hosted by Imelda Marcos, wife of the Philippine President, Ferdinand Marcos. Quite a few children had been invited for what was obviously a PR stunt. Ever since the incident at the Washington Embassy in 1964, Epstein's policy had been never to accept invitations to government soirees. An invitation from Imelda Marcos had been received, and a telegram had been sent politely declining it. The Marcos regime had simply ignored this.

Although he had been made aware of the situation, Epstein refused to wake his band. They were tired and needed rest. When the band did awake they were shocked to see on their televisions, pictures from the Palace relaying their non-appearance. To calm the situation, Epstein appeared on national television to explain the band's side of events. As he spoke, interference suddenly hit the nation's screens and his words were drowned out. Many think the TV editors scrambled Epstein on instructions from a higher authority. Still, that afternoon and evening, the band played two shows to 80,000 excited people.

NO POLICE ESCORT HAD BEEN PROVIDED SO THE BAND HAD TO RUN A GAUNTLET OF HATE, SEVERAL PEOPLE AIMING KICKS AND PUNCHES AT THEM

The next day they woke up to newspapers condemning them, hotel staff who would not serve them and a general atmosphere of hostility. The band headed for the airport. There they found several hundred angry citizens waiting for them. No police escort had been provided so the band had to run a gauntlet of hate, several people aiming kicks and punches at them.

Inside the terminal, all the escalators and elevators had been turned off. So had the message boards. The group desperately tried to find their gate without suffering further punches. Soldiers appeared and began roughly herding them towards passport control. Mal tried to put himself between the soldiers and the band and took several clouts from sticks and fists.

Brian and Ringo were also assaulted while Paul, John and George spotted some nuns and used them as a shield. As officials slowly examined each passport, locals appeared behind a huge glass screen and began banging on it, screaming insults. Finally, the band was allowed on to the plane. As they waited to lift off, the pilot came on the intercom and asked Tony Barrow, Mal Evans and Brian Epstein to leave the plane. Eventually, they returned – having been relieved of much of the money made at the gigs.

The plane was now heading to India where the band were looking forward to a four-day break. They were furious with Epstein, and the normally urbane manager now worked himself up into such a state of nerves that in India he was hospitalized for four days. India had been chosen as the perfect place to recuperate, as it was assumed this country was unaffected by Beatlemania. Not so. On landing, hundreds of Indians greeted the band and it became apparent that they would not be able to venture out at all. As George Martin had said, it was a hell of a life really.

The Beatles play their

LAST EVER
CONCERT

DATE 29 August 1966, Candlestick Park, San Francisco

The Beatles' last American tour was riddled with disappointment and upset. John's 'Bigger than Jesus' remark still haunted them, especially in the Bible Belt. On Friday 19 August 1966 the band played the Mid-South Coliseum in Memphis, Tennessee. A phone call prior to the show informed them that one or all of them would be shot while playing. During their second show, someone in the audience threw a firecracker on stage. When it exploded each Beatle looked at the others to see who had been shot.

The next day in Ohio, just as the band was about to go on, a massive downpour started up. The band refused to go on stage. There was no cover for their amps. The risk of electrocution was just too high. Thirty-five thousand fans had to be told to return the following day for a lunchtime show.

On 23 August they returned to Shea Stadium, the site of one of their greatest triumphs but in contrast to that amazing night in August 1965, the band found that 11,000 tickets had gone unsold. The same decrease in support happened in many American cities. Although they remained a huge act, many of their stadium shows did not sell out.

Although John's 'Jesus' comments had undoubtedly hurt the band's standing, the real reason was the fans' disillusionment. For the third time in as many years, they were being asked to pay a lot of money to stand in a field and watch four dots on the horizon. Worse, those four dots were now treating these engagements with real contempt. 'The Beatles were famous for doing 15-minute shows,' Lennon confessed.

FANS WERE BEING ASKED TO PAY A LOT OF MONEY TO STAND IN A FIELD AND WATCH FOUR DOTS ON THE HORIZON. WORSE, THOSE FOUR DOTS WERE NOW TREATING THESE ENGAGEMENTS WITH REAL CONTEMPT

'We got our kicks from seeing how fast we could do the whole show. And if we were really counting them in too fast ... we'd run off and realize we'd only been on for 15 minutes.'

NOW THAT THE BAND HAD STARTED WRITING SONGS OTHER THAN BOY MEETS GIRL, GIRL LOVES BOY AND HERE'S THE HAPPY ENDING, THERE WAS A DEFINITE LESSENING OF INTEREST IN THEM

If the songs were performed off key, they didn't care. And no one was there to censure them for their bad attitude. Although they had just released *Revolver*, their finest album to date, the band refused to play any songs from this groundbreaking work. To do so would have meant intricate tape effects and sounds being employed and the band could not be bothered. As Mark Lewisohn, their main biographer writes, 'The Beatles were playing these huge open-air stadiums in order to satisfy as many fans as possible with the minimum of effort and maximum income.'

Dwindling attendances were not their only problem. Beatles records were not selling in the quantities they once did. Their single 'Paperback Writer' (Paul's song and the first Beatles single not to concern itself with teenage romance) and the 'Nowhere Man' EP, which again flew against the grain, were the band's signals that change was afoot. And although both records sold well, sales were down. Now the band had started writing songs other than boy meets girl, girl loves boy and here's the happy ending, there was a definite lessening of interest in them.

The Beatles were a band that had to move on – their artistic impulses would not let them stand still for anyone. Everything they touched had to be fresh and innovative. Touring was anything but, and by undertaking such work, the band found themselves seriously upsetting their creative flow. The money was great and the girls were still willing but everyone in and around the band sensed the days of Beatlemania were drawing to a close.

Only Paul argued against the idea of never touring again. His point of view was that live work kept a band alive and driving forward. Except for The Beatles the reverse was true. Live work was actually damaging them as musicians. All the skill and power they had developed in Hamburg had been dissipated in huge stadiums all over the world, lost in a maelstrom of screams and hysteria. 'It got that we were playing really bad,' Ringo said, 'and the reason I joined The Beatles was because they were the best band in Liverpool ... On the last tour of America the most exciting thing was meeting people who came to the shows, not the shows themselves.'

Their last ever show took place at Candlestick Park, San Francisco, on 29 August 1966. It was apposite that it should be so. The hippy culture that was about to sweep the world and change The Beatles irrevocably was being shaped in this city. Lennon took a camera on stage to take photos of this historic event, McCartney asked press officer Tony Barrow to record the gig. Unfortunately, tapes in those days lasted only 30 minutes so Barrow missed the closing number 'Long Tall Sally'.

That they should end on this Little Richard song was also significant. The first stirrings of Beatlemania could be said to have begun on 27 December 1960 at Litherland Town Hall. This was the band's first Liverpool show since returning from Hamburg. The band came on stage dressed in leather, Paul went up to the microphone and screamed the opening lines, and for the first time ever the crowd did not carry on dancing but instead turned, faced the band and ran towards them.

The security thought a riot had erupted. The promoter Brian Kelly, meanwhile, locked all the doors going backstage and waited for the band with a pen and a new contract in his hand. And in such a fashion The Beatles' popularity had been born. How proper then that the band should finish the night with the very same song five years later.

The band had changed so much since the early days it was incredible. They had gone from grimy rock'n'roll covers to catchy pop tunes like 'Love Me Do' to LSD-inspired masterpieces like 'Tomorrow Never Knows' in a relatively short space of time, an amazing artistic leap. In fact, in 1966, it now felt as if there were two

THE MONEY WAS GREAT AND THE GIRLS WERE STILL WILLING BUT EVERYONE IN AND AROUND THE BAND SENSED THE DAYS OF BEATLEMANIA WERE DRAWING TO A CLOSE

Beatles in existence. One touring the world, shaking their heads and acting like mop-tops, the other Beatles ensconced in a recording studio, determinedly and fearlessly pushing back the boundaries of pop and sound. On the plane back to London, George Harrison sat down, broke into huge smile and said, 'Well, that's it, I am not a Beatle anymore.' And everyone breathed a sigh of relief.

John Lennon meets

YOKO ONO

DATE 9 November 1966, Indica Gallery, Mason's Yard, London

In early 1966, Yoko Ono was living in New York City with her husband, Tony Cox. She was an avant-garde artist and her parents were not at all happy with her choice of career. They observed strict codes of conduct, ruled their children with a firm hand and did not understand what the hell their daughter was doing with a bunch of Bohemians, Beatniks and deadbeats, expressing flowery theories about art and life.

'I just wasn't able to stand up to my mother and before I did anything at all I used to ask permission,' Yoko recalled, adding that she often felt 'weak' in her parents' presence. The family background was one of extreme wealth. Prior to World War II, Yoko's father was very high up in the banking game, running the San Francisco branch of the Yasuda Bank. Money came to him in sackfuls. It is said that at one time the Ono family employed 30 servants.

Yoko Ono was born on 18 February 1933 and did not meet her father until she was two years old; that fact alone delivers great insight into the bleak emotional landscape of her childhood. The family moved back to Tokyo in the early 1940s and then war broke out.

In March 1945 America launched a bombing campaign against Tokyo, now considered the most destructive raid in history. The family protected themselves from the incessant rain of bombs and bullets in a special bunker and then fled to the hills where they begged for food and shelter every day. Somehow, they survived. Fortitude was in their blood.

In the early 50s, they moved back to America. Yoko attended college and in 1956 went against her parents and married Toshi Ichiyanagi, a Japanese pianist who the family despised. The couple lived in New York, which is when Yoko hooked into the city's avant-garde scene. Those at the

IN NEW YORK YOKO HOOKED INTO THE CITY'S AVANT-GARDE SCENE. MANY RECALL THAT HER ART WAS ALWAYS DRIVEN BY AUDIENCE PARTICIPATION OF SOME KIND

time recall that her art was always driven by audience participation of some kind. At her shows, she would produce a blank canvas and ask people to paint anything they liked on it.

Yoko divorced Toshi in 1961 and in the same year hooked up with Tony Cox. Cox worked in the film, music and art worlds, and together they attempted to take Manhattan as conceptual artists. 'She was as much a star in her world as John was in his,' Dan Richter, an employee of the couple, later said. 'But it was a very small world.'

NATURALLY, SUCH AN AFFAIR HAD TO BE KEPT SECRET. JOHN WAS STILL MARRIED TO CYNTHIA AND TO LEAVE HER FOR YOKO WOULD HAVE BROUGHT THE WORLD'S MEDIA DOWN ON THEIR HEADS

In 1966, with her marriage to Cox finished but the couple staying together for work purposes, she was invited to London to participate in the Destruction In Art Symposium. At the event, Yoko invited members of the audience to come up and cut a piece of her clothing with scissors until she was naked. Yoko liked London. She and Cox stayed put. 'She was clearly an entrepreneur and absolutely brilliant at working things out,' said her friend Adrian Morris whose flat she and Cox crashed at.

Soon, Yoko was given her own show at John Dunbar's Indica Gallery in Mason's Yard. Dunbar, once married to Marianne Faithfull, was connected to The Beatles. It was he who invited Lennon along to the opening, which took place on 9 November 1966. John arrived at the show having been tripping for three days. It was the night before the grand opening and John had heard enough about Yoko on the grapevine to intrigue him. Plus, LSD had undoubtedly helped push John towards new artistic horizons. Where McCartney had enthusiastically thrown himself into London's avant-garde scene without the drug, Lennon retained his scepticism, especially around conceptual art. Like many, his idea of great art was based around certain parameters. Anything out of that remit was to be met with suspicion. LSD helped change that perception. Lennon now recognized (thanks maybe to McCartney) that in terms of helping his songwriting, everything in the art world was worth considering. Lennon stepped into the art gallery. There were a couple of students putting last-minute touches to the exhibition and Yoko and Dunbar were around somewhere, but to all intents and purposes on the night that his life would change forever, Lennon was alone.

One of the first things he saw, he later reported, was an apple. And it was

Yoko Ono with her second husband, Tony Cox, who was an art promoter and film producer. Both of them were prominent names on the avant-garde art scene in New York before they came to London, looking for further acclaim and success.

on sale – for £200. Lennon got the joke straight away and smiled. But what really caught his eye was a ladder placed in the middle of the gallery floor. At the top of the ladder, hanging off the wall, was what looked like a black canvas with a spyglass hanging off it. Lennon climbed the ladder and then looked through the glass. In very tiny letters he could make out one word and one word alone – 'yes'. Lennon was impressed. For him, the word was positive

and encouraging. It did not say 'go away and get lost'. It said, 'yes'. John Dunbar now brought Yoko over to meet John. John was waiting for this moment. He knew that despite all the smiles, the handshakes and the expressions of goodwill, Dunbar would be seriously slacking in his job if he did not arrange for his client to meet a very rich pop star. In that sense, John had not lost any of his inbuilt cynicism. On meeting the Beatle, Yoko handed Lennon a card that said 'Breathe' on it. Lennon took one look and he panted right back at her. The stage was set.

In Beatle Land the official story line is that John and Yoko circled each other for about 18 months before hooking up and becoming one of the world's most famous couples. According to John's chauffeur Les Anthony this timeline is incorrect. He states that within a month of their meeting John and Yoko were making out in the back of his Rolls-Royce. Naturally, such an affair had to be kept secret. John was still married to Cynthia and to leave her for Yoko would have brought the world's media down on their heads.

JOHN VIEWED LIFE WITH CYNTHIA AND JULIAN AS A TRAP. HE HAD NOT BECOME A BEATLE TO LIVE LIKE A NORMAL MAN

Despite John admitting to Cynthia that he had slept with hundreds of women (including some of her friends), his wife stayed resolutely by his side. Cynthia loved John, would have done anything for him. She understood the temptations offered to a Beatle on an hourly basis, and as long John came home and kept the relationship alive, all things were possible in her eyes.

John had no such feelings. He viewed life with Cynthia and Julian as a trap, something that constrained him from following his impulses. He had not become a Beatle to live like a normal man. His relationship with both his wife and his son was patchy and highly volatile. Away on tour for the best part of Julian's early years (the week he was born, John and Brian Epstein had holidayed in Spain), Lennon was not the greatest father or husband, something he would later acknowledge.

It was left to Cynthia to raise Julian as best she could. In later life, Julian would say, 'Sometimes I wish I had been born an average Joe.' For the press, however, Cynthia was the perfect wife – loving, devoted and a great mother. In their eyes she was the epitome of what every woman should aspire to, so for John to dump her and go off with an avant-garde artist would be an outrage.

What's more, Yoko was Japanese and that only deepened the sin. Britain had fought Japan in World War II and viewed their closed society with enormous mistrust. Stories of Japanese torture methods applied to allied troops were still being met with incredulity.

John didn't care. Yoko was unlike any other woman he had come across. She was interesting, attractive (John had a thing for Oriental women), but most of all she was artistically challenging. John later stated that all his life he had dreamt of meeting an artist woman that he could fall in love with forever. When he and Yoko started conversing, Lennon quickly realized that his dream had just been made reality. 'That's why when people ask me for a precis of my story, I put, "born, lived, met Yoko" because that's what it's been about.'

YOKO'S AVANT-GARDE THEORIES REIGNITED THE BEATNIK SIDE OF JOHN THAT HAD BEEN FORGED AT ART COLLEGE AND SUBSEQUENTLY BEATEN OUT OF HIM BY BEATLEMANIA

Yoko, he would later say, was not his equal – she was, in fact, his superior. He likened their relationship to a pupil–master one, always casting himself as the pupil lucky enough to have fallen into Yoko's orbit. For her part, Yoko unwittingly highlighted his increasingly unsuitable situation at home.

Lennon was hopelessly adrift in Weybridge. After spending hours engaged in intense conversation with Yoko, he would travel back to his suburban home, his suburban wife, his suburban life. He would ignore wife and child and lock himself away, Yoko playing endlessly on his mind. Theirs was a love not born out of physical desire but a meeting of two minds,

one firm and imaginative, the other highly distorted by years of Beatlemania.

Yoko's refusal to fawn or treat John in the way he had been accustomed to by the rest of the world both attracted and fascinated him. It was Yoko, he would later argue, who showed him that he had become a king whose ties to the throne had to be maintained by those around him, for once the king was dead the courtiers had no job. Thus began Lennon's abdication and his dismantling of Beatle Land, the country he had reigned over so gloriously these past few years.

Yoko's avant-garde theories reignited the Beatnik side of John, the side that had been forged at art college and subsequently beaten out of him by Beatlemania. He felt The Beatles had turned him into a puppet, and recalled, 'Yoko didn't give a shit about The Beatles. "What the fuck are The Beatles? I'm Yoko Ono. Treat me as me." From the day I met her she demanded equal space, equal time, equal rights.'

John looked at Yoko in amazement. Cynthia did not stand a chance. Their marriage had just entered its final stage and so – unknown to everyone – had John's relationship with The Beatles.

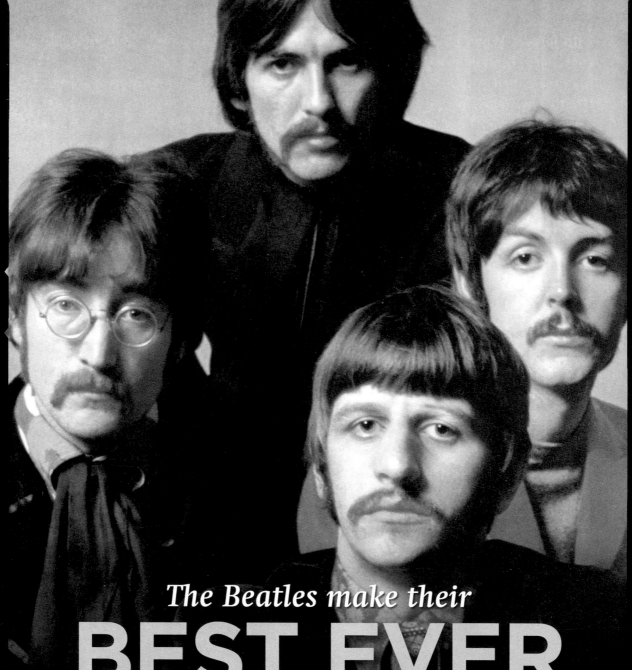

The Beatles make their

BEST EVER
SINGLE

DATE November 1966, Abbey Road Studios, London

The gang scattered and left each other to their own devices. For the first time since signing to EMI they would not see each other for at least a month. Previously during breaks they had holidayed together – Paul with Ringo, John with George, George with Paul. Tellingly, this time around they went off individually. As the gang dispersed one thought preyed on their minds: where do we go from here? No band had ever put an end to touring and become just a recording unit. Would the strategy work?

Ringo headed off to the sun, George went to India to study the sitar under Ravi Shankar, Paul stayed in London to compose the soundtrack for a film called *The Family Way* (1966) and then went to Africa, and John went to Spain to appear in Dick Lester's film, *How I Won The War* (1967). Lennon later said it was at this point that he first seriously considered quitting the band. He just didn't have the courage to make the first move. If being a Beatle had started to lose its appeal and no longer interested him, the same could be said of his home life. 'Instead of going home ... I immediately went to Spain with Dick Lester because I couldn't deal with not being continually on stage,' he confessed. 'And that was when the seed was planted, that I had to somehow get out of this without being thrown out by the others.'

Paul, ever the optimist, had no such qualms. He quickly began devising new strategies for the band. 'We were fed up with being The Beatles', he said. 'We really hated that fucking four little mop-top boys approach. We were not boys, we were men ... plus we'd got turned on to pot and thought of ourselves as artists ... Then on a plane I got this idea ...' And that idea

LENNON LATER SAID IT WAS AT THIS POINT THAT **HE FIRST CONSIDERED QUITTING THE BAND.** HE JUST DIDN'T HAVE THE COURAGE TO MAKE THE FIRST MOVE would lead to the making of the band's most famous work.

It was against this unsettled backdrop that Lennon began work on one of his greatest songs, 'Strawberry Fields Forever'. For the purposes of Lester's film Lennon had also spent time in Hamburg with Neil Aspinall visiting all the old haunts. When he returned to Almeria (Cynthia, Ringo and Maureen joined him two weeks into filming) he tapped into the past again and started writing a song named after the orphanage that stood close to his home

HE SUBVERTED THE FIGURES ON PENNY LANE: THE BANKER GOES COATLESS IN THE RAIN, THE FIREMAN CARRIES AN HOURGLASS, THE NURSE BELIEVES THAT SHE IS ACTING IN A PLAY

in Liverpool. The lyrics, he later said, were psychoanalysis, clever and cute but not saying a lot. One line – in which he sees himself alone and up a tree – alluded to his confusion about his character. Was he genius or madman? It was a question that he said had haunted him since he was five.

It was this ability to constantly change and challenge that served to keep his fellow Beatles on their toes. People were wary around Lennon, never quite knowing what he was thinking and feeling. This not only allowed him to control any given situation, but it also meant that any positive encouragement he gave had so much more meaning. Fourteen years after the band had split, Paul said of John, 'We all looked up to John. He was older and he was very much the leader; he was the quickest wit and the smartest and all that kind of thing ... He was certainly the one I looked up to most definitely.'

It is tempting to believe that McCartney wrote 'Penny Lane' in retaliation to Lennon's new song. Not so. In a November 1965 interview he mentioned that he was considering writing a song called 'Penny Lane' (probably in response to John's earlier masterpiece 'In My Life', which dealt with memories of the past). Like Lennon's offering, 'Penny Lane' harked back to the Liverpool of McCartney's youth.

Brimming with melody, verve and confidence, in 'Penny Lane' McCartney takes the listener on a vivid tour of the street stopping off to point out the barbers and the banker, the nurse and the fireman. These are traditional figures but McCartney subverts them; the banker doesn't wear a coat in the rain, the fireman carries an hourglass, the nurse believes she is acting in a play and the barber keeps photographs of all the customers he has ever served. Lennon, who helped him complete the third verse, used to meet Paul at Penny Lane so devising an ending was no problem.

John's was the first song the band recorded when they resumed work on 24 November 1966. As a measure of how times had changed 'Strawberry Fields Forever' took several days to record before it was considered anywhere near ready. 'Love Me Do' had taken two hours. The Beatles now had the run of Abbey Road Studios, allowing them to explore all kinds of sonic possibilities. From the original demo of John on acoustic guitar, the song mushroomed into a psychedelic masterpiece, using backwards tapes, tapes played at different speeds and all kinds of instrumentation such as the haunting Mellotron used for the intro.

Many versions of the song were tried out until Lennon asked Martin to take two differing versions and marry them together. That Martin was able to bridge two sections with different keys and emerge with a classic record is testament to the man's skill.

'Penny Lane' was next, taking up to nine days to record. Although this was the B-side, 'Penny Lane' had a much more commercial edge to it than 'Strawberry Fields Forever'. Its catchy piano riff, vivid imagery, bright sounds and musical adventurism made this song a much better candidate for a single.

On 27 January 1967 the band signed a new and better contract with EMI. The first thing the record company asked for was a new single. Without any thought, these two songs were handed to them and on 17 February 1967 this Beatles masterpiece was released. At the same time a promo was shot, which like the song it represented, also used backwards tapes (the band jumping in and out of trees) and surreal imagery. The band all sported moustaches and wore bright colourful clothing.

AS A MEASURE OF HOW TIMES HAD CHANGED 'STRAWBERRY FIELDS FOREVER' TOOK SEVERAL DAYS TO RECORD BEFORE IT WAS CONSIDERED ANYWHERE NEAR READY. 'LOVE ME DO' HAD TAKEN TWO HOURS

The song itself, however, was kept off the top spot by Engelbert Humperdinck's 'Release Me' thus prompting further speculation that the band's career was over. In fact, since the band had not toured the UK for over a year, media speculation over The Beatles' future had refused to abate. One programme called *Reporting 66* doorstepped all four band members as they each entered Abbey Road Studios. All of them laughed off the idea of a split then went to work on their new album, a thing provisionally entitled *Sgt. Pepper's Lonely Hearts Club Band*.

The Beatles launch
SGT. PEPPER

DATE 19 May 1967, Chapel Street, Belgravia, London

On 19 May 1967 the Belgravia home of Brian Epstein opened its doors to a select group of journalists, DJs and photographers. Unbeknown to his visitors, Brian had just spent several days at The Priory clinic recovering from his latest drug binge. After today's soirée he would return to rehab to continue his recovery. No one suspected a thing, and anyway they were not there to check on Epstein's wellbeing. They were there to hear an album that would change history. Its name – *Sgt. Pepper's Lonely Hearts Club Band*.

Present at the party would be the makers of this extraordinary work – The Beatles. The journalists and photographers (including a young American named Linda Eastman who would later become Mrs Paul McCartney) were excited. Many of them knew the band personally and were sympathetic to them (hence their invitation to attend) but had not spoken to them for quite some time.

Now that touring had stopped, access to the band had become limited. All anyone knew was that for the past five months they had been hidden away recording and that their last single, 'Strawberry Fields Forever', had not given them their customary number-one hit. As they sipped champagne and nibbled canapés, a noise suddenly came from above. The crowd looked up and there were The Beatles.

Paul was dressed in a grey pinstripe jacket and long scarf (very Small Faces actually), Ringo wore a thin pinstripe suit with huge lapels, George went for purple Edwardian-style jacket with a psychedelic patterned shirt but it was John who drew

IT WAS JOHN WHO DREW THE MOST ATTENTION. DRESSED IN A GREEN FLOWERY FRILLY SHIRT, MAROON CORDS, A SPORRAN AND BRIGHT YELLOW SOCKS, HE LOOKED GAUNT, HE LOOKED ELSEWHERE

the most attention. Dressed in a green flowery frilly shirt, maroon cords, a sporran and bright yellow socks, he looked gaunt, he looked elsewhere, he looked like he was on something. Biographer Ray Coleman would later write, 'John looked haggard, old, ill and hopelessly addicted to drugs. His eyes were glazed, his speech slow and slurred.'

GIVEN THE ENORMOUS PRESSURE ON THEM TO PRODUCE MAGIC, WHAT COULD THEY POSSIBLY DO TO SATISFY THE WORLD? ANSWER: DO WHAT PAUL HAD JUST DONE – ADOPT A DISGUISE AND CREATE AN ALTER-EGO BAND

The band posed for photos and then came down the stairs and started mingling with the guests. According to Coleman, Lennon kept enthusing about a record he could not stop playing. The only thing was he could not recall its name – it turned out to be 'Whiter Shade Of Pale' by Procol Harum. Lennon was also worried about the reception the band's audience would give their new work. 'Do you think they will like it, or have we gone too far?' he kept asking. He would know the answer within the week, and he would not be disappointed.

Sgt. Pepper was inspired by the art of disguise. On tour the band always carried wigs, glasses and hats for anyone wishing to deceive the fans or the press and go walkabout. Paul was always the most successful at getting away with this ruse. In fact, in Sweden, so good was his disguise that he fooled George and the press pack into thinking he was a photographer.

McCartney had holidayed in France, gone unrecognized among the locals, thanks to his use of hats and sunglasses. His success at doing this sparked an idea. Given that The Beatles were so successful, given the enormous pressure on them to produce magic, what could they possibly do to satisfy the world? Answer: do what Paul had just done – adopt a disguise and create an alter-ego band. In one stroke that idea opened up the world – The Beatles no longer had to be The Beatles. They could be who or what they liked.

The Beatles' debut album took a single day to make. By contrast *Sgt. Pepper* had taken five months. To turn their ideas into reality, they literally took over Abbey Road, working all kinds of hours, using all kinds of instruments and machines, turning the studio into their own personal playground to arrive at their dreams.

Interestingly, making their debut album in one of the other studios was a band called The Pink Floyd Sound. The Floyd were a major presence at London's leading psychedelic club, The UFO on Tottenham Court Road. Their unique mix of English whimsy and lengthy freak-out had won them a large following among many of the capital's serious LSD users. The Beatles would have taken note of The Floyd and their work, Lennon especially.

Despite frequently being under the influence of LSD, the drug had not yet subdued Lennon's fierce competitive streak. The band's demand that they forge ahead by creating new sounds had kept him busy composing songs such as 'Lucy In The Sky With Diamonds', inspired by a picture his son Julian had drawn at nursery; 'Being For The Benefit Of Mr. Kite!', inspired by a 19th-century circus poster; and 'Good Morning Good Morning', inspired by a cornflakes commercial.

As with *Revolver* the band looked to George Martin for extraordinary effects to create music never heard before. For example, Lennon wanted a fairground organ to feature on 'Being For The Benefit Of Mr. Kite!' and McCartney enquired whether it was possible to make his voice sound considerably younger on 'When I'm Sixty-Four'. The pressure placed on George Martin and his assistants was enormous.

The climax of all this creativity began the day John walked into Abbey Road in mid-January with a new song entitled, 'A Day In The Life'. This was his new 'Tomorrow Never Knows'. To realize the song's stunning potential, to really lift it out of the ordinary, 40 classical musicians were hired. Their job was to go from the bottom note of a scale to the top in just 24 bars. George Martin tried to explain. 'The orchestra just couldn't understand what George was talking about,' recalled Geoff Emerick. 'It didn't make any sense to them because they were all classically trained.'

It did not make much sense to them either when they were asked to don various masks. During the session, the band and entourage – also wearing novelty items such as joke spectacles and so on – wandered round with cameras, as did their guests for the night, which included the obligatory Mick and Keith from The Rolling Stones, Marianne Faithfull, Donovan, and Mike Nesmith from The Monkees. The presence of the latter musician was quite symbolic.

The Monkees, a band manufactured as America's answer to The Beatles, had supplanted The Fabs as the main object of UK female attention. The girls no longer swooned and screamed over The Fabs. They did that instead about The Monkees. In response to this shift, girls' magazines such as *Fab 208* had drastically reduced their coverage of The Beatles and filled their pages up with The Monkees instead. The Beatles had lost their place as the girls' favourite pin-ups. They were no longer cute, they were – well – weird.

After five months of toil the band declared their work ready for release. That the album had been driven forward by McCartney is evident in his absolute determination to create a sleeve to match the music. His initial ideas were mapped out in sketches and drawings, depicting the

Paul meets Linda Eastman for the second time at the press launch for *Sgt. Pepper's Lonely Hearts Club Band* at Brian Epstein's house on 19 May 1967. Not long after, Paul and Linda became an item, eventually forming a marriage that would last until Linda's tragic passing in 1998.

band holding clarinets and trumpets and wearing military-style jackets. The location would be an Edwardian living room with a picture of people they admired pinned to the wall behind them.

McCartney's next idea was to depict the band in front of huge floral clock being presented to a local Mayor with all their heroes and friends gathered round them. Paul showed these drawings to art dealer Robert Fraser who told him he should bring

in a real artist to execute the idea. Peter Blake, one of the founders of the Pop Art movement, was suggested. Together, Blake and McCartney came up with an image of The Beatles standing in front of a collage of their heroes. EMI Records were not pleased when they heard the idea. It would mean getting clearance from everyone the band selected. McCartney remained unfazed. He argued that everyone would be happy to be on a Beatles cover. And he was right.

'They gave us an indemnity for 10 million dollars royalties in the light of any legal action and set about contacting people,' recalled EMI head, Sir Joseph Lockwood. Leonard Bernstein was the first to receive the telegram, and said he would be 'delighted' to be on the cover. Astonishingly, considering The Beatles didn't bother to contact everybody, there has never been a claim on that sleeve.

Because of the cover, because The Beatles touted the album as a concept LP, and because the sleeve broke new ground by carrying the lyrics – the first LP ever to do so – many believe that *Sgt. Pepper* was the album that turned pop into art. Despite Bob Dylan's *Blonde On Blonde* and The Beach Boys' *Pet Sounds*, *Sgt. Pepper* grabbed that honour thanks mainly to its presentation.

Despite the album's weaknesses there is a mood and a style, a sense of purposeful imagination, which creates space and allows *Sgt. Pepper* to somehow triumph when it shouldn't. An album that has as its second track, Ringo – never the world's greatest vocalist – singing an average song ('With A Little Help From My Friends') should not work. But it does because there is huge goodwill behind every part of this album and therein lies its secret. On *Sgt. Pepper* there is no darkness, no aggravation, just fairytale lands where newspaper taxis take you away, and songs that talk about bettering yourself, songs that conjure up fairgrounds and circuses, all childhood fantasies that stir the mind positively.

At the photo session for the cover, McCartney urged his bandmates to gaze into Michael Cooper's camera and think the word 'love'. He later fought EMI to have cut outs inserted, for the cardboard to be thicker than on other albums, for the sleeve to be in full colour. And why? Because of his debt to music.

In the Barry Miles biography of McCartney, *Many Years From Now* (1997), Paul recalled how all of the Beatles had memories of being kids and taking their long-saved pocket money to the record department of Lewis's where they would rifle through the 45s and 78s to find the gems. Paul recalls how he was burnt by purchasing a record by The Ray Charles Orchestra, which he had assumed to be Ray Charles, whose records he loved. He was bitterly disappointed when the record turned out to be an instrumental. So when it came to *Sgt. Pepper* he was adamant that the band would create the record they had always wanted to make. 'We'll really do it all this time,' he said. 'We're in no hurry. There's no tour we have got to be on, we're getting stoned, we're feeling great; we were being cool about this whole thing. We wanted it to be very very full of value.'

Sgt. Pepper spent a total of 27 weeks at number one. In 1968 it was nominated for seven Grammys and won four. To date, it has sold 32 million copies worldwide, which certainly answers John's urgent question as to whether The Beatles had gone too far.

The band in their famous *Sgt. Pepper* outfits, which were hired from theatrical outfitter Berman's on London's Shaftesbury Avenue.

ALL YOU NEED IS LOVE

is sung to 400 million people

DATE 25 June 1967, Abbey Road Studios, London

The 60s had hit its stride. Youth culture in the form of hippies had started pushing forward ideas of peace and the BBC wanted in on it. Earlier in the year they met The Beatles, asking if they would be interested in participating in a groundbreaking project – the first ever global television link up. Entitled *Our World*, the 125-minute programme would be broadcast live to 26 countries. The BBC wanted The Beatles to represent the UK with a new song. Were they up for it?

They certainly were. John and Paul got to work. Actually, they left it until near the deadline before revealing their hand. Paul came up with 'Baby You're A Rich Man' but John trumped him with 'All You Need Is Love', a far more suitable song to take to the masses. 'All You Need Is Love' was sloganeering, catchy and simple to comprehend. It would have fitted perfectly on *Sgt. Pepper's Lonely Hearts Club Band*, the album that would dominate the charts all summer and showed that despite Lennon's leadership loosening due to excessive drug intake, he still had the power to slap down those snapping at his heels.

The song caught the spirit of the times. The first line consisted of the word 'love' being repeated nine times, the second line alluded to John's firm belief that nothing in life is impossible, that we are all capable of achieving whatever we want from life. The young man who had terrified Hamburg with his pill popping, his beer swilling and his aggressive nature was now decked out in flowery clothes, telling the whole world that love is all you need. 'So we had one message for the world – love,' Paul said, 'We need more love in the world.'

He had a point. Just days before the band laid down the rhythm tracks for the song, Israel and Palestine entered a Six-Day War, Greece fell to a military dictatorship and riots broke out in Tampa, Florida, when police shot a young black man named Martin Chambers. The Beatles in their new role as avatars (defined as an embodiment or personification of a principle, attitude or view of life) were the answer to the violence and the chaos.

For the occasion the band had commissioned a young Dutch design team

The band rehearse 'All You Need Is Love' in Abbey Road for their appearance on the groundbreaking *Our World* TV show, the first satellite-uplink performance broadcast worldwide on 25 June 1967.

who they had become friendly with (John especially) over the months leading up to the broadcast. The Fool was a collective made up of two women – Marijke Koger and Josje Leeger – and two guys – Simon Posthuma and Barry Finch. They were discovered in Ibiza by a photographer named Barry Ferris, whose pictures of their clothes were published in *The Times*. London fell for them so they arrived, opened up a studio and by frequenting various clubs tapped into many bands, including The Beatles. The Fool designed many of the outlandish clothes the band wore for the broadcast.

The band invited numerous friends and celebrities to the studio for the live event. These included Keith Richards, Mick Jagger, Marianne Faithfull, Keith Moon, Eric Clapton, Pattie Boyd, Jane Asher, Graham Nash and Mike McCartney. The idea was that the TV cameras would capture a party where The Beatles were performing. Along with the band was a 13-piece orchestra. To safeguard themselves, the rhythm tracks and other elements of the song had already been recorded. John's lead vocal, Paul's bass, George's guitar solo, Ringo's drums, the band's harmonies and the strings were played live and the rest was transmitted from George Martin's studio. Flower displays had been brought in and Martin conducted the orchestra himself, adding touches from the French national anthem, 'La Marseillaise', Bach's 'Brandenburg Concerto', 'Greensleeves' and music from American band leader Glenn Miller.

After the show the guests drifted away and the band stayed behind to put the finishing touches to the recorded version of the song, which they would release as their new single on Friday 7 July. The track was a first in that for the first time ever on a Beatles single, George Martin was given a credit. The song dominated the single charts that summer while *Sgt. Pepper* ruled supreme in the album charts. The band's musical output that year was again astonishing for its quality, inventiveness and sheer craftsmanship. Moreover, The Beatles had managed to change their image and outlook completely and still remain highly successful.

One reason for this great achievement was their consummate skill as songwriters. Whether they were mop-tops or acid-heads, it did not matter. Beatles records tended to be mini masterpieces of melody and sound and usually proved highly irresistible to most people. Incredibly, they had not finished there. In the year he wrote 'Strawberry Fields Forever', 'A Day In The Life' and 'All You Need Is Love', Lennon was also writing a new song, which he would call 'I Am The Walrus'.

The *Our World* event was a success, despite the USSR pulling out at the last minute (a decision that carried some irony, as it was the pacifism pushed forward by Russia's greatest writer Leo Tolstoy,

THE YOUNG MAN THAT HAD TERRIFIED HAMBURG WITH HIS PILL POPPING, HIS BEER SWILLING AND HIS AGGRESSIVE NATURE WAS NOW DECKED OUT IN FLOWERY CLOTHES, TELLING THE WHOLE WORLD THAT LOVE IS ALL YOU NEED

which had served to influence Gandhi and Martin Luther King and, in turn, The Beatles' generation) and was watched by a record-breaking audience of an estimated 400 million people. The event also proved significant to John. It showed him how to use his huge popularity as a musician to put forward his views on subjects such as world peace. He would become a master manipulator of the press. But first he needed to buy an island.

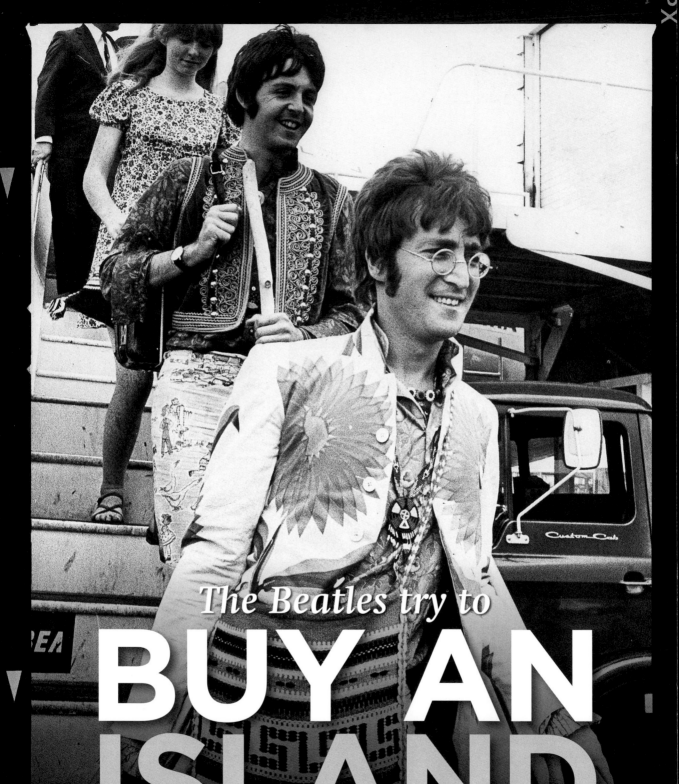

The Beatles try to

BUY AN ISLAND

DATE July 1967, Athens, Greece

Yanni Alexis Mardas was a young Greek man on the make. He arrived in London in 1965 and was soon friends with John Dunbar, who ran the Indica Gallery in Mason's Yard. In the early days, he and Dunbar got on so well that they moved into a flat together on Bentinck Street, Marylebone. Yanni started work as a TV repairman and then through Dunbar got to meet various celebrities, including Brian Jones of The Rolling Stones.

As he would do with all the big names he came to shake hands with, Mardas pitched an idea to Jones. It was a psychedelic light box and he was so good with the patter that it got Mardas a place on The Rolling Stones' 1967 European Tour, attempting to match the onstage lighting with the band's music.

Through Jones, Mardas met Lennon and for him Mardas pitched the Nothing invention, basically a small box that carried blinking lights. On LSD Lennon would spend hours gazing at this contraption (and this is the trouble with drugs – before they destroy you, they put you off your guard and leave you highly vulnerable). Lennon said, 'Wow', nicknamed him 'Magic Alex' and brought him into The Beatles' circle but never into the gang. Other ideas of Alex's that caught Lennon's attention were an X-ray camera

and a force field that would be installed around the band's homes, keeping them safe and sound. There was also talk of Alex building a flying saucer spaceship.

In July 1967, given the band's huge artistic triumphs, a holiday was required. Lennon by now was tripping most days and hated living in Weybridge. It was he who decided that the band and their close ones should build a commune and live happily

FOR LENNON, MARDAS PITCHED THE NOTHING INVENTION, BASICALLY A SMALL BOX THAT CARRIED BLINKING LIGHTS. ON LSD LENNON WOULD SPEND HOURS GAZING AT THIS CONTRAPTION

ever after in real life Beatle Land, free from other people and their constant demands. They could build their own houses, their own schools, even their own society. But most important of all they could ingest as many drugs as they liked and not have to worry about the police busting them.

THEY COULD BUILD THEIR OWN HOUSES, SCHOOLS, EVEN THEIR OWN SOCIETY. BUT MOST IMPORTANT OF ALL THEY COULD INGEST AS MANY DRUGS AS THEY LIKED

In the book *The Beatles Anthology* (2000), Derek Taylor outlined the master plan. Pretty soon, The Beatles and their entourage would cut themselves off from the straight world forever. They would buy and then develop a huge estate in which they could escape the world's eyes. In the middle of the estate would be the main building, a Modernist compound made of glass and iron, where the band and their manager, Brian Epstein, would live. No expense would be spared in providing the best of everything. On the outskirts of the main building, other houses would be built where the trusted inner circle (Taylor, Neil Aspinall, Mal Evans and families) would reside. There would be a creative

area set aside for the band to work and play in. The only problem was where to build the paradise? One of the suggestions was none other than Norfolk. Cold, wet and windy Norfolk. Taylor explained that weather conditions would pose no problem to the Fabs. 'We would set up a chain reaction so strong that nothing could stand in our way,' he explained. 'And why the hell not? "They've tried everything else," John said realistically, "wars, nationalism, fascism, communism, capitalism, nastiness, religion – none of it works. So why not this?"'

When this idea was again mooted one night, Magic Alex was present. He chipped in, told the band of an island in Greece he knew about. He added that he had connections high up in the Greek government and should the band want to buy it, he could speed up the process. George later recalled, 'Alex's dad was something to do with the military in Greece, and Alex knew all the military there, very strange.'

In fact Greece had just suffered a military coup so buying any real estate there would mean giving large amounts of money to fascists. Surprisingly, that idea did not faze Lennon at all. He argued that all governments were corrupt, whether they were fascist or communist, socialist or democratic. 'Look what they do here,' he pointed out. 'They stopped Radio Caroline and they tried to put The Stones away [Mick Jagger, Keith Richards and art dealer Robert Fraser had just been charged with possession of drugs] while they're spending billions on nuclear armaments and the place is full of US bases that no one knows about.'

The band with wives and assorted employees such as Alistair Taylor and Neil Aspinall flew to Athens where Magic Alex awaited them and they were whisked through passport control. Alex later claimed that he had struck a deal with the vice president of Greece to allow the band immunity so that they could bring their drugs in.

THE NEGOTIATIONS THAT WERE REQUIRED TO SEE THE DEAL THROUGH DRAGGED ON AND ON AND EVENTUALLY THE BAND DITCHED THE DEAL. THEY SOLD THEIR DOLLARS BACK TO THE GOVERNMENT AT A PROFIT

Lennon came off the plane tripping. Much to his horror he discovered that he had left his LSD back at home. A phone call was made to Mal Evans in London. 'John needs his medicine for his *acidity*...' Evans arrived the next day carrying John's stash. Their chartered yacht was detained for three days due to bad weather, so the party stayed in Athens where they were continually snapped by government photographers. The group then sailed on to view the island. George later remembered it as a wonderful trip, during which he and John tripped on acid and sat around in the sun playing ukuleles.

Back home, The Beatles' office was instructed to get the acquisition under way. The cost was £95,000 and The Beatles had to buy special export dollars from the British Government to make the purchase. Prime Minster James Callaghan personally wrote to them allowing the band to take the money out of the country but, 'Not a penny more. I wonder how you are going to furnish it?' he added.

The negotiations that were required to see the deal through dragged on and on and eventually the band ditched the deal. They sold their dollars back to the government and were pleasantly surprised to find the exchange rate had gone up and they had made £11,000 profit. 'It was about the only time The Beatles ever made any money on a business venture,' George said dryly. Still, at least hippy idealism carried some benefits.

The Beatles meet the
MAHARISHI

DATE 24 August 1967, The Hilton Hotel, London

George Harrison's spiritual journey began in the Bahamas on 25 February 1965. He was filming The Beatles' second film, *Help!*, when a man named Swami Vishnudevananda came up and handed the band copies of his book, *The Complete Illustrated Book Of Yoga*. The work contained several yoga exercises and an introduction to the Hindu religion. The book's thesis was that spiritual enlightenment could not be attained through the mind; one had to transcend all the senses and leave behind the intellect to discover true nirvana.

George was the Beatle most taken by the book. His nickname among the fans was 'The Quiet One'. Where John and Paul would laugh out loud on stage, basking in the craziness they were creating, George would just smile knowingly. At press conferences he often just mimicked John's humour or he kept silent, impatiently waiting for the moment he could leave.

In later years he would be the most irascible when it to came to the press. When *Reporting 66* asked the band about their future outside Abbey Road in November 1966, it was George who displayed the most irritability. He was certainly the most anxious to kill off Beatlemania for good, discovering that what he had attained in the form of money, girls and luxury was really not worth the incredible hassle that went with being a Beatle.

Before the Bahamas, before the meeting with Swami, the band had been filming at Twickenham Film Studios. In one scene they had to eat in an Indian restaurant, which had been furnished with the typical accoutrements. When filming finished, George picked up a sitar standing

GEORGE NOW BEGAN AN ENDURING FASCINATION WITH INDIAN MUSIC AND RELIGION AND IN DOING SO WAS ABLE TO CARVE OUT A DISTINCT ROLE WITHIN THE BEATLE GANG. HE WAS NOW THE INDIAN BEATLE

nearby and so began a lifelong relationship with the instrument.

At the party in Los Angeles in August 1965 when Peter Fonda had continually talked about his death and annoyed Lennon so intensely, Harrison had talked with the musicians Roger McGuinn and David Crosby of The Byrds.

As they spoke, the music of Ravi Shankar was brought up and the two Byrds began wildly enthusing about India's leading sitar player. Not long after, Harrison began buying Shankar's albums and loved every one of them. Soon, he purchased his first sitar and started to

THE BEATLES – MINUS RINGO – SAT AND LISTENED TO THE MAHARISHI'S THOUGHTS ON THE SPIRITUAL LIFE. AFTERWARDS, THEY WERE GIVEN A PRIVATE 90-MINUTE SESSION WITH HIM

figure the instrument out. At the recording session for John's new song, 'Norwegian Wood', Lennon claims he asked George to play the song's riff (as Lennon later put it, 'the dee, dee, dee diddly dee bit') on the sitar. George did, and so chalked up another first: The Beatles became the first band to feature the sitar on a pop record.

George now began an enduring fascination with Indian music and religion and in doing so was to carve out a distinct role within the Beatle gang. He was now the Indian Beatle. During the recording session for 'Norwegian Wood', one of the sitar strings broke. Unsure of where to go for a replacement, George called up EMI who in turn furnished him with the number of the Asian Music Circle in Finchley, London. George would spend three months being taught sitar by the teachers in the Circle before travelling to India in September 1966 to receive further tutelage from Ravi Shankar himself. Harrison spent a month with Shankar and became deeply impressed by the country's many religions and the manner in which music is used for spiritual purposes.

For George, sick of Beatlemania, sick of songs that went 'I love you, you love me, happily ever after', Indian music and religion were suddenly offering him something far more meaningful. Thrilled by this discovery, George's excitement was only tempered by the realization that mastering the sitar was not an option for him. Ravi Shankar told the Beatle that he and every other sitar player of note had risen to their position by practising 12 hours a day since childhood. Even without the touring, George's duties as a Beatle and his age easily prevented him from fulfilling such a dream. Still, Shankar was impressed by George's honesty and humility, by his willingness to adopt a new culture.

George was not the only one drawn to India. Despite her fame and money, his wife Pattie Boyd felt dissatisfied with her life and was seeking something extra, too. Browsing the Sunday papers one morning in February 1967, she came across an advert for transcendental-meditation classes in London and quickly enrolled herself in the Spiritual Regeneration Movement.

Boyd now became a regular meditator. In August, she read that the Maharishi Mahesh Yogi was giving a series of talks at the London Hilton. She invited George to attend. George – of course – invited the gang to come with him.

At the Hilton Hotel, The Beatles – minus Ringo whose wife Maureen had given birth to son Jason a few days earlier – sat and listened to the Maharishi's thoughts on the spiritual life. Afterwards, they were given a private 90-minute session with him. 'Maharishi was every bit as impressive as I thought he would be, and we were spellbound,' Pattie was later to say. 'At the end we went to speak to him and he said we must go to Wales where he was running a ten-day summer conference ... We leapt at it.'

Two days later the Beatle party jumped on a train at Euston Station and headed for the retreat in Bangor. Mick Jagger was also with them. Harrison later said in that typical dry manner of his, 'He was always lurking around in the background, trying to find out what was happening ...'

In the chaos of the occasion, with press and fans and security all converging on the band as they ran for the train (typically they were late), Cynthia Lennon was left behind on the platform. Neil Aspinall drove her to Bangor later that day. When she got there John's first comment was a biting one. 'Always late aren't you?' he snapped at her. Cynthia burst into tears. Years later, she confessed that was when she knew her marriage to John was over, her standing on a platform surrounded by strangers as John sped off into the future.

'The seminar was in a school,' Paul recalled. 'He would tell you how to meditate and then you would go up to your room and try it. And of course you can't do it for the first half hour ... But then I got good at it.'

The gang fell for meditation, big time. Lennon was quick to start endorsing its properties. 'Even if you go into the meditation bit just curious or cynical, once you go into it, you see. The only thing you can do is judge on your own experience. I'm less sceptical than I ever was ... You get a sniff and you are hooked.'

As John spoke a phone started ringing near to him. When it was answered a voice told them that Brian Epstein had just passed away.

The Beatles and friends with the Maharishi in 1967 after which they immersed themselves in meditation and withdrew from the LSD scene.

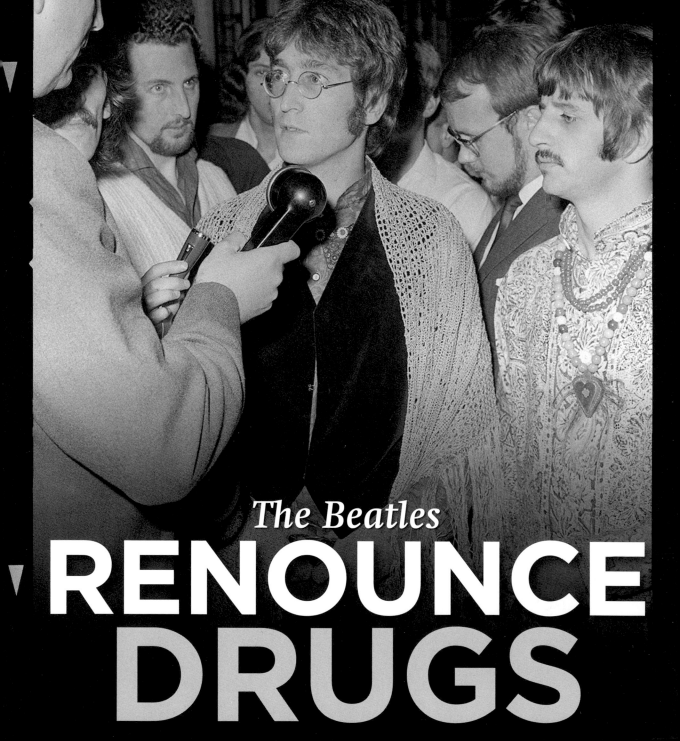

The Beatles
RENOUNCE
DRUGS

DATE 26 August 1967, Bangor, North Wales

On 19 June 1967, the day after his 25th birthday, a news crew arrived at Paul McCartney's house to ask him if he had taken LSD. Paul had been shouting the odds about drugs, telling *Life* magazine and *The People* newspaper about the trips he had been on, what he had seen, how it had changed him. Paul invited the men into his garden, sat down and told them, yes he had taken the drug, had taken it four times to be precise.

The interviewer asked if he felt that as a pop star, an icon to millions, perhaps he should not be telling the world about his usage? 'I don't think my fans are going to take drugs just because I did,' he replied. '... I was asked whether I had or not ... I am quite prepared to keep it as a very personal thing if you will too. If you shut up about it, then I will.'

LSD was proving to be problematic for the band, especially Paul. He was far from being anti-drugs and still enjoyed smoking pot, but he was always wary of anything that really took you out of control. John loved spiralling out of himself and losing all sense of reality but Paul was too focused to embark on that journey.

His refusal created one of the first significant fissures within the band. Normally, they moved as one. Not this time. Moreover, in the pop world of the mid-60s, LSD had acquired a badge of hipness. Either you were very cool and had taken the trip, or you were a square, someone on the outside. For a long while McCartney was on the outside but finally succumbed in late 1966. Gang thinking had won him over. 'I eventually thought,' McCartney recalled, 'we can't all be in The Beatles with me being the only one who hasn't taken it.'

In *The People*, McCartney said of his trip, 'It was truly a religious experience. I had never realized what people were talking about when they say God is within you, that He is love and truth ... God is a force we are all part of.'

The rest of the band read the above quote with a sense of real astonishment. For a year and half they had been trying to get Paul in on the trip and when they finally did, what did he do but go and tell the whole world about it? For them, there were compelling reasons to keep quiet about LSD. For one, the drug had been made illegal and such a disclosure would attract the attention of the infamous Detective Sergeant Norman Pilcher of Scotland Yard. Pilcher's harrying of pop stars was a cause for concern. He determined to use every method – legal or illegal – to catch his fish and did so. The Rolling Stones had been famously busted for drugs at Keith Richards' house in February of that year.

Second, the band knew the kind of press storm such an admission would bring and they could do without the hassle. It was hard enough being a Beatle without adding needlessly to the load.

Yet here was McCartney without even consulting them breaking cover and informing the world what he (and therefore by extension, the gang) had been up to. John and George were furious. John was, of course, even more scathing of Paul's actions. 'He always times his big announcements right on the letter doesn't he?' (Lennon's last comment carries much weight. To this day, McCartney's press announcements invariably fall on significant Beatle-related dates.)

It is also possible there was another force at work, one that perhaps demonstrates McCartney's constant desire to usurp his rivals. At the time of his announcement Keith Richards and Mick Jagger were facing prison sentences for possession of drugs. Richards had thrown an LSD party at his Redlands Estate in West Wittering, in the south of England, the police caught wind and 18 policemen had descended on the house. Their haul was negligible but their determination to prosecute was not. Battle lines were drawn.

Many people saw this trial as the Establishment taking on the new pop aristocracy although interestingly the one band that seemed immune to prosecution was The Beatles. George Harrison and Pattie Boyd had attended

FOR A YEAR AND HALF THEY HAD BEEN TRYING TO GET PAUL IN ON THE TRIP AND WHEN THEY FINALLY DID, WHAT DID HE DO BUT GO AND TELL THE WHOLE WORLD ABOUT IT?

the Redlands party but left early having decided not to trip out with the rest of them. When Harrison drove out of Redlands, the police moved in. It has long been assumed that they had been waiting for the Beatle to depart, which gives you some idea of the standing they still enjoyed as national treasures.

The following year, thanks to events such as this, that privilege would be stripped away and John and George would be busted. McCartney's admission therefore was not only provocative – catch me if you can – but allowed The Beatles to leapfrog The Stones as the leaders of the counterculture movement.

In a show of great solidarity Brian Epstein publicly supported his friend, adding he had tried LSD and found it had helped him enormously. Epstein's actions backfired on him. He was rebuked by an angry McCartney – who thought Epstein was trying to steal his thunder – and then by such favourites of his as Cilla Black, who demanded to know what the hell he thought he was doing, as the last thing she wanted was her manager linked to dirty drug takers. Epstein said sorry and then privately wondered why he had bothered trying to cover for his clients.

Meanwhile, George had travelled to San Francisco, the city where hippy drug culture had started, to see such trendy areas as Haight-Ashbury. Expecting to find a place peopled with right-on youngsters and groovy shops, George found himself instead walking round a rundown area, surrounded by freaks for whom drugs were not playing a liberating role but were wreaking physical and mental harm.

Offered tabs of LSD and tokes on huge joints, George refused everything and got out of there as quickly as possible, swearing never to take LSD again. John carried on as normal but the pace he was setting himself was just too much to bear. The acid he was taking, smuggled in from America, was pure and incredibly strong.

The highs may have been unbelievable but the lows were the worst.

In August, The Beatles came into the Maharishi's orbit and on 26 August decamped to North Wales to attend a meditation course. On their second day there, the band held a press conference where they turned 180 degrees and renounced the use of all illegal substances. 'You cannot keep taking drugs forever,' McCartney told the world. 'We are looking for something more natural. This is it. It [drugs] was an experience we went through. Now it's over and we don't need it any more. We think we're finding other ways of getting there.'

George added, 'LSD is not the real answer. It doesn't give you anything. It enables you to see a lot of possibilities that you may never have noticed before, but it isn't the answer.' The rest of the band agreed with him. Meditation would now replace the function of drugs as an artistic conduit and the pursuit of its powers and gifts would bring about one of the band's finest works with their next album, simply entitled *The Beatles* but known the world over as *The White Album*.

BRIAN EPSTEIN DIES,

aged 32

DATE 27 August 1967, Chapel Street, Belgravia, London

How long was the road that led from The Cavern to a spacious house in Belgravia where he drew his last breath, thus beginning the band's journey towards the break-up. And how long a time from the days when desperation consumed his soul as yet another company turned him down, to the night he stood at Shea Stadium and looked at all those people screaming their love for *his* boys. These moments and so many more led to the tragic passing of Brian Epstein.

Epstein was the best manager for The Beatles but he was not a businessman, he was not a shark. He was a gentleman and he expected others to act in the same fashion. Big mistake. Promoters in Liverpool were always slightly astonished when the band showed up to fulfil engagements booked six months previously that they were now far too big to undertake. In turn, Epstein was always somewhat astounded by their attitude. If he and the band committed to something then they saw it through. That was the proper way.

Under Epstein, The Beatles could have earned millions more than they did. He gave away their merchandise and signed away their first soundtrack album. Yet one quality overruled his mistakes – his absolute honesty. The band could trust him 100 per cent. In the era of Larry Parnes and Don Arden, of unscrupulous operators at every level of the business, honesty was a valuable asset. Unlike so many of his peers, Epstein was not in the hunt. He came from money and thus he expected money to come to him; cash was never that big a motivator in the way it was for others. Plus, Brian Epstein had to have had something about him for the band to open up and let him into Beatle Land.

Lennon famously said, 'Would The Beatles be where they are today if it weren't

> UNLIKE SO MANY OF HIS PEERS, **EPSTEIN WAS NOT IN THE HUNT.** HE CAME FROM MONEY AND THUS HE EXPECTED MONEY TO COME TO HIM

for Epstein? Not the same as we know it, no. But the question doesn't apply, because we met him and what happened, happened ... he helped us and we helped him.'

Brian loved the band, 'the boys', far too much to ever hurt them. He started off their superior with his cars and his handmade suits but pretty soon he was as much in awe of them as the rest of the world was. 'One of the biggest hang-ups I ever had was to categorize people,' he said, months away from his passing, 'and one of the things The Beatles have taught me is not to. They do not categorize people, things or music.'

BRIAN LOVED THE BAND TOO MUCH TO EVER HURT THEM. HE STARTED OFF THEIR SUPERIOR BUT SOON HE WAS AS MUCH IN AWE OF THEM AS THE REST OF THE WORLD WAS

Of course, it was John he loved the most and that was because of John's capricious nature. Epstein (like everyone else) never knew where he stood with John. One minute Lennon would be snapping at him to shut up, count the money and leave the music to the professionals, the next he would be hugging him. John was the one who fascinated, who teased, who showed glimpses of his soul and then shut up shop, always leaving you wanting more, always making it about him, never about you.

The others were quite straightforward, really. Paul moaned a lot and constantly questioned things, George kept a beady eye on the money and Ringo was down to earth and lovable. But John stood out because his unpredictability was the only predictable thing about him, and it was that quality – keeping people on their toes – that drew people such as Brian to him, desperate to understand this mercurial man. Moreover, Lennon tapped into the heart of Brian's sexuality. Epstein's excellent manners and demeanour were in no way reflected in his sexual preferences. He liked rough sex with rough boys, and Lennon was as rough as they came.

At the start of the adventure, Epstein managed the band. He got them to smarten up and act professionally. Yet by the time of Beatlemania what advice could he give them? Musically they were sprinting away and on stage they bowed, smiled and acted cute. They had it all in the palms of their hands. What on earth could Epstein say to the Kings of the World? 'Great show, lads, and here's the cash'?

By 1965 Epstein was more of an administrator than a manager, booking world tours, working like an agent. But that was OK because Epstein loved Beatle Land – in Beatle Land he could escape the straitjackets that his background, religion and sexuality had placed around him. Would he have danced to Motown and dropped acid without The Beatles in his life? It seems fairly unlikely.

Epstein's major flaw was his many insecurities. After the band quit touring Epstein believed he had been rendered obsolete. This was their way of saying 'Farewell, Mr Epstein'. His paranoia was deepened by LSD and various other chemical concoctions. So bad were these binges post-touring, post-Beatlemania, that Epstein often went into rehab to recover. In fact, the night before the *Sgt. Pepper* album launch at his Belgravia house was spent at The Priory clinic.

Yet it can be safely stated that at no point did the band ever discuss relieving him of his duties. The Beatles were a gang, they were loyal, first to themselves and then to others that had helped them along the way. Epstein – along with Neil Aspinall, Mal Evans, Derek Taylor, Peter Brown and Geoffrey Ellis – was at the centre of the group who had proved themselves to The Beatles. With his contract with the band now up for renewal, Epstein became convinced he would be sacked. Not so. At a party he gave two weeks after the *Sgt. Pepper* bash, John and George hugged him and told him never to worry about a thing. They were high on acid but the depth of their feelings had to have been there already in order to be heightened by the drug.

On 27 August Epstein's butler and housekeeper found him in his bedroom – the drugs had taken the life out of him and he was no more. The Beatles did not attend his funeral, knowing that their presence would detract from the occasion. Instead, they attended a memorial service a few weeks later at the New London Synagogue on Abbey Road.

THE BEATLES DID NOT ATTEND BRIAN'S FUNERAL, KNOWING THAT THEIR PRESENCE WOULD DETRACT FROM THE OCCASION. INSTEAD, THEY ATTENDED A MEMORIAL SERVICE A FEW WEEKS LATER

The truth was by now dawning on them. First they abolished the manager's position as an acknowledgment that no one could replace Brian. Then they tried to do his job and suddenly the world seemed a much more difficult place. 'We collapsed,' Lennon recalled. 'I knew that we were in trouble then. I didn't really have any misconceptions about our ability to do anything other than play music, and I was scared. I thought, "We've had it now."'

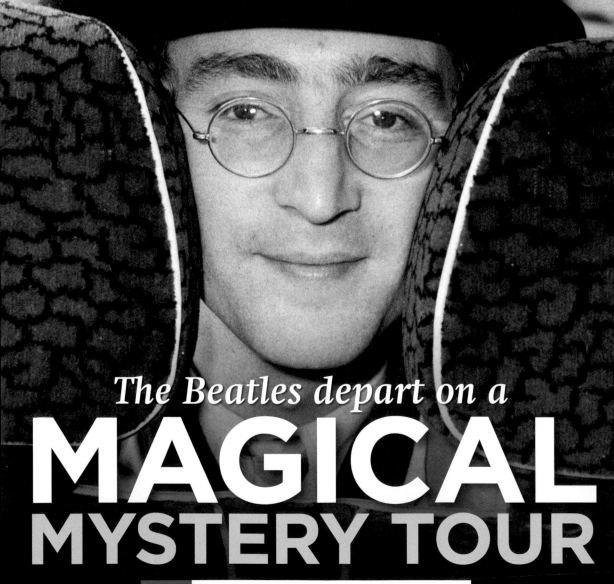

The Beatles depart on a

MAGICAL
MYSTERY TOUR

DATE 11 September 1967, Baker Street, London

With Epstein dead, workaholic Paul had to ensure that the group stayed together. He knew they could not afford to sink into depression over Brian's loss, for that way led to oblivion. They needed to work. From now on, all of the band's main ideas would emanate from McCartney. For Lennon the gang was no longer his only concern. He had started questioning the band's usefulness, and in doing so planted the seed that would cause him to kill that which he had once loved above all else.

The gap opened up by not touring now allowed other elements to catch Lennon's obsessive attention, namely meditation and Japanese avant-garde artist Yoko Ono. Music still drove him forward, but it wasn't to the exclusion of other influences. Soon, he would using one force in particular to break the gang up for good.

When the recording of *Sgt. Pepper* wound down, Paul flew to America as a 21st-birthday surprise for his girlfriend Jane Asher, who was touring in a production of *Romeo And Juliet*. Paul took Mal Evans and his movie camera along for the ride. He began shooting in various American locations and from this came the idea for a film in which a group of people would board a bus and travel round the country, the camera capturing their adventures and dialogue.

'I used to do a lot of amateur filming,' McCartney recalled, 'So, the idea tumbled together that we'd hire a bus, take a bunch of people out and start trying to make up something about a magical mystery tour.'

Part of the drive behind the film was a pressing need for the band to sustain their relationship with the fans through mediums other than the live concert. We must remember that in the Britain of The Beatles the media for pop music was extremely limited. For fans who could not see the band in the flesh now, television would be their only chance to see them. Tony Barrow, the band's press officer at the time, recalled, 'Paul made it clear to me that his aim was to make a feature-length film for full-scale theatrical release and he felt that a successful screen "tour" would go a long way towards plugging the gaping hole left by the axing of the Fab Four's concert trips.'

McCartney's idea brought together two very disparate elements – he mixed the band's northern working-class culture with LSD. That they were able in part to make this work is testament to the band's genius. The Beatles were always working from a huge palette of influences and brilliantly weaving them into fresh, unique works of art. McCartney once recalled them adopting a studious pose as another band walked into the dressing room, his mates pretending to listen to some poems McCartney was reading out of a book. The point he was making was that they were able to pull off the stunt because he had a book of poems on him. The other band didn't.

Magical Mystery Tour echoed writer Ken Kesey's famous 1964 trip around America with his band of friends and associates he named The Merry Pranksters but it also had roots in the Liverpool of The Beatles' collective childhood when bus companies ran mystery tours. Customers would pay to get on and not be told what their destination was until arrival. Blackpool was the usual endpoint.

'John and I remembered mystery tours,' McCartney later recalled, 'and we always thought this was a fascinating idea: getting on a bus and not knowing where you are going ... So we took that idea and used it as a basis for a song and a film.' Using their experiences on LSD and the general psychedelic zeitgeist, the idea developed to become a magical mystery tour, with the film being the cinematic equivalent of an acid trip.

The film's songs contain many drug references. The title song opens with the shout of, 'Roll up, roll up', an evocation of the circus master's cry and a knowing wink to marijuana smokers. The film's narration meanwhile continually makes references to 'the magic starting to work', just as a trip would unfold itself.

PART OF THE DRIVE BEHIND THE FILM WAS A PRESSING NEED FOR THE BAND TO SUSTAIN THEIR RELATIONSHIP WITH THE FANS THROUGH MEDIUMS OTHER THAN THE LIVE CONCERT

Brian Epstein was involved in the film's early stages. Coming back from America, McCartney had sketched out the film in the form of a pie chart, which he showed to his manager. One of the first ideas was that each member of the band be given a 20-minute slot to film a segment of their own devising. Brian liked the idea and made some calls on Paul's behalf, sounding out various people who could contribute to the project. His death in late

August meant the band would now have to make some serious decisions.

On 1 September a band meeting was held at McCartney's house where it was a decided they would manage themselves, push on with the film, and then head to India for a two-month meditation break. Four days later, work on the film's music started and the band recorded several new songs including the title track, 'Your Mother Should Know', 'I Am The Walrus', 'Flying' (their first ever instrumental) and 'The Fool On The Hill'.

It is interesting how Lennon and McCartney had again worked the same magic as earlier in the year, Lennon producing a fantastic psychedelic song in 'I Am The Walrus', Paul again replying with a song brimming with a melody and style that was unique to his talents with 'The Fool On The Hill'.

'I Am The Walrus' was recorded nine days after Epstein's death. The lyrics are part religious inspired, suggesting that God is within us all and therefore we are all brothers and sisters, and part derived from LSD trips with some truly surreal imagery. The song's remarkable musical changes allied with Lennon's powerful vocal, provides an unsettling reflection of the man's mind.

Lennon would later admit that he was writing obscurely at the time, à la Dylan, as he put it. He wanted his words to give the impression of profundity when in fact there was none. Or very little. 'Dylan got away with murder,' he revealed, 'I thought, I can write this crap too. You just stick a few images together, thread them together and you call it poetry.' Yet 'I Am The Walrus' remains an incredibly powerful record.

Paul's 'The Fool On The Hill' is by contrast sublime pop music, inspired in part by the Maharishi and the idea of a man who sees the world in a completely different way from others. The song's clever musical changes, moving from wistful to joyous in a second, is the work of a man at the top of his game.

As recording proceeded the band began working on the film's casting. 'We got Neil and Mal our trusty roadies to hire a driver and coach and paint our logo on the side: Magical Mystery Tour. We hired a bus full of passengers, some of which were actors. I got a copy of *Spotlight* and selected all the actors from there,' Paul recalled. Noted names who joined the cast included Ivor Cutler, Victor Spinetti and Nat Jackley, a music-hall star who specialized in funny dancing and who the band adored.

Called in for advice was Denis O'Dell who had worked on *A Hard Day's Night*. He was now employed full-time by the band and was worried about the ramshackle approach they were taking. 'Getting involved in producing and directing their own film was a brave step for a pop group,' he recalled. 'It was unprecedented at the time, unfortunately their attitude was to learn as they went along rather than find out about the job before taking it on.'

On 11 September 1967 the Magical Mystery Tour bus pulled up at Allsop Place off Baker Street and the weird and wonderful got on board. To their surprise, there were no scripts. McCartney explained that everyone would have to improvise. The point of a mystery tour, after all, was that you didn't know where you were going – making the film would be the same kind of journey.

THE TITLE SONG OPENS WITH THE SHOUT OF, 'ROLL UP, ROLL UP', AN EVOCATION OF THE CIRCUS MASTER'S CRY AND A KNOWING WINK TO MARIJUANA SMOKERS

Filming took place in London, Devon, Cornwall and Kent. On one occasion the band got stuck on a bridge and had to call the AA and police in to help them over. One morning, Lennon told McCartney about his dream the night before in which he was dressed as a waiter and piling spaghetti on to the plate of a fat woman. McCartney said great, and the entire sequence was filmed that very morning.

As no one had thought to book a proper studio to film the band performing their songs, Denis O'Dell booked West Malling Royal Air Force station near Maidstone, Kent and the band performed 'I Am The Walrus'. The footage is remarkable, the band dressed in full-on psychedelic clothing are gathered round John's white piano in the late-summer sunshine and their performance is interspersed with all kinds of surreal imagery, such as dancing policemen and shots of the band wearing animal-head costumes. As Paul would later say this footage alone is worth entering the Magical Mystery Tour.

Due to take two weeks, the editing process stretched to nearly three months. There was ten hours of material to carve into an hour-long film. Worse, someone had forgotten to use clapperboards at the start of each scene, which made editing a real nightmare.

In December McCartney took the finished film to the BBC. They had already banned 'I Am The Walrus' for the crime of using the word 'knickers'. However, the band had a secret and radical agenda. They wanted to use their popularity to get the film shown over Christmas. Christmas TV was traditionally based around comedy and light entertainment. The Beatles wanted to gatecrash the nation's party and push counterculture right into their homes. They wanted to mess with people's minds and if possible turn them on.

'We wanted to take over the Bruce Forsyth slot,' Paul later recalled. 'He was always on, "Hello everyone, Happy Christmas, had enough Christmas dinner?" We thought we'd had enough of all that. We wanted to make a change, so we wanted the big audience slot. Which we got.' The film was shown by the BBC on Boxing Day at 8.35 p.m. It was screened in black and white as most people did not possess colour TVs and in doing so stripped the film of its charm and great inventiveness. The nation sat and watched in bemusement as the band they knew as The Fab Four starred in a drab-looking formless film with no storyline, plenty of surreal images and improvised dialogue.

The papers were indignant. 'Blatant rubbish,' cried the *Daily Express* summing up the general press reaction. The Beatles were now in a very peculiar position. They were still deemed front-page news but in reality they did not merit such mainstream acceptance. If The Beatles had formed in 1966, only the music and counterculture magazines, such as *International Times,* would have been interested in them. They certainly would not have featured in the gossip columns.

What is striking about this film now is how close it feels to *The Prisoner* TV show that would air in September 1967 and captivate the nation. There was something in the air. Both show and film take a collection of disparate people and put them in a particular environment. The Beatles chose a coach; the TV show's star Patrick McGoohan had the unique Welsh village of Portmeirion. Both works of art set out to challenge the viewer and make them think about the world they live in.

Not surprisingly The Beatles became fans of *The Prisoner* and hooked up with McGoohan one night. *The Prisoner*'s final episode used the band's 'All You Need Is Love' to amazing effect.

THE BEATLES WANTED TO GATECRASH THE NATION'S PARTY AND PUSH COUNTERCULTURE RIGHT INTO THEIR HOMES. THEY WANTED TO MESS WITH PEOPLE'S MINDS

Beatles fans by contrast were left rubbing their eyes. They had seen the band on television three times in 1967 and in all three sections – the 'Strawberry Fields Forever'/'Penny Lane' promotional films, the *Our World* 'All You Need Is Love' event and this new film – the band were either dressed in psychedelic clothing and singing about love or making 'wink, wink' references about drugs to the nation.

As Her Majesty The Queen herself remarked about the band at an EMI board meeting, 'Yes, they have gone a little weird, haven't they?' The Beatles didn't care. They had gone to India and started chanting 'Hare Krishna' at one another.

The Beatles dressed up for their surreal film, *Magical Mystery Tour*. With Epstein dead and Lennon losing interest, McCartney played an even greater role in the band. It was he who directed and edited the film.

The Beatles open the
APPLE
BOUTIQUE

DATE 7 December 1967, Baker Street, London

In his early Beatles days, John Lennon was a Tory, brought up to believe – as were so many – that the Conservatives were the party best suited for power. Only they had the education and the class for the job. All the others were lacking. Later Lennon changed sides, calling himself a Labour man. But, of course, this being Lennon there had to be some kind of contradiction in his thinking.

Money obsessed Lennon from an early age, dominated a lot of his Beatle life. To Lennon, pop music was the new and best way to make cash. It was 'a modern form of success'. In 1964, he was asked if he thought himself a good role model for young people, he said, 'Only how to make money quickly, which is a good example, I think.'

In 1965, with the other band members gathered around him, John told *Playboy*, 'We're money-makers first; then we're entertainers.' Ringo corrected him. It was still viewed as unseemly to be so openly naked about money. 'We are entertainers first, John.'

'That's right, of course,' John said hastily, then, desperately covering his tracks, he added, 'It's just that the press drives it into you, so you say it 'cuz they like to hear it, you know.' Yeah, right.

In 1966 in the famous *Evening Standard* interview in which John made his 'Beatles are more popular than Jesus' comment, John showed journalist Maureen Cleave around his house, proudly pointing out all his acquisitions. Chief Beatle and journalist then went for a drive. In the car, Lennon showed Cleave the vehicle's luxuries such as a television, folding bed, refrigerator, writing desk and telephone. If Lennon had chosen to, he could have conducted all his business from the back of his Rolls-Royce. Lennon did complain about the phone, though, informing Cleave that despite numerous attempts, he had only been able to make one call from his car. Technology had not yet caught up with him.

Lennon then started the car up and took Cleave for a ride in the countryside. As they drove through the green Surrey landscape Lennon described himself as 'famous and loaded'. He also confessed that despite his huge earnings, he constantly worried about money. Although his accountants kept telling him his finances were buoyant and healthy, Lennon was truly frightened that by the age of 40 he would have frittered away the lot. It explained his recent decision to sell off some of his other cars. However, he then revealed, when he was told there had been no need to make such a move, he went out and bought them all back again.

APPLE WAS LAUNCHED IN 1967, THE DAY ACCOUNTANTS BRYCE HAMMER & CO. TOLD THE BAND THAT THEY COULD EITHER HAND THREE MILLION POUNDS TO THE BRITISH GOVERNMENT OR USE IT THEMSELVES. THEY CHOSE THE LATTER

Money to Lennon represented power and the only way for a man like him to attain that power was to work terribly hard, or be born into a rich family. Then displaying some of the political nous he would become famous for during the 70s, he stated that in the end the only winners were the government. 'That joke about keeping the workers ignorant is still true; that's what they said about the Tories and the landowners and that; then Labour were meant to educate the workers but they don't seem to be doing that any more.'

A year later his thinking – like the rest of the band's – had been radically altered, turned on its head by exposure to radical anti-capitalist ideas, his generous use of LSD, and by undertaking meditation. Suddenly, his deep-seated belief that he was of the Left surfaced and it was this that helped contribute to the band's new Utopian ideal – Apple.

Apple was launched in 1967, the day accountants Bryce Hammer & Co. told the band that they could either hand three million pounds to the British Government or use it themselves. They chose the latter and decided to set up an umbrella organization that would turn people's ideas into reality. Be it a book, a film, a song or even a gadget, if the band liked it then you would be given the money to realize it. Not only that, Apple would not use commercial traditions but would set up an alternative model to capitalistic enterprises. Who else but The Beatles would have the imagination, the talent and finally the courage to execute such a scheme? Chalk up another first. This was the hippy dream made real.

Their first venture was into the world of fashion. Some of their money had already been used to acquire property on the corner of Baker Street and Paddington Street in Marylebone. Apple offices were installed on the top floor while the downstairs was turned into a shop they would name the Apple Boutique. The band gave The Fool collective £100,000 to design and produce a range of clothing and to decorate the outside of the building. They came up with an amazing design that lasted only a few weeks before they were asked to paint over it by the building's landlords. Lennon, who had bought his close friend Pete Shotton a supermarket on Hayling Island, Hampshire, gave him the job of shop manager.

However, this would not just be a clothes shop, per se. It would also sell other things such as books, records, bric-a-brac and anything else that caught the eye. Paul wanted the shop to sell white china, which was not readily available in London, while George of course wanted spiritual objects to be sold. Jenny Boyd, Pattie's sister, took up employment there.

A party was held on 6 December 1967 to which John and George showed up munching apples, and on the 7th the shop opened for business. It was a success at first, with people digging deep into their pockets with Christmas just around the corner. But by mid-January the reality was setting in. The Fool's designs were striking and individual but they had not been cut to fashion-standard sizes. Potential buyers simply could not wear them or indeed afford them.

The shop had started to haemorrhage so much money that McCartney stepped in and asked John Lyndon, a former NEMS employee and theatrical producer, if he would turn the venture around. Lyndon agreed and set about looking for fashions that were accessible and affordable. His mission was just gaining ground when at a meeting in July at the new Apple offices at 3 Savile Row, John read an article in *Melody Maker* written by DJ John Peel asking why The Beatles were acting as rag-trade merchants. John instantly ordered the shop to be closed, much to Lyndon's shock.

BE IT A BOOK, A FILM, A SONG OR EVEN A GADGET, IF THE BAND LIKED IT THEN YOU WOULD BE GIVEN THE MONEY TO REALIZE IT

The night before closure the band showed up with their partners and took everything they wanted. The next day, 31 July 1968, word was put out that everything left was being given away for free. A mass of people descended on the shop and stripped it bare. 'The idea of it was much better than the reality,' George said after the venture collapsed. 'It was easy to sit around thinking of groovy ideas, but to put them into reality was something else. We couldn't because we were not businessmen. All we knew was hanging round studios making up tunes.'

The Beatles
GO TO INDIA

DATE 15 February 1968, Rishikesh, India

It would be the last time that they moved as one: after two months at the Maharishi's meditation course in Rishikesh, near the foot of the Himalayas, the long and bitter dissolution of the best gang in town would begin. It would take a year and a half and in that time The Beatles would produce one of their greatest albums, lose a fortune, become enemies, bring in the lawyers and finally blow up Beatle Land. The Maharishi's advice when Brian died – 'Stay calm' – was not adhered to at any point.

George had already spent a week in India before the band arrived in Rishikesh. He had been asked to produce the music for a film called *Wonderwall* (1968). At first he refused, but when the producer gave him a blank canvas and said that whatever he did they would use, George grabbed the opportunity to record and release what he described as 'an Indian music anthology'.

In early January, George spent five days with Indian musicians at the EMI Recording Studios in what is now known as Mumbai. While there he wrote and recorded one of his best Indian-influenced songs, 'The Inner Light', which stated his current point of view – that God is within us all and that is where you should be looking if you want life to have meaning.

On his return, the band decided to record a single to be released while they were in India. Paul's song 'Lady Madonna' was the first to be taped followed by a new song of John's entitled 'Across The Universe'. After laying down the vocal and instruments Paul and John both agreed the song needed falsetto harmonies but where could they find such voices at seven o'clock on a Sunday evening? The answer was simple. Outside Abbey Road there was always a group of girl fans waiting patiently to see their heroes. The Beatles simply went outside and invited Lizzie Bravo and Gayleen Pease in to lay down backing vocals.

On the following Thursday, at the invitation of George Martin, the comedian Spike Milligan (an ex-Goon) attended another session for 'Across The Universe'. Lennon was unhappy with the day's work so the band selected George's song 'The Inner Light' for the B-side and shelved 'Across The Universe' for future use.

Milligan now made a suggestion. Would they consider placing the song on an album he was involved with to raise cash for the World Wildlife Fund? The Beatles agreed to the proposition.

The song is not only a great Lennon song, bathed in warmth and intimacy, but it also reveals the great effect of meditation on John. Sung on acoustic guitar, John imagines the wonders of the universe calling to him. His line about the undying

MEDITATION HAD WORKED WONDERS FOR THE BAND. IT HAD INSTILLED A REAL SENSE OF CALM INTO THEIR LIVES, WHICH WAS DESPERATELY NEEDED AFTER THE CHAOS OF BEATLEMANIA

light of a million suns would fit in any psychedelic song but here it is framed in a non-LSD context. Meanwhile, the chorus line mentions the meditation teacher Dev who taught the Maharishi.

Meditation had worked wonders for the band. It had instilled a real sense of calm into their lives, which was desperately needed after the chaos of Beatlemania. The Beatles wanted more of it and were going to India to fling themselves head first into the discipline. The answers they had been

searching for might well be answered by meditation. There was even talk of starting up a meditation school, of enticing their fans to follow suit, so convinced were they of meditation's great benefits.

'We want to learn [Transcendental Meditation] properly so we can propagate it and sell the whole idea to everyone.' Lennon said. 'This is how we plan to use our power now – they've always called us leaders of youth, and we believe this is a good way to lead.'

John and George went out first, Paul followed, Ringo landed last. All Beatles brought their wives or girlfriends along with various friends. Their days followed a similar pattern. The Beatles, plus other celebrity guests, such as Mike Love of The Beach Boys and Donovan, would rise and breakfast in the open. They would then return to their bungalows and meditate. In the afternoon and evening, lectures were given by the Maharishi.

Everyone put on Indian clothes, wore flowers around their necks, relaxed and smiled – all except Cynthia. John was pining after Yoko and she was taking the brunt of his dissatisfaction as the Beatle set about acting in a brusque manner whenever his wife approached him. 'I hoped we would meditate together, grow in mutual understanding, talk, go for walks and rediscover our lost closeness,' she recalled. Lennon did not give her dream a chance. After a week, he demanded a chalet to himself and from then on ignored his wife. The others observed but kept quiet. No one criticizes the leader.

Cynthia later discovered that every morning, John was going to the post office to see if a letter from Yoko had arrived. Cynthia's response to his behaviour was to paint, write poetry and suffer. John's was to get out his guitar and write some of his most downbeat songs. In 'Yer Blues' he writes of a black cloud crossing his mind, a blue mist round his soul.

Despite the meditation, the healthy vegetarian food and the tranquil surroundings, John complained of being unable to sleep. His song, 'I'm So Tired' pinpoints the absence of his woman as the cause of his insomnia.

McCartney, as ever, was having no such trauma. He liked Rishikesh and the ambience, and he liked meditation and the creativity it inspired. He wrote two exquisite classics in 'I Will' and 'Mother Nature's Son' and also added 'Wild Honey Pie', 'Rocky Raccoon' and 'Back In The USSR' (with Mike Love helping out on the chorus) to his canon.

Paul stayed a month and then came home. Paul found meditating hard, his mind always settling on the next album, the next song, the next move. George took the event far more seriously. He would rebuke Paul when he began talking about the band, telling him to drop all worldly considerations. Then he would adopt familiar gang behaviour by challenging John as to who could meditate the longest.

George turned 25 during this period and a party was thrown for him; everyone wore paint on their faces and the Maharishi persuaded George to give a sitar recital. And then Magic Alex, John's new best friend, landed. Cynthia was always wary of this man, as she knew that he wanted control of John, just as the whole world did.

The Maharishi's influence on John was quite firm at this point. One night Alex informed John and George that the Maharishi had been rumoured to have shared inappropriate moments with an American girl from the West Coast. A night was spent discussing the accusation and then John and George went to see the Maharishi and confront him. The encounter was classic Lennon. When the Maharishi asked them why they were leaving, John tartly replied, 'Well, if you're so cosmic you'll know why.'

In later years regret at their actions began to surface, especially their refusal to let the Maharishi defend himself, which suggests that John had had enough and wanted to get back to Yoko as soon a possible. Alex's accusation gave him the perfect get-out clause. Last word goes to George: 'There were a lot of flakes there, the whole place was full of flaky people. Some of them were us.'

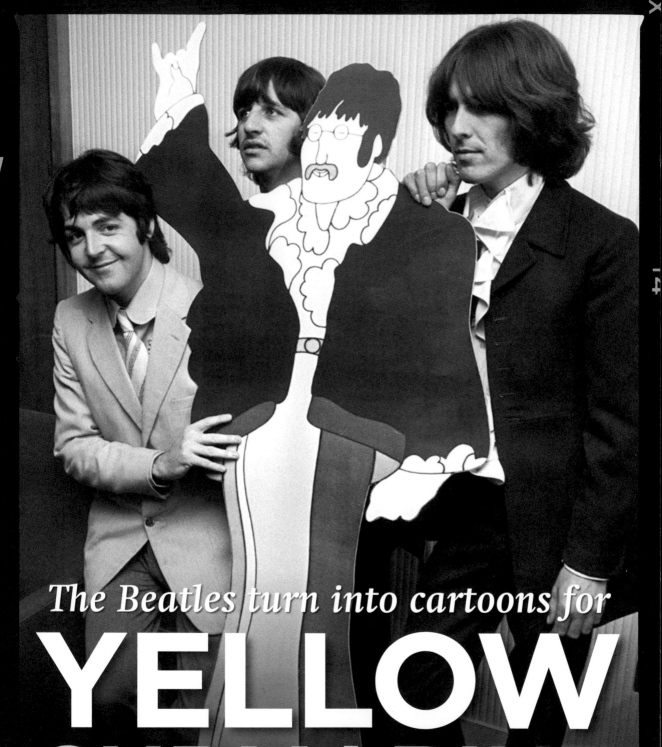

The Beatles turn into cartoons for

YELLOW
SUBMARINE

DATE 17 July 1968, The London Pavilion, Piccadilly

And still the people loved them. The press might now have turned against them, the police might have started to circle the band, picking up on the whiff of marijuana smoke that seemed to surround them everywhere they went, but people still loved The Beatles. In scenes reminiscent of Beatlemania, thousands gathered at the London Pavilion cinema in July to greet the band at the premiere of their animated film *Yellow Submarine*.

Why the love? Simple – because of the music. The Beatles' music cut through everything. Whether the band wore short or long hair, smoked joints or cigarettes, went off with models or avant-garde artists from the other side of the world, it didn't matter. The records were always special and always had a magical, generous spirit behind them. The Beatles were still viewed by many as 'one of us' and because of this they were granted the love of the people.

Yellow Submarine unexpectedly added to the band's appeal. They were lucky that it did. If the truth be told, they had as much interest in the film as they did in the football results. In other words, very little. By the end of the year that attitude would have changed.

Epstein, although gone a year now, was involved in the project in its infancy. In 1964 a Hungarian-American by the name of Al Brodax had contacted Brian with an idea. Brodax ran King Features, a cartoon-making company; would he be interested in producing a Beatles cartoon? Epstein and the boys agreed. They quickly came up with a deal and in 1965 the American network ABC started screening *The Beatles* animated series.

'YELLOW SUBMARINE' UNEXPECTEDLY ADDED TO THE BAND'S APPEAL. IF THE TRUTH BE TOLD, THEY HAD AS MUCH INTEREST IN THE FILM AS THEY DID IN THE FOOTBALL RESULTS: VERY LITTLE

Artistically it was a disaster. Cheap-looking, bereft of any good story lines, and featuring a cast whose idea of a Beatle accent was to speak in their own voices, the series was hugely popular in America. But that was no surprise – it had the band's name on it. How could it not sell?

AT FIRST THE BEATLES WERE FIRMLY AGAINST THE FILM AND WERE CONVINCED THAT A CHILDREN'S FILM WOULD BADLY DAMAGE THEIR CREDIBILITY AS HIP COUNTERCULTURALISTS

In the contract for the series it was agreed that if successful Brodax could commence work on a Beatles animated film, which would also contain new Beatles material. Brodax now instigated that part of the contract and in 1967 production began. The director appointed was a Canadian named George Dunning. He began working from a script inspired by the band's 1966 song 'Yellow Submarine', which had been written by Paul and sung by Ringo.

The song came to McCartney in what he described to his biographer Barry Miles, as the 'twilight moment', that space between wakefulness and sleep.

After writing the song, Ringo became the obvious candidate to sing it. His lugubrious voice suited the words perfectly plus there was now a tradition of handing the drummer a song to sing. With that in mind, McCartney made sure the song was suitable for Ringo's vocal range. Lennon helped out with the lyrics, thus explaining – McCartney says – why they turn more and more obscure as the song progresses.

The script had many writers including Erich Segal, the author of *Love Story* (1970), one of the 70s biggest-selling books and films. The brief was simple. 'The goal,' wrote fellow writer Lee Minoff, 'should be nothing less than to take animation beyond anything seen before in style, class and tone but avoiding the precious and the pretentious.'

Two hundred animators were employed worldwide to meet that challenge, to turn the story of The Beatles versus the evil Blue Meanies, who seek to invade the happy state of Pepperland. Interestingly, the band were portrayed in their Edwardian-style clothes, with lots of moustaches and ties and stripy jackets on display.

At first The Beatles were firmly against the film. They had all hated the American series (apart from the cheques it brought in) and were convinced that a children's film would badly damage their credibility as hip counterculturalists. Yet Dunning proved more than hip to the trip. He encouraged the film's numerous animators to utilize modern techniques and create striking visuals that would encapsulate styles from Bridget Riley to Andy Warhol, from Peter Blake to Richard Hamilton. Although McCartney would have preferred them to adopt a Walt Disney style, it soon became apparent that Dunning was attempting to match the band's musical ambitions and create art of a lasting nature.

ITS AMAZING VISUALS AND WARM HUMOUR MADE IT PERFECT FOR KIDS AND PERFECT FOR THE DOPE-HEADS WISHING TO SPARK UP AND FLOAT DOWNSTREAM INTO PEPPERLAND

For most people's money, he did exactly that. The colours, the style and the imaginative scene changes allowed *Yellow Submarine* to work on other levels, an artistic ploy the band always approved of. *Yellow Submarine* can be read as a classy children's film, a classic fairy story of good triumphing over evil. Yet it also works as a tale of the liberators (the underground army represented by The Beatles) overpowering the staid forces of the Establishment. Its amazing visuals and warm humour made it perfect for kids and perfect for the dope-heads wishing to spark up and float downstream into Pepperland.

As promised the band made a cameo appearance at the end, where they joked a lot, looked as much a gang as ever in their matching shirts and shared smiles. They also donated four songs to the project, two of which, 'Hey Bulldog' and 'It's All Too Much', were fine creations.

The film made the band further thousands thanks to *Yellow Submarine* merchandising such as alarm clocks, models and toys, and in January 1969, the *Yellow Submarine* album was released featuring the four new Beatles songs plus 'All You Need Is Love' and the title track 'Yellow Submarine', as well as seven instrumental cuts written and performed by The George Martin Orchestra. Despite the paucity of new Beatles material, the album sailed straight into the top ten.

In the year that the band tried to launch the impossible dream of Apple and fell into heavy bickering during *The White Album*, the *Yellow Submarine* project they had been so dismissive of proved to be a real highlight.

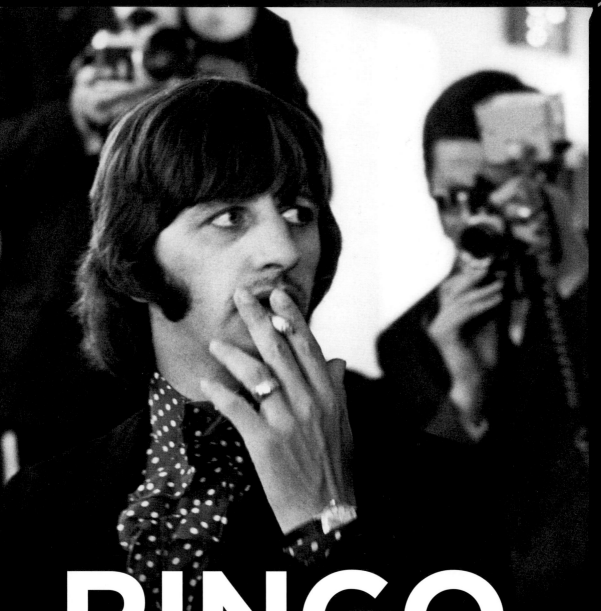

RINGO
LEAVES
The Beatles

DATE 22 August 1968, Abbey Road Studios, London

In later years, John and Paul would argue over who was the first Beatle to quit the band and destroy Beatle Land, each claiming it was them, but in fact they were both wrong. Ringo Starr was the first to leave The Beatles. On 22 August 1968 he walked out of Abbey Road and headed for Peter Sellers' yacht on the Mediterranean. That happy-go-lucky Ringo should be the first to crack speaks volumes about the sour, soul-sapping tone of *The White Album* sessions.

It was John's fault – to start the dissolution of the gang he knew he had to make a huge statement. Obviously appearing naked with Yoko on the *Unfinished Music No. 1: Two Virgins* album sleeve was not enough. Time then to smash forever the band's cardinal rule and once that had been broken, things were bound to unravel. And so it proved.

John walked into the studio with Yoko on his arm and acted as if nothing was wrong. At Beatles recording sessions, no outsiders were allowed. It was the gang and nothing but the gang in that studio.

In his fine memoir, *An Affectionate Punch* (1986), Justin de Villeneuve, Twiggy's manager, describes the day he went to visit the band on business at Abbey Road and found them having a break. At the time he considered himself a friend to Paul, George and Ringo but when they were together it was as though there was

a glass wall separating the band from everyone else. 'Paul, my pal, blanked me completely,' Justin recalled, 'Ringo looked elsewhere, George gave me a long stare ... After ten minutes of talking to myself I turned round, calling them "fucking Scouse gits ..."'

Every time they recorded, the invisible barrier descended and Justin was not the

JOHN WALKED INTO THE STUDIO WITH YOKO ON HIS ARM AND ACTED AS IF NOTHING WAS WRONG. AT BEATLES RECORDING SESSIONS, NO OUTSIDERS WERE ALLOWED

only one to notice this, as many other Beatles books and reports testify. John had now smashed through that barrier, cut it in two by bringing in Yoko, who sat by John and giggled and whispered in his ear and then – unbelievably – started giving her opinions on the music, as if she were a member of the band.

RINGO WAS EVERYMAN. RINGO SUGGESTED THAT GOOD THINGS REALLY DO HAPPEN TO GOOD PEOPLE AND THAT KNOWLEDGE WARMED THE HEARTS OF THE NATION

The other three Beatles were stunned, confused and angry. Paul retaliated by first bringing in his current beau, an American called Francie Schwartz and then later his wife-to-be Linda Eastman. Arguments erupted on a daily basis. Cutting remarks flew back and forth across Studio Two.

It didn't help that the band had some 30 or so songs to deal with. And the recording of some of them, if not all, drove the band crazy. 'Ob-La-Di Ob-La-Da' will never be recognized as McCartney's finest hour but the hours it took to record it successfully sent the band insane. With John and Yoko giggling like teenagers in lust for most of the sessions, Paul's school-

teacher persona had surfaced with George and Ringo – but never John – taking the brunt of his instructions.

Ringo's frustration was compounded by the fact that invariably he was always the first Beatle to arrive at Abbey Road. There then ensued hours of waiting until the others finally sauntered in. Once that happened, Ringo would sit there, enduring the arguments and the backbiting until finally work began, all in a bad temper. No one thought to say 'all you need is love' then. On 22 August he fluffed a drum fill, McCartney started lecturing him and suddenly the red mist descended. He quite simply had had enough. Beatles or no Beatles, for the first time in his life it did not matter to him. Ringo stormed out of Abbey Road.

Ringo's work in The Beatles has always been somewhat overshadowed by a flippant and arrogant John Lennon quote; when asked if he thought Ringo Starr the best drummer in the world, Lennon replied, 'He is not even the best drummer in The Beatles.' Starr detractors have used that quote against him ever since without stopping to wonder why two of the greatest songwriters of their century employed a lousy drummer for years to help realize their music? Of course they didn't. 'Rain', 'Tomorrow Never Knows' or 'Come Together' are all that one has to point to in any debate about his skills.

'Until *Abbey Road*,' Paul would point out later, 'there was never a drum solo in

The Beatles' act, and consequently other drummers would say that although they liked his style, Ringo wasn't technically a very good drummer. It was a bit condescending and I think we let it go too far.'

Ringo was the smile of The Beatles, the sound of the gang's laughter. He was the one element that carried an unassuming vulnerability, and that made him lovable. Ringo was everyman. Ringo suggested that good things really do happen to good people and that knowledge warmed the hearts of the nation. Plus, he was not just a drummer, he was the best actor in the band (John came a close second) and was the one the producers came knocking for.

In 1968 he took time off from the band to appear in a soft-sex farce masquerading under the term entertainment, called *Candy*. It was absolutely dreadful and he should never have done it, but he was paid for his efforts and got to see his name alongside Marlon Brando, Richard Burton and Walter Matthau.

The following year he starred in another film, *The Magic Christian*, and that too did not carry much greatness but this time his name ran alongside Peter Sellers, Spike Milligan, Richard Attenborough, John Cleese, Laurence Harvey, Christopher Lee, Roman Polanski, Raquel Welch, Hattie Jacques, Graham Chapman, Yul Brynner and Harry Carpenter.

In both films he did not disgrace himself, which is not bad going for a man who did not attend drama school. By the time of *Candy* he had endeared himself further to the British public by appearing in the *Cilla* TV show special, screened in February 1968. The show saw him indulging in spots of tap dancing, ventriloquism and singing.

WHEN HE CAME BACK TO THE BAND HIS DRUMS WERE COVERED IN FLOWERS AND THERE WAS A HUGE BANNER SAYING 'WELCOME HOME RINGO' HANGING HIGH ON THE CEILING

Six months later he was out of the band and lazing around on Peter Sellers' yacht with his family. It was there that he completed his first self-composition that would be performed by the band (although he had co-written 'What Goes On' on *Rubber Soul*). Suitably, given the events of the past week, it was called 'Don't Pass Me By'.

When he came back to the band and entered Abbey Road, slightly nervous at meeting the mates he had cursed to high heaven, his drums were covered in flowers and there was a huge banner saying 'Welcome Home Ringo' hanging high on the ceiling. And at that Ringo smiled, and at that Ringo laughed, and thus did The Beatles continue.

John and George get

BUSTED
FOR DRUGS

DATE | 18 October 1968, Montagu Square, London

In the old days, before the drugs and Indian culture got hold of them, the police understood that a Beatle was not to be busted. They were national treasures, Members of the British Empire. The country – hell, the world – adored them. Whatever nonsense they got up to, you turned a blind eye to it – within reason. Not any more. By 1968 the band had lost all protection. The Queen thought they were weird, the public agreed and the world wondered what on earth had happened to the mop-tops.

In times gone by, The Beatles used to be defined by human characteristics. Paul was cute, George was shy, Ringo was happy-go-lucky, John was bolshie. Now Ringo was an actor, Paul was a druggie, George was spiritual and John, well, John was just plain nuts. Look at him and Yoko wearing identical clothes and haircuts and travelling to Coventry Cathedral in June 1968 to plant acorns for world peace. One acorn to symbolize East (Yoko) meeting West (John), and one acorn for world peace. The pair of them were clearly 'out there'.

For some, the time was finally ripe for The Beatles to get their comeuppance. They'd had it easy for far too long. The detective sergeant charged with bringing down pop stars was named Norman Pilcher. After The Rolling Stones were busted in February 1967, Pilcher now placed The Fabs at the top of his list. He may well have done so because of Lennon's song 'I Am The Walrus', especially the promo, which portrayed policeman as robots. He probably did so because Paul McCartney spat in the face of justice by admitting to taking LSD on prime-time television.

On 18 October 1968, Pilcher and the police arrived at Ringo's flat at 34 Montagu Square. Inside, John and Yoko were sleeping. John slept well, for he had been prepared for this eventuality. Weeks before, he, along with Yoko and Pete Shotton, had swept the flat for drugs. 'That thing was set up,' Lennon later said. 'The *Daily Express* was there before the cops ... Don Short had told us, "They're coming to get you," three weeks before. So, believe me, I'd cleaned the house out ... I'm not stupid. I went through the whole damn house,' Lennon told *Rolling*

Stone magazine. Even so, Lennon still had one problem – he had no idea on which day the police would launch their search. All he could do was wait.

Lying in bed with Yoko one morning, Lennon was startled by a knock on the door. A woman's voice started shouting for him. Realizing what was happening, Yoko ran into the bathroom to get dressed, John pulled on some trousers and shouted for Yoko to ring his lawyers. Instead, Yoko called Apple much to John's later bemusement. Apple in turn called John's solicitor Nicholas Cowan who rushed round to the flat. He got there at about midday by which time the police were busy overturning the apartment under the supervision of Pilcher. He had already threatened to arrest John for obstructing the course of justice when Lennon had asked for identification and warrants to be shown. Cowan noted in one room masses of recording equipment, which seemed as if it had just been used. He moved to the next room where to his alarm he saw the police dog taking particular interest in a large trunk. The police opened the trunk and searched it thoroughly. Sure enough, in it they discovered a small lump of hash. At first Lennon was puzzled by the discovery and became convinced that the police had planted it. Thanks to zealous detectives this was not an uncommon practice in those days. But he was wrong.

The dope had not been planted. Months before this event, John had asked for possessions of his to be sent over from his old house, Kenwood. He had left the boxes unopened. Fatal mistake. 'It had just been there for years,' he admitted. 'My driver brought binoculars, which I didn't need in my little flat. And inside the binoculars was some hash … Somewhere else in an envelope was another piece of hash. So that was it.'

FOR SOME, THE TIME WAS FINALLY RIPE FOR THE BEATLES TO GET THEIR COMEUPPANCE. THEY'D HAD IT EASY FOR FAR TOO LONG

Six weeks later John pleaded guilty to a charge of unauthorized possession of 19 grams of cannabis. He was fined £150 with 20 guineas costs. Five months later they went for George. Why Paul was immune to the law's attentions remains obscure. Maybe his house with its locked gates and high walls persuaded the boys in blue that a raid would prove pointless. The Beatle would have more than enough time to wash his stash down the basin before they could grab him.

On 12 March 1969, the day Paul McCartney married Linda Eastman and did not invite any of The Beatles to the ceremony, George was at the Apple offices when he got a call from his wife Pattie who was at their house in Esher, Surrey. (When George and Pattie married in 1966, Paul was the best man.) In *The Beatles Anthology* (2000) book George recalled, 'He [Pilcher] came out to my house with about eight other policemen, a policewoman and a police dog, who happened to be called Yogi ... They took us off, fingerprinted us and we were busted.'

According to Derek Taylor, George remained calm – George was always calm; he sometimes got in a grump, but he was always calm. He called Pete Shotton who went round to their house to look after Pattie. As he and Pattie sipped vodka and tonics, Pilcher walked in the room with a lump of dope. As they now waited for George to arrive, a policewoman asked for a cup of tea. Pattie refused so the woman went and made tea for everyone else. In her autobiography *Wonderful Today* (2007) (published in the US as *Wonderful Tonight*), Pattie recalls the police standing around with their tea not knowing what do to until eventually George arrived home. 'He was still calm but he wasn't happy,' she remembered. 'The police were obviously excited to meet him. They stood to attention and were almost elbowing each other out of the way to get closer to him while Sergeant Pilcher went into his "I am arresting you..." bit.'

George always maintained that the dope had been planted simply because he was methodical and tidy and therefore always kept his stash in his stash box. The police's claim that they discovered the drugs in one of his shoes simply does not ring true at all.

On 31 March 1969 at Esher Crown Court, George and Pattie were fined £250 for possession of cannabis and ordered to pay 20 guineas court costs. For both Lennon and Harrison the fines were mere trifles. Where these arrests hurt them was when they applied for American visas. The USA has a very dim view of drug-takers, even if you are a Beatle.

FOR BOTH LENNON AND HARRISON THE FINES WERE MERE TRIFLES. WHERE THESE ARRESTS HURT THEM WAS WHEN THEY APPLIED FOR AMERICAN VISAS

As for the UK, both brushes with the law affirmed that The Beatles had given up all rights to be considered national treasures. They were still loved by many and still sold records in impressive quantities, but their place at the heart of national life had now been obliterated. 'I guess they didn't like the way the image was looking,' reflected Lennon. 'The Beatles thing was over. No reason to protect us for being soft and cuddly any more – so bust us! That's what happened.'

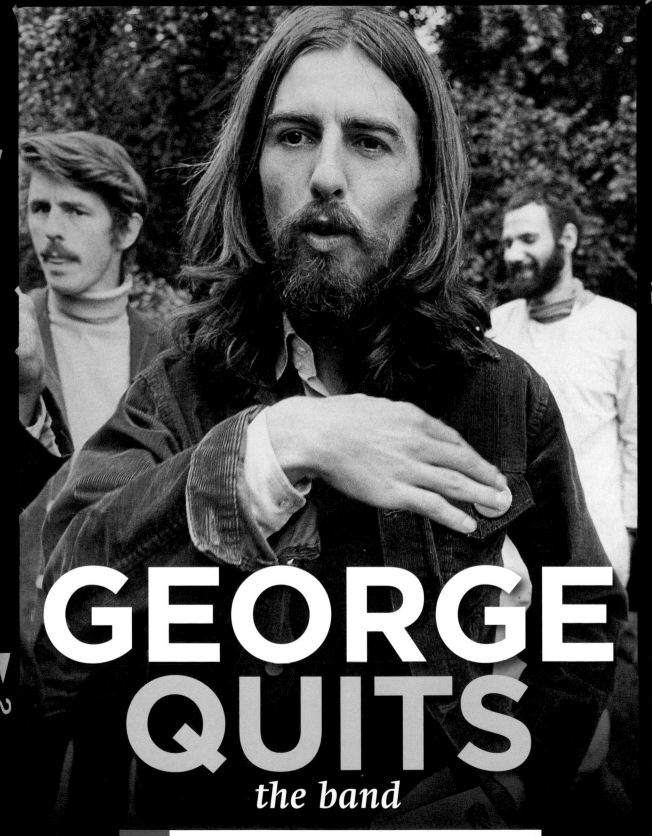

GEORGE QUITS
the band

DATE 10 January 1969, Twickenham Film Studios, Middlesex

On Thursday 2 January 1969, The Beatles arrived at Twickenham Film Studios to shoot a documentary. The subject was a live concert the band was now planning to undertake, their first in three years. The idea was to film the band rehearsing and then playing the gig itself. What made the concert special was that the set list would comprise solely of material from their new album. That album would then be released as a live document.

This was typical of Beatle thinking. Other bands released live albums of old material. As ever, this band went the other way. The end was approaching but they still wanted to break new ground. Only things did not work as planned. At Twickenham, the band began bickering to such an extent that on 10 January George Harrison, having viciously argued with Paul and later John, announced that he was quitting the band. He suggested the band place ads in the music papers to find a new guitarist.

The Beatles' recent single 'Hey Jude' was partly to blame and so were many other things, ranging from John's disillusionment to the precarious financial state of the band. By the end of 1968 'Hey Jude' had sold five million copies. It had hit number one all over the world and given the band their longest ever stay at the top of the US singles chart. Clocking in at seven minutes, it was the longest single ever to chart. It also reminded the band of their power to create sublime pop music that spoke to millions.

The song had been inspired by John and Cynthia's divorce. Driving to John's house to work one morning, Paul began thinking about Julian, John and Cynthia's son. It was typical of him to do so. Paul had grown close to Julian. John, like his father before him, had never paid his son the attention he deserved and that pushed Paul into acting almost like a surrogate dad to Julian.

'Paul and I used to hang out more than Dad and I did,' Julian Lennon once confirmed. 'We had a great friendship going and there seems to be far more pictures of me and Paul playing together at that age than there are pictures of me and Dad.'

To promote the single the band travelled to Twickenham to perform it for the popular TV show *Frost On Sunday*. An invited audience watched as they ran through both 'Hey Jude' and its B-side, 'Revolution'. After the highly tedious time spent making *The Beatles* double album (*The White Album*), the band were pleasantly reminded of the joys of performing.

Meanwhile, 'Hey Jude' was released on 30 August 1968 and dominated the rest of the summer. McCartney even took it to the party thrown by The Rolling Stones to launch their new *Beggars Banquet* album and had the DJ play the single. In doing so, he totally usurped Mick and the boys' evening. Everyone went home talking about the amazing new Beatles single.

John was not too happy, though. He had put forward his song, 'Revolution', as the A-side but the band did not think it strong enough. Lennon felt they missed the point. John was not too concerned with chart positions. He was now very keen to produce art of an instant nature, and communicate through song his current thinking on the political upheavals that had swept the world in 1968.

Lennon's position was, for once, muddied. Although his natural instincts were against authority, he was also set against violent revolution, arguing that, 'if you want peace you won't get it with violence'. Ironically, as Lennon looked for ways as a pop star to create an equal society, money came to haunt him. Money had always been a source of worry for Lennon. Even at the height of Beatlemania, he felt insecure about his earnings. He told journalist Maureen Cleave in *that* interview, that he had taken some of his cars back to be re-sold, until his accountant had assured him that he was rich enough not to have to take such an action.

> GEORGE HAD NO INTEREST IN APPLE WHATSOEVER. IN FACT THE WHOLE OPERATION MUST HAVE BEEN AGONY FOR HIM. AFTER ALL, IN DAYS GONE BY, GEORGE WAS THE MAN WHO KEPT HIS EYE ON THE FINANCES

Lennon always felt money would slip away from him as so much in his life already had – mother, father, best friend, manager. Furthermore, to his – and the band's – great annoyance, he could never fully understand how Beatle money worked. Accountants told him he was a millionaire – on paper. What did that mean? Is the money in the bank? Well, it is – and it isn't. Uh?

One thing he did understand was a note an accountant had recently slipped him which stated that if the Apple organization carried on in the same manner, The Beatles would be broke in six months. Apple was haemorrhaging money. It was a mess. Every week, new ventures were announced. An Apple School, run by John's old gang member, Ivan Vaughan, was put on the To Do list. As was Apple Publicity, Apple Management, Apple Books, Apple Films, Apple Fashions. There was also Apple Electronics, headed by Magic Alex, who recommended a young man named Caleb be brought in to read the I Ching before any major business decisions were made.

In hindsight, it is perhaps unfortunate that Caleb was not able to foresee the defective nature of Magic Alex's schemes. Despite the talk, he had not been able to create a force field to protect the band's homes nor had he been able to make loudspeakers out of wallpaper. He was now building a new 16-track studio in the basement of their offices at 3 Savile Row. The building was expensive and seemed to be full of people taking all the drink and drugs their Beatle expense accounts could handle. Only Apple Records was in profit. The singer Mary Hopkins had scored a serious chart hit with her song 'Those Were The Days' (adapted from a Russian folk song McCartney admired).

George had no interest in Apple whatsoever. In fact the whole operation must have been agony for him. After all in days gone by George was the man who kept his eye on the finances. It was he who badgered Epstein constantly about monies

owed and money due. Now Apple was eating up all that cash and he could only stand by and watch. 'I was still in India when it started,' he explained. 'I think it was basically John and Paul's madness – their egos running away with themselves or with each other.' Note the use of the word 'ego'. If Yoko had changed John, then India had changed George. His enthusiasm for its people, its music and its religious practices knew no bounds. His discovery of meditation had now brought him to the same understanding that John had taken from Timothy Leary and his LSD-inspired teachings; the ego must be dissolved before nirvana can be achieved.

Yet, as George sought to rid himself of worldly goods and desires, he was also attempting to remain a Beatle. The two were not compatible. The lengthy bouts of meditation that George undertook – sometimes up to eight hours – had convinced him that the world and its ways were meaningless. Suddenly Beatle Land seemed silly compared with finding God. The problem Harrison had was that he was human and sometimes not able (or willing) to put aside all pleasures. By all accounts George seems to have vacillated between clean living and the rock'n'roll lifestyle, a duality that would last all of his days.

Meditation and India also changed his relationships within the band. George was always third in the hierarchy. To John and Paul, George was the little kid who had followed them round hoping for attention. In The Beatles they still treated him as such. That changed in 1965 when John and George took LSD together and bonded. Then John met Yoko and problems developed. George like Paul was aghast at losing the gang leader to a woman, an avant-garde artist of all people. (George viewed the avant-garde scene and then uttered the phrase, 'Avant garde a clue.')

George was not at all happy to be in Yoko's company at work. He was not too keen about Paul being there either. During the sessions for *The Beatles* double album, with John wrapped up in Yoko, Paul had taken charge, taking the band through endless takes of his songs until he was satisfied. George saw his behaviour as ego driven and felt that Paul's anger and frustration at the recent dissolution of his relationship with Jane Asher, plus John's relationship with Yoko, was now being taken out unfairly on both him and Ringo.

It also did not help that throughout his Beatle career George had always struggled to have his compositions accepted by John and Paul; both men often considered themselves superior in that department and often put his songs down or refused to record them. George took their attitude on the chin. The gang moved as one back then. Dissent in any way hindered its progress. But now ...

For the *Let It Be* sessions, George had written 'All Things Must Pass', 'Hear Me Lord' and 'I Me Mine'. Only the last of these songs would be recorded by The Beatles.

The other two, plus many more the band had passed on, would go on to make up his highly acclaimed debut solo album, *All Things Must Pass*.

It did not help that George had recently spent time with Bob Dylan up in Woodstock and written a song with Dylan called 'If Not For You'. John and Paul had never once offered to write a song with him. They had helped him with his compositions but not reached out to him like Dylan had. That rankled badly.

Perhaps the problem John and Paul had with George's new material was the mystical nature of the songs. Indeed, George's spiritual development was now starting to put down roots. Since 1965 George had explored all kinds of different religions but had settled of late with the Hare Krishna movement, the International Society for Krishna Consciousness. He was impressed by the followers' humility and lack of interest in Western consumerism, unlike the Maharishi who swanned around in a private helicopter. George befriended them, gave them money and wrote his most famous song, 'Something', with Krishna in mind. One evening at home, George explained that he had to change the lyrics. A Beatle singing about 'he' rather than 'she' would be likely to cause misunderstanding and so the lyrics were changed.

On the day he stormed out of Twickenham, the band plus Yoko spent the afternoon jamming: Ringo played weird drums, Yoko did her screaming bit, John supplied feedback guitar and Paul rubbed his bass up and down his amplifier. Two days later, the band plus Yoko arrived at Ringo's house to try to sort out their differences. George instantly raised his objections, saying that it had been agreed that the meeting should be limited to the four band members only. John said he had not been told that and George said he didn't believe him and walked out, heading up to his parents' house in Liverpool.

AS GEORGE SOUGHT TO RID HIMSELF OF WORLDLY GOODS AND DESIRES, HE WAS ALSO ATTEMPTING TO REMAIN A BEATLE. THE TWO WERE NOT COMPATIBLE

On the Wednesday, all four Beatles convened again at the Apple offices. Progress was made. George agreed to return but only on the condition that they agree to drop the live-concert idea, get out of Twickenham and head into the studio that Magic Alex had built for them to make a new album. With the band back in harmony, they marched downstairs to the studio only to find that Magic Alex's plans had proved faulty and the studio would have to be taken apart and rebuilt. As Harrison looked at the mess, he must have thought this was the perfect metaphor for Apple, a beautiful idea, realized at great cost and unable to function properly.

Given the tensions between the band, one has to ask why they did not split up there and then. Why carry on with this unwieldy beast that was only causing grief? Part of the reason was that sometimes there were moments of real magic, moments that reminded them of their special nature, moments that returned them to much happier times.

On 30 January the band finally hit on the perfect venue for their gig to be filmed. They would play unannounced on the roof of the Apple building. Traffic would stop, chaos would ensue – it was perfect. The band set up and started playing. As they went through tracks such as 'Get Back' and 'Don't Let Me Down', obviously enjoying the situation, word reached them that the police were on their way. All of them had the same thought, great, let's get busted, what an ending to the film that will make. However, this was not Hollywood. The police did not drag Ringo screaming and kicking from his drums. They did not frog march the other three into vans. They simply tried to turn the electricity off.

The event served to reunite the band temporarily but it did not last. The fact was that although most of them were ready to quit, financially they could not afford to do so. It was ironic; the band that had help liberate the world was now the band that held its members prisoners.

The Beatles last live performance was on the rooftop of the Apple building, on 30 January 1969. They played for about 45 minutes, and then the police stopped the show.

Paul McCartney marries
LINDA EASTMAN

DATE 12 March 1969, Marylebone Register Office, London

On 12 March 1969 Paul McCartney married Linda Eastman at London's Marylebone Register Office. No Beatle was invited to the ceremony although George and Pattie (fresh from being busted) showed up at the reception at The Ritz Hotel. Paul later admitted to being a bit of a bastard on that one. 'Maybe it was because the gang was breaking up,' he said. 'We were all pissed off with each other. We certainly were not a gang any more. That was the thing. Once a group's broken up like that, that's it.'

He had first met Linda at The Bag O'Nails club in Kingly Street, Soho. He spotted her in an alcove and got chatting to her before taking her on to the Speakeasy to watch the band Procol Harum. Linda was American, upper middle class, a photographer and in London working on a book called *Rock And Other Four Letter Words* (1968).

Linda had a New York brashness about her. Hearing of the launch party for *Sgt. Pepper* at Brian Epstein's house, she wangled herself an invite. She also regularly bumped into Paul at the clubs and eventually started invading his dreams. 'I was starting to have those sort of thoughts,' Paul admitted. 'I was thinking back over all the girls I'd known and wondering who was the favourite to get serious with, and she was the one who always came to mind.'

Linda had a daughter, Heather, from a previous relationship, and given the tendency of Paul's heart to melt in the presence of children, it was no surprise that he and Heather drew close during his courtship of her mother.

Linda certainly had her work cut out with Paul. His only major relationship in

GIVEN THE TENDENCY OF PAUL'S HEART TO MELT IN THE PRESENCE OF CHILDREN, IT WAS NO SURPRISE THAT HE AND HEATHER DREW CLOSE DURING HIS COURTSHIP OF HER MOTHER

Beatle Land had been with the actress Jane Asher. They had met after the 1963 Beatle performance at The Royal Albert Hall, which had been broadcast by the BBC. Also appearing were The Springfields, Rolf Harris, Del Shannon, Kenny Lynch and George Melly. For the show's finale the band appeared with all the other acts to perform the song, 'Mack The Knife'.

ONE DAY, JANE RETURNED FROM AN APPOINTMENT, WALKED INTO PAUL'S HOUSE IN CAVENDISH AVENUE AND FOUND HIM IN BED WITH ANOTHER WOMAN

Jane Asher had been commissioned by the *Radio Times* to interview the band. A strikingly good-looking girl, when she appeared in their dressing room, all four Beatles suddenly got very interested. It was Paul she eventually chose. He certainly seemed a better bet than John who began his move by crudely questioning her about her virginity.

After moving down to London, Paul moved in with Jane at her parents' house in Wimpole Street. Quite properly, he had his own bedroom. The Ashers were a compelling family to McCartney – wealthy, artistic and not given to judgemental behaviour. Jane's mother Margaret was a music teacher and taught Paul the recorder. Jane's father Richard was a well-known physician.

The Ashers allowed McCartney to realize his mother's dictum and improve himself. He loved the lively talks round the dinner table and drawing on their cultural knowledge. What he was not so comfortable with was Jane's fierce drive and independence. She wanted to be recognized as an actress in her own right. The last thing she wanted was to be seen as just Paul McCartney's girlfriend.

Although Paul was stimulated by the family, he was also very traditional when it came to women. He had been raised in a city where men were men and women were expected to know their place. Paul and Jane often clashed over her refusal to bow down to him. She went her own way whether he liked it or not, taking on engagements he would rather she didn't. Moreover, McCartney displayed no guilt about sleeping around, be that on tour or elsewhere. When questioned about his promiscuity, he would exclaim, 'Well, I'm not married to Jane, am I?'

A great insight into their relationship is captured in Michael Braun's book *Love Me Do* (1964). In early 1964, Jane arrived in Paris to visit the band during their two-week engagement. Naturally, she was keen to see the city but Paul wanted her to stay in her hotel room, as she might be recognized on the street. 'That's typical of Paul,' she told Braun. 'It's so silly of me to stay at the hotel. It's just that he is so insecure ... He can't see that my feelings for him are real and that the fans' are fantasy.'

Paul and Jane dated until Christmas Day 1967 when they announced their engagement. It lasted just six months. One day when Jane returned from an appointment, she walked into Paul's house in Cavendish Avenue and found him in bed with another woman, just as Cynthia had done with John a couple of months before. She swept out of the house and in a TV interview announced that their engagement was over.

By all accounts, Paul was devastated by her departure and began losing himself in drink and drugs. The woman in Paul's bed was an American named Francie Schwartz. She claims that when Paul later dumped her, he told he was sorry but he was a complete bastard and did she mind making him some dinner before she left?

With Linda, Paul seems to have pulled no such stunts. Like Jane, Linda had her own career and the great ability to move between the differing worlds of Ivy League and rock'n'roll with consummate ease, which over time Paul would become fascinated by.

For a working-class Scouser like Paul, Linda's effortless grace was captivating. So was her ability to understand and navigate situations. When her relationship with Paul deepened, people began gossiping about her in a malicious manner. Linda simply ignored the barbs and got on with her life. She would later introduce McCartney to vegetarianism and launch her own brand of vegetarian foods. McCartney was certainly besotted by her.

FOR PAUL, LINDA'S EFFORTLESS GRACE WAS CAPTIVATING. WHEN THEIR RELATIONSHIP DEEPENED, PEOPLE BEGAN GOSSIPING ABOUT HER. LINDA SIMPLY IGNORED THE BARBS AND GOT ON WITH HER LIFE

Two years after meeting her they were married. He later said that during their 29-year marriage (Linda sadly died of cancer in April 1998) they only spent one night apart. He had written 'Yesterday' but found his tomorrow.

Yet on the day they married, Paul's estrangement from the gang he loved with all his heart was about to take a terrible turn. In a month's time John would again trump him and announce his departure from The Beatles.

HAIR
PEACE.

BED
PEACE.

John and Yoko
BED IN
for world peace

DATE 25 March 1969, The Hilton Hotel, Amsterdam

In 1969 Lennon contributed a verse to McCartney's new song, 'I Got A Feeling'. In it, John talked about having a hard year, no doubt thinking of the tedious sessions that accounted for *The Beatles* double album. If he had written the verse about 1969 he would have said, everybody had a busy year. He certainly did. In 1969 John released six albums, left The Beatles but kept it a secret, staged bed-ins for world peace, returned his MBE to the Queen, had two number-one singles and married Yoko Ono. And he also played his second live gig of the year, but without The Beatles.

After the debacle at Twickenham (in which time the album *Yellow Submarine* was released) where John's heroin use had rendered him a mostly mute onlooker, the band headed into new studios at Savile Row where they spent ten exhausting days trying to record *Get Back*, their live album of new material (later aborted).

As they had decided not to use any overdubs, the quality of the songs rested with the quality of the performance. And on that none of them could agree. Lennon later referred to these sessions as 'hell on earth'. On 30 January they played their last ever gig as a band but despite their enjoyment of it, the rot had set in. Four days later Lennon, Starr and Harrison appointed Allen Klein as their new manager and McCartney refused to go along with the idea. The gang was at war.

In early February, John proposed to Yoko. She accepted. The couple decided a

> **THE LENNON OF 1961 WOULD HAVE SNEERED AND CUT DOWN THE LENNON OF 69 WITH HIS ACID TONGUE AND WIT. THE LENNON OF 69 USED THAT WIT TO PUT FORWARD THE CONCEPT OF WORLD PEACE**

UK wedding would cause too much hassle, so they headed for Paris. There they tried to get hitched but were unsuccessful. As Pete Brown worked on the problem, the couple honeymooned. The last time John had been on holiday in Paris was with Paul back in 1961 and how different a man he was then. The changes were astonishing. In just eight years John Lennon had transformed himself from a snarling angry young thug into a man who fiercely supported world peace and women's liberation. The Lennon

THEY DECIDED THAT JOHN'S HIPPY APPEARANCE MIGHT CLOSE PEOPLE OFF TO THEIR MESSAGE. THUS BAGISM WAS BORN. IN VIENNA JOHN AND YOKO GAVE ALL THEIR ANSWERS HIDDEN INSIDE A WHITE BAG

of 1961 would have sneered and cut down the Lennon of 69 with his acid tongue and wit. The Lennon of 69 now used that wit and intelligence to put forward the concept of world peace.

Pete Brown contacted them and said they could marry in Gibraltar – which they did, with Savile Row tailor Tommy Nutter's brother taking the wedding photos. The couple then flew to Amsterdam, booked in

to the Hilton, and put out a press release announcing they were holding a bed-in for world peace.

As expected the world's press hurried to their room to be greeted by John and Yoko in bed, in their pyjamas, granting interviews in which they put forward their wish for world peace. 'Our life is our art,' Lennon later recalled. 'That's what the bed-ins were. When we got married we knew our honeymoon was going to be public anyway, so we decided to make a statement. We sat in bed and talked to reporters for seven days. It was hilarious.'

They moved on to Vienna, to the Hotel Sacher. They had now decided that John's hippy appearance ran the risk of closing people off to their message. Thus Bagism was born. At their Vienna press conference John and Yoko gave all their answers hidden inside a white bag. It was 1 April, April Fools' Day.

The couple came back to London where they resumed work on the *Abbey Road* sessions for a month before catching a flight to America. No joy there. John's drug bust prevented him from entering. They moved on to Canada and Montreal where after a two-and-a-half-hour wait, they were granted a ten-day stay. The couple headed for the Hotel Le Reine Elizabeth where they staged another bed-in. Back in London John and Yoko's second album, *Unfinished Music No. 2: Life With The Lions* was released on the Zapple label, the offshoot of Apple Records designed to promote challenging music. (George's album *Electronic Music* was also issued that day.)

On 1 June at the bed-in in Montreal, with the press and well-wishers looking on, John recorded his new song 'Give Peace A Chance'. The couple then spent a further five days in Canada before heading home. By now 'The Ballad Of John And Yoko' had hit number one. On 7 July 'Give Peace A Chance' was released, credited as Lennon and McCartney. 'We all have Hitler in us,' John said, 'but we also have love and peace. So why not give peace a chance for once?'

From July through to August John helped write and record the band's final album *Abbey Road*. On 22 August the band undertook their final photo session posing for the cameras of Monte Fresco, Ethan Russell and Mal Evans in and around John and Yoko's Tittenhurst Park abode. Yoko and Linda were also photographed with the band and separately. They even posed together in couple of shots.

In early September Lennon was at the Apple offices when the phone rang. He answered. Many callers to Apple were often astonished to hear a real live Beatle on the other end of the line. It was a young Canadian promoter with a proposal. In four days' time he was staging a Toronto rock and revival show starring Chuck Berry, Little Richard and Gene Vincent. Would John Lennon or The Beatles be interested in attending it? Lennon said he'd do more than attend it, he'd play it. Lennon promised a band would come

over with him, Yoko, Eric Clapton, Klaus Voormann and drummer Alan White. They would be called The Plastic Ono Band.

The promoter could not believe his luck. He had sold only 800 tickets in a 20,000-seater stadium. When news of Lennon's appearance broke, 10,000 tickets were sold in a day. On the flight over, with Allen Klein in tow, the band took out their guitars and rehearsed. On arrival, John's personal habits were such that phone calls had to be made. (Interestingly, it is claimed that the man who attended to John was named David Schneiderman. By all accounts Schneiderman was a major presence at the Redlands party when Keith Richards, Mick Jagger and Robert Fraser were busted. It was his acid that the party was sampling. Schneiderman later claimed to have given Lennon the phrase 'instant karma', which he used for a famous single the following year.)

Finally, the band walked out on stage. Lennon, with a white bag placed next to his microphone, told the crowd they had not really rehearsed and then launched into the songs he had spat out in Hamburg with teenage rage – 'Blue Suede Shoes', 'Money' and 'Dizzy Miss Lizzy'. This time around his voice was croaky, devoid of vigour. Then he played three of his own songs, 'Yer Blues', a new haunting song about drug withdrawal called 'Cold Turkey' and 'Give Peace A Chance'. So far, so ragged. It was then that Yoko struggled out of the bag next to John's microphone, said hello to the crowd and then screamed into the microphone for about 20 minutes. The band played on as best they could.

The crowd now turned hostile but John was exhilarated. After the show, he told Allen Klein that he had made his mind up. John Lennon was leaving The Beatles. Life was so much more fruitful and exciting without them.

On 20 September 1969 at a board meeting John Lennon made his move and finally killed off the gang. Paul McCartney had arrived full of new ideas to push the band forward. The main idea was one he had been trying to make them realize for months now. He wanted them to go back on the road, but to do it under a pseudonym. The idea was to start all over again, hitting the colleges and small venues to whip up some excitement, play some rock'n'roll and discover the magic that once bonded them together. As he spelt out his reasons, Lennon kept saying, 'I don't want to do that. I don't want to do that.'

Finally, an exasperated McCartney went into a speech, the kind of up-and-at-them spiel Lennon used to use back in the old days when they were playing half-filled halls to uninterested audiences. 'Come on,' he urged Lennon. 'After all, we are The Beatles aren't we?'

And that was when Lennon delivered the words they had all been secretly dreading they would hear, the words that would tell them once and for all that the Beatle dream was over.

From Twickenham onwards The Beatles had brought up the subject of splitting up but none of them had acted on their words. Even George and Ringo who had walked out had returned within two weeks. John was different, though. 'I'm not [a Beatle]. Don't you understand? It's over. I want a divorce, like the one I got from Cynthia. Can't you get it through your bloody head? I wasn't gonna tell you this until after our new record deal, but I'm leaving the group.'

YOKO STRUGGLED OUT OF THE BAG NEXT TO JOHN'S MICROPHONE, SAID HELLO TO THE CROWD AND THEN SCREAMED INTO THE MICROPHONE FOR ABOUT 20 MINUTES. THE BAND PLAYED ON AS BEST THEY COULD

There was stunned silence. Lennon continued. He expressed his relief at having finally smashed the gang in two. Then he stood up and looking at his forlorn gang members, smashed home his departure. 'It's over. Finished,' and then he and Yoko swept out of the building. It had taken the leader to finally kill off the best gang in the world – and in a way that was right and proper.

In October the *Abbey Road* album was released and sold millions worldwide. Three weeks later John and Yoko released their third album, *The Wedding Album*, along with another Plastic Ono Band single, 'Cold Turkey'. Lennon had offered this harrowing song to The Beatles but they had turned their collective nose up at it. A song about the pain of withdrawal set to violent ragged guitars did not a number one make, they reasoned. So Lennon said he'd do it himself.

That he should have written such a major composition in this year of such frenetic activity tells us much about the new artistic energy he was now working with. This was the number-one pop star in the country laying bare to all the world his heroin addiction. This was the number-one musician in the country baring his soul.

The theme of self-revelation he had been developing in The Beatles was now allowed to flourish and would go on to produce one of the great Beatles' solo albums, *John Lennon/Plastic Ono Band*. 'Cold Turkey' reached number 14 in the charts in the week beginning 11 November. The following week it dropped one place to 15. Lennon took immediate action. He took his MBE off Aunt Mimi's mantelpiece and put it an envelope, which also contained a letter. The letter was to the Queen and it read: 'I am returning my MBE as a protest against Britain's involvement in the Nigeria-Biafra thing, against our support of America in Vietnam and against "Cold Turkey" slipping down the charts. With love, John Lennon of Bag.'

His actions of course made front-page news, most of it anti-Lennon. Lennon just smiled and moved on. In December Apple released The Plastic Ono Band's performance in Canada under the title *Live Peace In Toronto*. It contained their whole show complete with Yoko's contribution.

To sign off the year, Lennon dipped into his own pocket to the tune of US$72,000 and in 11 major cities put up huge posters that read 'WAR IS OVER! IF YOU WANT IT. Happy Christmas from John & Yoko'. Ritchie Yorke, who helped with John and Yoko's peace campaign, later said this about John and his commitment to peace: 'John totally believed that love could save us. He thought that if one person really stood up things could be changed. I have never seen anyone so committed to a cause regardless of the cost.'

At the end of the year Lennon sent out a humorous book to all of his friends. It was called *The John Lennon London Diary 1969*. In it he had made handwritten entries for every day and they all pretty much read the same; 'Got up, went to work, came home, watched telly, went to bed.' He may no longer be a Beatle, he may have been a long-haired hippy prattling on about love and peace and Yoko for breakfast, but he was still a major comedian.

John and Yoko's famous bed-in at the Amsterdam Hilton in March 1969. Lennon had now decided to quit The Beatles and use his fame for political ends.

John and Paul record
THE BALLAD OF
JOHN AND YOKO

DATE 14 April 1969, Abbey Road Studios, London

John Lennon and Yoko Ono figured a wedding in the UK would be too much hassle, so they went abroad and tied the knot in Gibraltar on 20 March 1969. It was John's second marriage and of course he had to write a song about it. John brought the song round to Paul's house in April and told him how keen he was to get it out as a single. He did so at a time when Ringo was making *The Magic Christian* film and George was on holiday.

The song was originally entitled 'The Ballad Of John And Yoko, Christ They're Gonna Crucify Me'. McCartney was aghast. He knew they could never get away with such a provocative title without upsetting a lot of people. And quite frankly it just wasn't worth the hassle. Had they not been through this already with John's infamous 'more popular than Jesus' quote and the huge furore that it had caused. One death threat was one death threat too many, as far as he was concerned. Despite his mate's reservations Lennon was insistent that they cut the single without any delay: they could talk about the title later.

The next day found John and Paul together at Abbey Road studio starting work on the next Beatles single. Despite the business wranglings that were now starting to consume them, onlookers at Abbey Road all remarked at how happy John and Paul seemed as they leapt from instrument to instrument with huge enthusiasm. Paul played drums, bass, piano, maracas and did the backing vocals. John looked after the guitars. They recorded the rhythm session first and then added the vocals and instruments on top. At one point, John shouted to Paul behind

ONLOOKERS AT ABBEY ROAD ALL REMARKED AT HOW HAPPY JOHN AND PAUL SEEMED AS THEY LEAPT FROM INSTRUMENT TO INSTRUMENT WITH HUGE ENTHUSIASM

the drum kit, 'Go faster Ringo.' 'OK George,' Paul shouted back. They booked the studio for six and half hours and finished with an hour to spare, that is how quick and how fun the whole enterprise was.

Paul later confessed that during the session, he became increasingly anxious about what George and Ringo's attitude would be when they discovered that they were not going to feature on the band's next single. 'We did it and stood back to see if the other guys would hate us for it – which I'm not sure about. They probably never forgave us. John was on heat, so to speak. He needed to record it so we just ran in and did it.'

THIS WAS 1969 AND BEATLEMANIA WAS LONG DEAD. JOHN'S COMMENTS ON RELIGION WERE NO LONGER POTENT ENOUGH TO TRIGGER DEATH THREATS OR WORLDWIDE CONDEMNATION

He need not have worried. Both George and Ringo were not unduly fussed by this turn of events. Lennon later recalled, 'The story came out that only Paul and I were on the record, but I wouldn't have bothered publicizing that. It doesn't mean anything. It just so happened that there were only two of us there.'

As for the song itself, John's view of music had been radically altered by Yoko. He had started off life wanting to be Elvis – a tough rock'n'roller with a sneer and a punch. Then he wanted to write love songs à la Goffin and King. Then he wanted to be the Acid King. Now, Yoko had persuaded him that he was an artist and therefore his life was a work of art. His music would now report on that life and on that artist.

Paul was right about the chorus line that mentioned Christ and crucifixion, though. On the song's release on 30 May 1969, quite a few American radio stations refused to play it, while others put a noise over the offending part. But this was not 1966 anymore. This was 1969 and Beatlemania was long dead. John's comments on religion were no longer potent enough to trigger death threats or worldwide condemnation.

Perhaps if they had heard what John did in 1968, they would have reacted far more strongly. At the height of an LSD binge, John reportedly called a meeting at Apple and announced to the band and their entourage that he was in fact the new incarnation of Jesus, come back to save them all. Luckily, everyone realized what was happening and played along with him. It was John. On acid. Not to worry. He would come down soon.

For Paul, the reaction of the world to this new Beatles single did not matter.

What mattered, what really mattered, was that the magic had been rekindled. John had brought him a radical song and the two of them had joined forces and turned it into a fine piece of work. Despite everything they could still work together, still create meaningful music.

FOR PAUL, THE REACTION OF THE WORLD TO THIS NEW BEATLES SINGLE DID NOT REALLY MATTER. WHAT MATTERED, WHAT REALLY MATTERED, WAS THAT THE MAGIC HAD BEEN REKINDLED

Music had achieved that, music had brought them together – just as it did when they were skinny teenagers in Liverpool and hungry for success, when John would come to Paul's house and ask him why he was not more assertive with his dad. Paul would make up some lame excuse and then they would get some tea out of the tea pot and put it in a pipe belonging to Paul's dad and smoke it, all the time coughing their lungs up. Then Paul would tune John's guitar and John would joke about the guitar because he had bought it from an advert which said it would never split. Paul would laugh, and take their exercise book out and write at the top of the page, 'A Lennon And McCartney Original' and then Paul would write some words like, 'They said that our love was just fun...' and the boys would try and find chords and a vocal melody line and spend hours trying to finish the song.

When Jim, Paul's dad, finally came home, he would brusquely nod at John because he did not approve of him hanging out with his son, and John would take the hint and get up and leave. Jim would tell Paul he would get nowhere hanging out with the likes of him. Paul would smile and change the subject and start thinking about the next day's writing session, and John would be sitting at the bus stop at the top of Paul's road, smoking a cigarette and playing music in his head as a sneer drew across his lips. And this is what music did, this is what John Lennon and Paul McCartney had between them, a shared all-consuming love, a musical gift from the gods that took them out of this world and bound them together – forever.

'The Ballad Of John And Yoko' would prove to be the band's final number-one single in the UK, and in some sense that was quite fitting. It is the only Beatles record to feature just John and Paul. And, ironically, it is about the woman many believe came between these two men and finished the band.

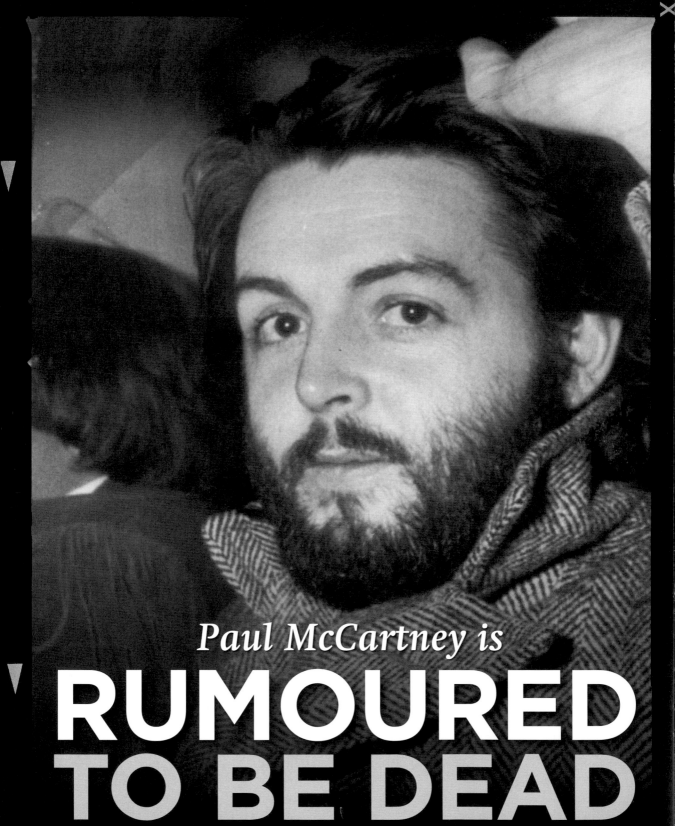

Paul McCartney is
RUMOURED
TO BE DEAD

DATE 17 September 1969, UK

Once upon a time Paul McCartney died. He was driving his car very fast on a wild and windy night and he smashed headlong into another car. The reason he was driving very fast is because he'd had a big argument with his best mate, John. John had been vicious with him, so Paul got into his car and he angrily drove off, telling John to 'eff off' before he left. When Paul McCartney died, there was a girl named Rita sitting next to him in the passenger seat. She was dead too.

Paul had picked up Rita because she was hitchhiking and she looked very wet and miserable. Paul pulled up beside her. He opened the door said, 'Hop in, love.' Rita got in, thanking her knight in a dark Aston Martin. As Paul's car sped off Rita glanced over and suddenly realized who her driver was – and she went crazy. She could not believe it. She loved The Beatles. More than that, she loved Paul McCartney. She began showering him with kisses, telling him how great he was. Paul tried to fend her off but it was too late. Another car came hurtling round the corner and the two vehicles smashed into each other, head to head. Paul, Rita and the other driver were instantly killed.

When word of the tragedy reached The Beatles, they quickly held a meeting. This was tragic news. Without Paul they stood to lose millions. There must be a solution. 'Well,' said one Beatle, 'do you remember that Billy Shears? He looks a lot like Paul. Maybe we could bring him in as a double?' 'Really?' asked another Beatle.

> WITHOUT PAUL THEY STOOD TO LOSE MILLIONS. THERE MUST BE A SOLUTION. 'WELL,' SAID ONE BEATLE, 'DO YOU REMEMBER THAT BILLY SHEARS? HE LOOKS A LOT LIKE PAUL. MAYBE WE COULD BRING HIM IN AS A DOUBLE?'

'Yeah, why not? You write the songs, John, we will teach him how to talk and walk and act like Paul and maybe, just maybe, we will get away with it.'

'You know the other thing we could do,' another Beatle suggested. 'What?' 'We could lay clues on album covers, on records, as to Paul's passing. That way if we do get caught we can say, we told you all along.' 'Great idea,' said the other three ... two, rather.

IF YOU LOOK AT THE PHOTO OF McCARTNEY IN HIS SATIN UNIFORM, HE IS WEARING ON HIS ARM A BADGE CARRYING THE INITIALS 'OPD'. IN THE USA THOSE INITIALS STOOD FOR 'OFFICIALLY PRONOUNCED DEAD'

The first clues to Paul's death came with the album *Sgt. Pepper's Lonely Hearts Club Band*. If you look at the photo of McCartney in his satin uniform, he is wearing on his arm a badge carrying the initials 'OPD'. In the USA those initials stood for 'Officially Pronounced Dead'. Look at the people they have chosen to surround the band on the cover – Marilyn Monroe, James Dean, Jayne Mansfield, all killed in the prime of their lives. Turn the sleeve over. Look at Paul standing with his back to the camera and look at the lyrics that run over his back. Only the words from George's song 'Within You Without You' which refers to people hiding themselves behind illusion and not glimpsing the truth until it is too late when they pass away.

Listen to the music on the *Sgt. Pepper* album, listen to the band singing about Billy Shears, the cat you have known for all these years, and lovely Rita the meter maid (a subtle reference to the car, get it?), and listen to 'I Am The Walrus', which uses the death speech from the Shakespeare play *King Lear* at the end in that cacophony of noise and distortion, which in itself suggests death.

On their *Magical Mystery Tour* album the band dressed in animal suits. Paul was the walrus, the symbol of death. As everybody knows. More clues followed with the *Abbey Road* album sleeve. The band are depicted in a funereal procession. Left-handed Paul (who is really Billy Shears) holds a cigarette in his right hand! He has bare feet and is out of step with he rest of the band. John wears white (the angel), Ringo wears black (the undertaker) and George is dressed like a gravedigger in his all-denim clothes. For two years The Beatles, along with their new member, Billy Shears, fooled the world. And then the secret got out and all hell broke loose in Beatle Land.

The first the world heard about The Beatles' dastardly plot was in September 1969 when Tim Harper, an American college student-paper editor, wrote an article entitled 'Is Beatle Paul McCartney Dead?' His article was picked up by the popular Detroit radio station WKNR-FM. A listener responded to the story and called in and listed all the clues in the band's records, including John at the end of 'Strawberry Fields Forever', saying, 'I bury Paul'. (He didn't really, he said 'cranberry sauce' but let's not allow a fact to get in the way of a good story, eh?)

American journalist Fred LaBour picked up the story and ran with it. A satirical article appeared in *The Michigan Daily* in which he pointed out the clues on the covers, including the newly released album, *Abbey Road*. LaBour was absolutely astonished when the rest of the press picked up his story. He had made up all the clues. Such was the fuss, the band's press officer was forced to issue a statement denying Paul's death.

'Recently we've been getting a flood of enquiries asking about reports that Paul is dead. We've been getting questions like that for years, of course, but in the past few weeks we've been getting them at the office and home night and day. I'm even getting telephone calls from disc jockeys and others in the United States.'

Paul McCartney himself went on the radio to deny the story and then agreed to be interviewed by *Life* magazine to verify to the world that he was in fact alive and not dead. Trust John to blow his cover. On his 1971 solo album *Imagine*, John recorded a bitter diatribe against Paul called 'How Do You Sleep?'. He did not like his best mate any more. He had been nasty to him. So John was nasty right back. In retaliation for Paul's songs on his *Ram* album '3 Legs' and 'Too Many People', and the bad feeling that had been generated by a bitter court case, John sang that the freaks were right when they said Paul was dead. And a million conspiracy theorists said, see, John says so – it must be true.

> JOHN RECORDED A BITTER DIATRIBE AGAINST PAUL CALLED 'HOW DO YOU SLEEP?'. IN IT, HE SANG THAT THE FREAKS WERE RIGHT WHEN THEY SAID PAUL WAS DEAD. AND A MILLION CONSPIRACY THEORISTS SAID, SEE, JOHN SAYS SO – IT MUST BE TRUE

The iconic picture on the *Abbey Road* album cover. Paul's bare feet helped spark rumours that he had been killed two years previously.

THE
BATTLE
to manage *The Beatles*

DATE 27 January 1970, The Dorchester Hotel, London

Two Americans dropped down into London to fight for control of The Beatles, and they could not have been more different. Lee Eastman was elderly, Ivy League educated, a cultured, assured man, and father, of course, to Linda. Allen Klein was raised in an orphanage. He was brash, spoke tough and was driven by money. The choice divided the band. McCartney was loyal to his father-in-law while John, George and Ringo felt far more affinity with the streetwise Klein.

Lee Eastman had been called to London by his son-in-law. McCartney believed The Beatles were the best in the world and therefore everything round them should be at a similar level – for him Lee was the perfect person to take over as manager.

Allen Klein on the other hand was rough and ready. His obituary said of him, that he had the, 'Gun rattle of Brooklynese argot, liberally sauced with ripe invective'. He had been called to London to meet John Lennon. The ensuing face-off between Eastman and Klein was akin to tough Brooklyn taking on suave Manhattan: there was only going to be one winner.

In 1967 Allen Klein was driving his car through New York when the news broke that Brian Epstein had died. Klein slapped his steering wheel hard. 'I've got them, I have fucking got them,' he thought to himself and pushed his foot down harder

on the gas pedal. He had met Epstein back in 1964, at the time of the band's first American tour, and offered to renegotiate the band's recording deal and get them a much higher royalty rate. In return, he would get 20 per cent of the money earned by the higher royalty rate. Epstein took one look at this character with his raw

MANAGERS MANAGED. THEY GOT THEIR ACTS MONEY AND FAME. THEY RARELY STOPPED TO LIKE OR UNDERSTAND THE MUSIC THEY WERE SELLING. KLEIN DID AND THAT MADE HIM VERY ATTRACTIVE TO LENNON language and dishevelled appearance, and showed him the door.

Klein shrugged his big shoulders and went to Plan B, The Rolling Stones. Their manager Andrew Loog Oldham loved hustlers and shakers, mainly because he aspired to that status himself. His favourite film was *The Sweet Smell Of Success* starring Tony Curtis and Burt Lancaster. He loved the film's smart language, the clothes, the betrayals. Oldham saw Klein in a similar light and was enthralled.

McCARTNEY DID NOT TRUST KLEIN AT ALL. HE FELT THAT THE EASTMANS WOULD BE FAR MORE OLD SCHOOL, FAR MORE TRANSPARENT THAN THE HUSTLER KLEIN

Mick Jagger recalled, 'Andrew sold him to us as a gangster figure, someone outside the establishment. We found that rather attractive.'

Klein read the signs and played his part to a tee. 'Andrew liked having me portrayed as this shadowy American.' Klein later said. 'That was Andrew. He just created it, that I was like a gangster. He said they'd love it in England.'

Klein had previous. Back in the day he had worked with Sam Cooke and Bobby Darin, and had extracted money from Mafia-owned labels where no one thought money could be extracted. He also liked all things British. Along with The Stones, he also helped out The Animals, The Kinks, The Dave Clark Five and Donovan. For Klein, the road was only leading one way – towards the gates of Beatle Land.

Derek Taylor brought him to Lennon in 1969. The flow of money pouring from Apple had to be stemmed. Tough measures were needed. Phone tough-guy Klein, then. A January meeting was held in a plush London hotel. John and Yoko, Allen Klein. They hit it off well. Lennon warmed to Klein's background, the lost mother and the time spent in an orphanage all chimed with him. Plus, Klein had done his homework. He knew the best way to a songwriter's heart is always through his songs.

Klein started telling Lennon about his lyrics and songs he adored. Not obvious numbers that any Joe could have heard, but B-sides and album tracks that few people spoke about. Lennon's ego lapped it up. Klein may have been a hard-hearted businessman but he was also a music man and in those days the two were not that compatible. Managers managed. They got their acts money and fame. They rarely stopped to like or understand the music they were selling. Klein did and that made him very attractive to Lennon.

The next day, Lennon told his gang that they had a new manager. 'Do we?'

asked McCartney. After the last year or so, Paul was no longer prepared to follow the leader. That is why he too had been working behind the scenes. When the band had signed a new contract with Brian Epstein, they had actually signed

KLEIN WOULD LOOK INTO ALL THE DEALS TO DATE AND UNCOVER ALL HIDDEN MONIES. THE EASTMANS WOULD HANDLE ALL NEW DEALS, THUS GIVING THE BAND SECURITY ON TWO FRONTS

to Epstein's company NEMS. On Brian's death his brother Clive had taken over but just two years into the job he wanted out. He announced he wanted to sell NEMS. McCartney phoned his father-in-law to ask for advice. He told him to buy NEMS. Borrow the money required from EMI and then that way you own the company that owns you.

Lennon organized for the band to meet Klein at Apple. George and Ringo followed the leader, and took to Klein, 'Because we were all from Liverpool,' George noted, 'we favoured people who were street people.' McCartney did not trust Klein at all. He felt that the Eastmans would be far more old school, far more transparent than the hustler Klein. The band argued differently. They pointed out that Eastman would be on Paul's side in whatever negotiations took place.

The gang divided itself and battle lines were drawn up. Things came to a head at a session for the *Abbey Road* album. It was a Friday night. McCartney arrived early and was playing an instrument when the rest of the band showed up, with Klein in tow. They asked McCartney to sign a contract giving Klein 20 per cent. Paul refused. He told them they were a big act – he should get 15 per cent. No way, 20 said the others. Only fair for what he was going to do for them. McCartney did not pick up the pen that night.

The band went ahead anyway and ordered Klein to begin shaking up Apple. Out went Ron Kass, Tony Bramwell, Denis O'Dell. In came Klein's people. An uneasy compromise was also put into place. Klein would look into all the deals to date and uncover all hidden monies, his speciality. The Eastmans would handle all new deals, thus giving the band security on two fronts. It didn't happen. Within two weeks Eastman and Klein had clashed over important documents. Then in late March, Dick James the director of Northern Songs, the company that owned the Lennon and McCartney catalogue, announced he was selling his share to Sir Lew Grade of Associated Television.

And so it went, headache after headache, the band spending days and

The legendary producer Phil Spector who Lennon asked to salvage the band's *Get Back* session tapes. McCartney was angered by Spector's treatment of his song 'The Long And Winding Road' although the song did go on to win a Grammy award in 1972.

days and days – and oh such long days – around the table at Apple, arguing over money and management, over lawyers and shares. And they should never have done so for they were musicians. They should have been making music, recording, performing, doing that which all bands must do.

Instead, they spent their time totally out of their depth. In reality, they were far too young to understand the complexities of the money world they were trying to control. They had no real head for business and money. John would later admit, 'We were naive enough to let people come between us,' he said. But then added, 'But it was happening anyway.'

If the truth be told, it had happened the day John met Yoko really – that was the day the gang began to fall apart. Everything since had been a long and painful death throe. With Lennon off promoting world peace and filled with obsession for Yoko, Paul, George and

Ringo all started making solo albums. In April McCartney announced the imminent release of his solo album *McCartney*. He was furious. Through Klein, Lennon had handed over the tapes of the *Get Back* sessions to producer Phil Spector. He had gone through them and produced the album, *Let It Be*.

THEY WERE MUSICIANS. THEY SHOULD HAVE BEEN MAKING MUSIC, RECORDING, PERFORMING, DOING THAT WHICH ALL BANDS MUST DO. INSTEAD, THEY SPENT THEIR TIME TOTALLY OUT OF THEIR DEPTH

To McCartney's disgust, he had added strings, a harp and female backing vocals to McCartney's major composition 'The Long And Winding Road'. Lennon supported Spector the whole way. 'The tapes were so lousy and so bad none of us would go near them. They'd been lying around for six months and none of us could face remixing them. But Spector did a fantastic job.'

McCartney fired off a letter to Klein and Spector, which began, 'In the future no one will be allowed to add to or subtract from a recording of one of my songs without my permission ...' He then filled in a questionnaire supplied by Derek Taylor, designed to answer all press enquiries that would accompany his solo album. His answer to the question as to whether The Beatles broken up was, 'Yes, we won't play together again'.

As soon as the press saw the statement phones started ringing all over the world. John in particular was annoyed. He had split the band up so he wanted the credit. It was kids' stuff really, but typical of where The Beatles were now at with each other. George agreed. 'In that period everybody was getting pissed off at each other for everything ... He had that press release, but everybody else had already left the band. That was what pissed John off ... It was, "Hey, I've already left and it's as if he's invented it!"'

On 10 April 1970 the headlines arrived. 'The Beatles Split Up'. The gang was no more and the game was up. 'I absolutely did believe – as millions of others did – that the friendship The Beatles had for each other was a lifesaver for all of us,' Derek Taylor said with typical insight. 'I believed that if these people were happy with each other ... life was worth living. But we expected too much of them.' These words are so true, but the spirit of the gang would live on, refusing to wither or to die.

PAUL SUES

The Beatles

DATE 18 February 1971, High Court, London

All his life Paul recalled his mother's cry to better himself. He had always followed that order, and in doing so he had helped The Beatles become the wondrous magical band that they were. Yet after the split, he became deaf to his mother's entreaties and went the other way – worsened himself in fact. He sought oblivion in drink and anything else that he could get his hands on.

He became such a nightmare to live with that later on he felt obliged to write a song called 'Maybe I'm Amazed', as good as anything he did in The Beatles, for his exasperated wife Linda by way of apology for his behaviour. And then he wrote another song called 'Every Night', in which he detailed his drunkenness and it too was a wonderful song.

Why the bad behaviour? Because Paul McCartney was no longer a Beatle and that fact killed him. McCartney believed that however bad things got there would never be a world without The Beatles for that was the promise of the gang; no matter what, they would stick it out forever and ever, Amen. That is why in later years he had cajoled them into films and albums, urged them to get into a little van and under the name Rikki And The Red Streaks (the name taken from one of their very minor rivals back in The Cavern days) go out and play village halls. All to no avail.

The gang were simply not interested in being a gang anymore and that badly wounded McCartney. He felt angry and horribly betrayed. 'Talk about traumas!' he exclaimed. 'Not only were The Beatles broken up... these true buddies of mine from way back, were now my firmest of enemies overnight. Ever since a child I had been in this group ... this was my school, my family, my life ...'

He did not yet know that the thing that does not kill you serves only to make you stronger. It would be in later life that McCartney would absorb this lesson. At the time, he was inconsolable. He either stayed in bed or hit the bottle, or both. This was so unlike him. Paul was the strong Beatle, the Beatle with the drive, the ambition. His mother's words had become his constant mantra – better yourself, son, better yourself. Now he was lazy, slothful, and often drunk. Everything he once knew to be solid, relied upon implicitly, had been removed, sending him into free fall. For the first time in his life, his talents were not required. For McCartney, this was a huge shock to the system. Even a year ago he had a purpose in life. He was a Beatle. Now there was just a void. Linda tried her best to console and encourage him but her entreaties fell on deaf ears. All he had left was his money.

McCartney was always proud of his wealth. Songwriters tend to measure their talent by their money and sales and on that count McCartney had every right to feel good about himself. Allen Klein was about to take a huge chunk of that money. The gang be damned, he was not going to allow him to do that without a fight.

In 1971 Paul McCartney sued The Beatles. He wanted the band dissolved so that Klein would lose his power base. The other three stood against him. McCartney put forward three charges, that Klein had tried to delay the release of his solo album, *McCartney*, that his songs on the *Let It Be* album had been altered without permission, and that Klein had also transferred the rights to the *Let It Be* film (which had been released in May 1970) from Apple to United Artists.

The other band members did not appear in court but McCartney turned up frequently. And when Allen Klein walked in, he turned his face away in disgust. The case centered on Klein's ability to manage The Beatles. To prove that he did not have the band's best interests at heart,

McCartney's lawyers examined thousands of documents. And good that they did because there in one folder was a cheque from Capitol Records, The Beatles' US label, showing that Klein was taking a much bigger percentage than he should have done (in this case half a million pounds). The judge handed McCartney the victory.

McCARTNEY WANTED THE BAND DISSOLVED SO THAT KLEIN WOULD LOSE HIS POWER BASE. THE OTHER THREE STOOD AGAINST HIM

How did John react? He recorded 'How Do You Sleep?', even singing the 'C word' in one version. On hearing it, Paul acted with restraint. He knew John inside out, knew that he always went with whatever was in his head at the time. John hated him. He also knew that the very next day John might love him again.

Two years later McCartney started making peace signals and of course Lennon made him jump through hoops. 'I used to actually have some very frightening phone calls …' Paul revealed. 'I went through a period when I was so nervous to ring him and so insecure in myself that I actually felt like I was in the wrong.'

By 1974 there was loose talk of a Beatles reunion floating round both Lennon and McCartney camps. Paul jammed with John in LA and John suggested visiting him in New Orleans. John never made the visit. Yoko called, and John hotfooted it to New York.

For his part, McCartney was overjoyed to be back in Lennon's orbit. He took to dropping by the Dakota building whenever he could. One night while watching the comedy show *Saturday Night Live* with John, the news that The Beatles had been offered 230 million dollars to re-form for a gig in New York was used as a skit. The announcer said he would give them three grand. Both men looked at each other with the same idea. Shall we go downtown and do it, get the three grand? Then they said, nah, rolled another joint and carried on watching TV.

By this stage, Paul McCartney was back doing what he did best: making hit records. His band Wings had finally made it big, especially with the *Band On The Run* album where he forcibly pushed himself back into the spotlight; he is yet to leave it. After Wings came solo albums and from their successes, McCartney bounced himself into many other areas of expression. He wrote oratorios. He wrote music for films and played director. He wrote poetry and children's books. He made avant-garde experimental albums under pseudonyms. He exhibited his own paintings, a discipline he took up only

in 1983. He opened up a talent school in Liverpool and was knighted. He has lived a life full of creative adventure and honour. And yet, in a recent interview to promote a ballet he had written music for he admitted that all his art should be judged by his work in The Beatles; that was the gold standard.

As for John, although Paul would still try to compete with him, even after John's death, Paul probably summed it up the best in a 1984 *Playboy* interview. Asked about the man who he had shown the chords to 'Twenty Flight Rock' all those years ago at Woolton Village Fete, McCartney's mind instantly fixed on one particular incident. It was March 1965. The band were in Austria filming *Help!*. John and Paul were sharing a chalet and after a day's filming were getting ready for dinner. As they dressed, Paul put on a tape of the new songs both men had written for the band's next album. Three of the songs were Paul's, three of them were John's. At the end of the tape, John wistfully said, 'I probably like your songs better than mine.'

Paul couldn't believe his ears. John rarely praised his fellow bandmates. For one thing a leader knows that silence from the top keeps the followers on their toes. For another, John always felt actions spoke louder than words and therefore praise was not required. The fact that he had just gone against the grain and casually given Paul the validation he had sought all these years was something Paul would remember for all time.

John Lennon is
ASSASSINATED

DATE 8 December 1980, Dakota building, New York City

In his last years on earth, John Ono Lennon finally faced up to the trauma and tragedies that had shaped his character, atoned for his sins and started to find some serenity about who he was, where he had been and where he was going. That is what some said. Others chose to believe the opposite. They believed Lennon was a mess right up until his dying day, unhappy, unfulfilled and taking out his frustrations on both Yoko and his son Julian. As in all these cases, the truth is no doubt to be located somewhere between those two extremes.

His talent had not diminished. Wonderful songs such as 'Beautiful Boy' and 'Woman' proved that beyond doubt. The trouble was that because Lennon had locked himself away in the late 1970s, speculation about his life had grown.

The case for the defence was launched by Lennon himself. In a series of major interviews round the time of his last album, *Double Fantasy*, he asserted that he had been at home 'baking bread and looking after the baby', that he had identified the demons of his past and slain them. He had rid himself of his macho tendencies and saw Yoko as a partner on the level of his relationship with McCartney.

The case against Lennon was provided by Albert Goldman's 1988 biography *The Lives Of John Lennon*, which examines Lennon with a ferocious attitude. Apart from digging up all kinds of negative events in his life – including an alleged near-rape incident that involved Lennon

WHEN HE STEPPED OUT OF THE CAR A YOUNG MAN WAS WAITING FOR HIM WITH A GUN. HE CALLED HIS NAME AND THEN **THE WORLD FROZE** AS MARK DAVID CHAPMAN SHOT JOHN LENNON

John Lennon with fan Paul Goresh, taken on the day of Lennon's death. Goresh also took a photograph of Lennon signing a copy of his *Double Fantasy* album for Mark Chapman.

and a female fan prior to a show – the opening chapter on John's life in the Dakota building portrayed a man with very little purpose in life, a man at the beck and call of his wife, unable to make a move without the help of a tarot-card reader and unable to seek a way out of his misery and torpor.

One thing we do know is that Lennon's last thoughts on earth were not for himself but for his five-year-old son. John and Yoko were in the limousine returning home from the studio when she suggested they go for a meal. John said he would prefer to go home and say goodnight to Sean before he went to sleep.

When he stepped out of the car a young man was waiting for him with a gun. He called his name and then the world froze as Mark David Chapman shot John Lennon and then dropped the gun and waited.

Lennon remained conscious for about 30 minutes, and then passed away in the hospital he had been rushed to. His fellow gang members were absolutely distraught. Two of them, George and Ringo, could not talk to anyone except immediate family. Paul managed to put out a release in which he said, 'I can't take it in at the moment. John was a great guy. He's going to be missed by the whole world.'

Chapman told the police he had killed John Lennon because the voice in his head told him to and because he thought Lennon was a real phoney. A phoney was a concept Chapman had absorbed during his growing obsession with the J.D. Salinger novel, *The Catcher In The Rye* (1951). The main character, Holden Caulfield, spends a lot of his time lambasting those he perceives as phonies. Chapman felt the same way about Lennon. How could he sing about imagining he had no money when he had piles of the stuff stashed away? That made him a liar, a phoney, and for that Lennon had to pay. In this thinking, Chapman actually becomes a little more human in his actions; when they don't like the message, it is a sad fact that humans often attack the person bringing it. Chapman literally did shoot the messenger.

Since quitting The Beatles, Lennon had been giving out many messages. In his early years after quitting the gang, he had delved into radical politics, hung out with Black Panthers and characters such as Michael X, moved to America, attacked discrimination, put forward agendas of peace and had even undergone Primal Scream Therapy to rid himself of his childhood demons.

OF ALL THE CURES HE HAD TRIED IN HIS LIFE TO DISCOVER HAPPINESS, IT WOULD SEEM THAT LOVE – A FATHER'S LOVE FOR HIS CHILD, HIS LOVE FOR YOKO – WAS THE ONE THAT GAVE HIM THE MOST COMFORT

Lennon's emotional stability was erratic. And so too was his chart life. His debut solo album *John Lennon/Plastic Ono Band* was by far his most sustained solo album, an intense descent into his soul, a harrowing howl of pain and bitterness that was the logical culmination of his previous solo work.

He had a number-one single with 'Whatever Gets You Thru The Night' but saw double albums such as *Some Time In*

New York City savagely attacked. He worked with David Bowie and Elton John but still kept in contact with Beatle Land. He gave Ringo a song called 'I Am The Greatest' for his solo album while George played guitar on his acerbic attack on Paul, 'How Do You Sleep?'

THE WORLD MOURNED HIS DEATH TERRIBLY. AS MANY POINTED OUT, WHATEVER YOUR POLITICAL STANDPOINT, LENNON'S COMMITMENT, UNLIKE MANY OTHER POP STARS, COULD NEVER BE QUESTIONED

Within two years of that song Lennon had changed his feelings towards the man he had shared so much with, and friendship was resumed. In 1974 Lennon started producing Harry Nilsson's album, *Pussy Cats*. Nilsson was a talented musician and major drinking buddy of Lennon's. On 31 March Paul and Linda McCartney dropped into the session and jammed with Lennon, Stevie Wonder, Harry Nilsson, Jesse Ed Davis and Bobby Keys at Lennon's Los Angeles beach house. It sounds amazing – except it wasn't, as a bootleg from the session testifies. It is called *A Toot And A Snore*. Enough said. On John's 35th birthday Yoko gave birth to Sean, and John took on a far greater parental role that he had with Julian. In the same year he was also given permission to live in America after a long and bitter struggle with the authorities. Putting aside his guitar for a while, he stayed out of the limelight, stayed out of politics and stayed at home.

Of all the cures he had tried in his life to discover happiness, it would seem that love – a father's love for his child, his love for Yoko – was the one that gave him the most comfort. In 1979 he and Yoko commenced work on an album entitled *Double Fantasy*. John no longer had the appetite to slug it out with his contemporaries over the number-one slot. If he made it, great, and if he didn't, so what. Lennon had bigger fish to fry now.

And then he met Mark Chapman. Like Lennon, Chapman's childhood was troubled. His father had abused both him and his mother. He was bullied at school. The Beatles came along and saved him. Chapman lost himself in their music. By the time he was 14, Chapman was dressing like Lennon, mimicking the man that he would one day murder.

The infatuation did not last long. Chapman threw away rock'n'roll and embraced Jesus. He worked with children at a summer camp and won an award from his employers. He hooked up with a girl he quickly grew to love, but the girl ditched him and Chapman tried to commit suicide. Incarcerated in a secure hospital, Chapman spent his time serenading fellow patients with Beatles songs on his guitar.

A year later he took out his savings and went on a six-week round-the-world trip. He visited the Far East, India and Europe. When he came back to America, he met a Japanese-American woman named Gloria Abe and the couple soon got married. He also started getting very high and began hearing voices in his head.

JOHN LENNON'S CHARACTER, HIS MOOD SWINGS, HIS OBSESSIONS, BUT ABOVE ALL HIS ARTISTIC DARING IS WHAT DROVE THE BEATLES AND STILL FASCINATES TO THIS DAY

Chapman's plan to murder someone famous soon developed but several people are said to have featured on his shortlist. To make the decision, Chapman is reported to have gone to the biography section of his local library, to have closed his eyes and selected a title at random from the shelf. Whoever the book was about would be the person he killed. The book he picked was about John Lennon.

The world mourned his death terribly. As many pointed out, whatever your political standpoint, Lennon's commitment, unlike many other pop stars, could never be questioned. 'I'll tell you something that no one should forget about John Lennon,' the sports commentator Howard Cosell said, 'he was never, ever a hypocrite about anything he ever did or said or believed … he was a man of conviction and commitment. I am proud to have known him.'

Since his death, Lennon's stature has risen and risen. There is an airport in Liverpool named after him, statues of him have been erected, polls still place him as a leading icon and Beatles records still sell in their millions. The man who once revelled in violence, who stood in dance halls in rough areas of Liverpool watching with morbid delight as Teddy Boys viciously tore into one another, who openly laughed at drummer Tommy Moore's stitches splitting open on stage, his blood flowing everywhere, who punched his girlfriend in the face and booted customers in Hamburg clubs in the head, was now an icon of world peace.

John Lennon's character, his mood swings, his obsessions, but above all his artistic daring is what drove The Beatles and still fascinates to this day. It is one of the reasons why he remains as popular as ever and thus it is only right and fitting that we look to him for final enlightenment on this matter. 'Everybody loves you,' Lennon once said, 'when you're six foot in the ground.'

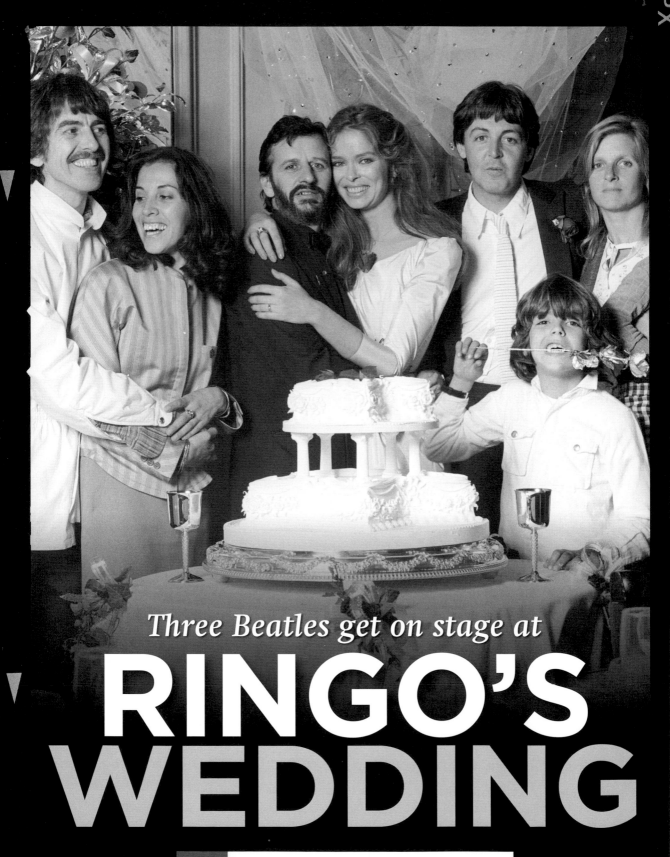

Three Beatles get on stage at

RINGO'S
WEDDING

DATE 27 April 1981, Rags Club, Mayfair, London

Incredibly, after the gang fell apart and dispersed, Ringo got to be busier than George and nearly as busy as Paul. In the year of their break-up – 1970 – Ringo recorded two albums, *Sentimental Journey* and *Beaucoup Of Blues*. On the former, the big boys helped out – Paul McCartney, Quincy Jones, George Martin and Maurice Gibb – and on the latter, he indulged the country-and-western instincts his Beatles composition 'Don't Pass Me By' had displayed.

He scored two hit singles with 'It Don't Come Easy' and 'Back Off Boogaloo' in the UK and played on Lennon's stark debut album, *John Lennon/Plastic Ono Band*. That gesture alone tells you how highly he was rated by John. The sound of that album is haunting, and the drums had to be spot on for the music to work.

George Harrison was also of the same persuasion – he invited Ringo to play on his highly acclaimed *All Things Must Pass* album. Ringo then played with George at his Bangladesh fundraiser and befriended Marc Bolan, directing a documentary on his band, T. Rex, called *Born To Boogie*. He also started up a furniture company. His third album *Ringo* featured all three Beatles (the gang owed him) on different tracks and gave him number-one singles in the USA with 'Photograph' (co-written with George Harrison) and his rendition of 'You're Sixteen'. His next album *Goodnight Vienna* spawned three more hit singles and he got to date singer-songwriter Lynsey De Paul after divorcing Maureen in 1975. While married to Ringo, Maureen had a fling with George Harrison. Bizarrely, George had informed Ringo upfront of his intentions. It certainly didn't help Ringo and Maureen's relationship.

AT THE RECEPTION AFTERWARDS THE THREE OF THEM GOT ON STAGE AND PLAYED, PAUL ON PIANO, GEORGE ON GUITAR, RINGO ON SPOONS. 'FANTASTIC,' SAID ONE GUEST

In the late 70s his recording career started to falter. Ringo responded by starting up his own label, Ring O'Records, which issued albums by the likes of Rab Noakes and David Hentschel. They did as well as those names would suggest.

THE CITY RESPONDED IN KIND. A PARK TOPIARY RECREATION OF THE BAND WAS ATTACKED AND RINGO'S HEAD WAS CUT OFF

In the early 80s Ringo staged something of a comeback. His album *Stop And Smell The Roses* was a critical success. He later revealed that he was due to record two Lennon originals for the project, 'Nobody Knows' and 'Life Begins At 40', but after his dear friend's murder he backed off. The album did not sell well but any financial worries were soon obliterated when in the mid-80s he began narrating the incredibly popular children's TV show, *Thomas The Tank Engine And Friends*. His lugubrious voice was the perfect tool with which to enchant children the world over.

By now he was married to actress and model Barbara Bach (ironically she appeared on the cover of the *Playboy* issue that contained one of Lennon's last ever major interviews) who he had met while filming *Caveman* in 1980. Drummer and model hit it off straight away. They married a year later on 27 April 1981. Paul and George both attended with their wives and posed for pictures, the first time the gang had done so since the photo session at Tittenhurst Park 12 years previously. At the reception afterwards the three of them got on stage and played, Paul on piano, George on guitar, Ringo on spoons. 'Fantastic,' said one guest. The world looked on enviously.

By 1988 the couple were in a detox clinic and fighting alcoholism. Both have since fully embraced sobriety. The following year, Ringo launched his new group Ringo Starr & His All-Starr Band. It had taken him that long to get over the demise of the gang and start a new band. Not that the gang ever goes away ...

In 1997 Paul made a call to Ringo and asked him to come to London and drum on some tracks for his new album *Flaming Pie*. The album included a song Paul had written about Maureen, Ringo's ex-wife, called 'Little Willow'. Maureen had died of leukaemia in 1994. She and Ringo had fallen apart around the time The Beatles did and it later emerged that Ringo had not been the best husband in the world. He later defined himself as, 'a drunk, a wife beater and an absent father'. This was not the happy-go-lucky Ringo the world had come to smile on. Yet love endured. Ringo was there the night Maureen passed away as were the three children their marriage had produced, Zak, Jason and daughter Lee.

At the session for 'Little Willow', Paul said he needed drums for another song of his called 'Beautiful Night'. Ringo stayed on, and one night the two men jammed in the studio and in doing so came up with a third song called 'Really Love You'. For the first time ever the songwriting credit McCartney/Starkey appeared on an album.

Ringo maintained his own recording career by linking up with a songwriter named Mark Hudson. For nine years they worked together issuing several albums, though with little chart presence accompanying them.

EVER SINCE HE WAS A YOUNG BOY RINGO STARR WANTED TO BE IN A BAND. TODAY, RINGO STARR STILL WANTS TO BE IN A BAND. THE FACT THAT HE DRUMMED FOR THE MOST REMARKABLE GANG EVER HAS NOT DIMINISHED THAT DESIRE BY ONE IOTA

Hudson and Starr fell out in 2008, a year that will not be fondly recalled by Ringo. Twice, he shot himself in the foot. After helping launch the celebrations to mark Liverpool's new status as European Capital of Culture, a week later Ringo appeared on the highly popular *Jonathan Ross Show*. Ross asked Starr about Liverpool and he remarked that there was nothing there to interest him. It was probably not the best thing to say when promoting a new album he had named *Liverpool 8* after the district he hailed from.

The city responded in kind. A park topiary recreation of the band was attacked and Ringo's head was cut off. It was the second time Ringo's figure had been attacked. In that same year, Ringo made an announcement: from now on he would be no longer signing any autographs. It seemed a petulant act and one unbecoming of a man whose public image had been forged in the arts of fun and positivity. He also bemoaned the fact that whenever people interview him all they want to do is talk about The Beatles.

Drummer and solo artist Ringo Starr is still touring, a remarkable feat for a 70-year-old. He is sitting on an absolute fortune now that all Beatle financial matters have been successfully resolved. Yet, still he persists. The reason is quite simple; ever since he was a young boy Ringo Starr wanted to be in a band. Today, he still wants to be in a band. The fact that he drummed for the most remarkable group ever has not diminished that desire by one iota.

ANTHOLOGY
The Beatles re-form

DATE February 1995, Paul McCartney's Studio, West Sussex

Suddenly they became hip, really hip. After years in the wilderness of not being talked about, The Beatles sprang to life again. Two elements combined to bring about their new hipness. In the music press, magazines such as *Mojo*, *The Word* and *Uncut* emerged to service an older music-loving audience, brought up on bands such as The Fabs. The success of these publications lay in their ability to examine the past as they did the present. Suddenly, The Beatles were being placed on front covers, just like the old days.

At the same time a new generation of bands emerged. They had names like Oasis and Ocean Colour Scene and seemed to have followed a similar musical path to each other. They had rejected the music of their teenage years – which meant most of the 1980s apart from the likes of The Stone Roses, The Happy Mondays and The Smiths – and delved back to the 1960s for their inspiration. There they found the wonders of The Beatles waiting for them.

Oasis in particular were highly vociferous about The Fabs, ending each show with a full-on ten-minute assault on 'I Am The Walrus'. Lead singer Liam Gallagher spoke constantly about being 'Lennoned up', while brother Noel, the songwriter, often inserted cheeky little riffs and samples of Beatles music into songs such as 'Don't Look Back In Anger'.

At the same time as this revival started to take place, The Beatles themselves started moving closer to each other. Soon there was talk of reviving an idea that Paul McCartney (as ever) had put place some years before. When it looked

THE BRIEF FOR THE REMAINING BEATLES WAS TO **SCOUR THEIR PRIVATE COLLECTIONS FOR FOOTAGE.** THIS ACTION WAS THEN FOLLOWED BY AN AGREEMENT BY ALL THREE TO BE INTERVIEWED increasingly as if their future was coming to an end in 1969, McCartney had instructed Neil Aspinall to gather up as much Beatles footage as he could lay his hands on.

THE ONE BEATLE WHO HAD ALWAYS POURED SCORN ON SUCH PROJECTS WAS GEORGE. YET HIS WORSENING FINANCIAL SITUATION NOW MEANT HE WOULD HAVE TO BITE HIS LIP AND GET INVOLVED

Thus the idea of a documentary entitled *The Long And Winding Road* was born. That idea was put into operation in 1992. Initially, the brief for the remaining three Beatles was to scour their private collections for footage. This action was then followed by an agreement by all three to be interviewed both together and separately.

The one Beatle who had always poured scorn on such projects was George. Yet his worsening financial situation now meant he would have to bite his lip and get involved. Quite simply, the spiritual Beatle desperately needed cash. His only stipulation was that the documentary not be named after a McCartney song.

The Beatles Anthology, a TV series of ten episodes that covered the band's life, was put in motion. Meanwhile, George Martin was sent back to the vaults to start compiling albums to accompany the TV series. Martin reported back that none of the unreleased material was up to scratch for release but that there were enough interesting versions of songs from right across their career to make up at least three albums. Meanwhile, their old press officer Derek Taylor was given the job of scouring every Beatles interview ever written or recorded to create a massive new biography complete with pictures and new interviews.

At some point the suggestion that the three remaining Beatles could write some instrumental music for the show was made. To many people's surprise, the band accepted the job. Paul called Yoko. Grief over John's terrible passing had bought him and Yoko closer together. He had since written one very moving song about John entitled 'Here Today', which he had placed on his 1982 album *Tug Of War*. Paul told Yoko what was being planned. But even as he spoke, doubts crept into his head. Did the world really need a new Beatles record with only three of them on it? Did that not betray the gang ethos they had forged in their youth of 'all for one and one for all'? Was it possible then to include John somehow? 'I talked to Yoko about it and she said she had these three tracks...'

On 19 January 1993 at the ceremony to induct The Beatles into America's Rock'n'Roll Hall of Fame, Yoko handed over a tape to Paul of three songs that John had made rough demos of, one of which was called 'Free As A Bird'. A month later the band along with Jeff Lynne as producer (Harrison and Starr had insisted on Lynne's involvement) the band set to work. Tensions crept in quite quickly. The unfinished nature of John's demo allowed for all kinds of musical developments. McCartney heard the song as a 1940s Gershwin-type affair. Harrison and Starr disagreed.

DID THE WORLD REALLY NEED A NEW BEATLE RECORD WITH ONLY THREE OF THEM ON IT? DID THAT NOT BETRAY THE GANG ETHOS THEY HAD FORGED IN THEIR YOUTH OF 'ALL FOR ONE AND ONE FOR ALL'? WAS IT POSSIBLE THEN TO INCLUDE JOHN SOMEHOW?

In the end they played it straight, disguising the ragged nature of the tape with harmonies and soaring guitars. Lennon's demos were digitally processed and the three remaining Beatles were overdubbed to create a virtual reunion of all four musicians. Throughout the rest of the year they worked on the *Anthology* TV series and the following February reconvened to attempt to record John's second song, 'Real Love'. This session, plus further sessions in March and May, yielded nothing worthwhile. Typically, George Harrison, the wit, said of the time spent together, 'It's just like being back in The Beatles.' He was not being complimentary.

Finally the single, the album, the book and the TV series were ready. It had taken three years to put together. On its release, *Anthology 1* (containing the band's earliest recordings) and 'Free As A Bird' hit numbers one and two respectively. The album went on to sell millions, reaching number one in America and several other countries. The TV series was a huge commercial success.

It was like the old days and for a while there it seemed that Beatlemania was back. To accompany *Anthology 2* 'Real Love' was released and again both album and single soared high into the charts. Despite this, McCartney was unable to persuade George and Ringo to cut a third single to accompany *Anthology 3*. Soon after the latter's release, the band announced they would never work together again. The Beatles reunion had been and gone.

THE DEATH
of George Harrison

George Harrison
1943   2001
Mission Complete
R.I.P.
with love osmo

When the knife plunged into his chest George Harrison felt blood spurt up into the back of his throat, heard air escape from his lungs. At that moment his primary thought was that he was about to die, just like his friend John did, at the hands of an assassin. According to reports, however, George was saved when his wife Olivia picked up a lamp and brought it down on the assailant's head, knocking him out. Later reports asserted that George had sustained one stab wound in the chest but no further injuries.

This was the story that broke on 30 December 1999. But it wasn't true, said Rolling Stones drummer, Charlie Watts. He claimed later on that he had spoken to Ringo who told him that the attack actually lasted ten minutes and that George had suffered forty wounds to his body. Despite Olivia hitting the attacker on the head repeatedly, he refused to go down, and kept maniacally slashing at George. 'The man was slashing him everywhere,' Watts revealed. 'George's wife hit him again and again on the head with the brass lamp, but he just wouldn't stop. There was blood everywhere.'

The attacker, Michael Abram, was a disturbed ex-heroin addict from Liverpool who had spent time at a psychiatric unit. He had recently become obsessed with the music of The Beatles, his mother revealed, and became determined to hurt one of them. 'He has been running in pubs shouting about The Beatles. He started to wear a Walkman to play music to stop the voices in his head. He talked about Paul McCartney more than George Harrison.'

Because of its huge size, George's house was accessible. Locals reported that

UNSURPRISINGLY, THE ATTACK SEVERELY TRAUMATIZED GEORGE AND OLIVIA. HARRISON HAD TO HAVE SOME OF HIS LUNG REMOVED AND FOR MONTHS AFTERWARDS WAS A SHELL OF A MAN teenagers in the area often scaled the walls just to look at the amazing gardens that Harrison and his family had created. One of the gardeners said that around the house there were places where people could easily enter undetected. Security was low, there were no guards and no dogs prowling the estate.

HARRISON HAD SUFFERED NONE OF THE TRAUMA THAT McCARTNEY WENT THROUGH WHEN LEAVING THE BAND. IN FACT, HE WAS HAPPY AND RELIEVED TO QUIT

The night that Abram entered the house he did so by smashing a window. It was this that alerted Harrison to an intruder in his house, not his alarm system, which failed to trigger. Harrison told Olivia to phone the gardener who lived on the estate, and then came downstairs wearing only pyjama bottoms to confront Abram. That was when Abram plunged his knife into Harrison's chest.

When the police arrived, they found Olivia cradling George and Abram walking round in a dazed and confused manner. To play down the seriousness of what had occurred, Harrison put out a statement saying that Abram 'was not a burglar and had not come to audition for The Traveling Wilburys either', the latter a reference to the supergroup Harrison had helped form in the late 80s.

Unsurprisingly, the attack severely traumatized George and Olivia. Harrison had to have some of his lung removed and for months afterwards was a shell of a man. He would spend hours sitting at the kitchen table going over the events of that terrible night. Not long after came the second major blow.

In 1997 a lump had appeared on his neck, which was dealt with by doctors. George told the world not to worry, all was well. However, in 2000 doctors diagnosed George with cancer. Many believe that the Abram attack had left him so vulnerable, physically and mentally, that the return of the disease was inevitable. And so it proved. As he came to terms with the cancer, his mind must have replayed the events of his life as a former Beatle.

Harrison had suffered none of the trauma that McCartney went through when leaving the band. In fact, he was happy and relieved to quit. He'd had quite enough of Paul's bossy ways and not being taken seriously as a songwriter.

That had all changed by 1971 with the release of his triple album, *All Things Must Pass*. Using all the songs that he could not place with The Beatles, plus adding an album consisting solely of George jamming with friends such as Eric Clapton, the album received great reviews and established Harrison as a talented singer-songwriter. The album sales were buoyed further by the huge success of George's single, 'My Sweet Lord', a number-one hit all over the world.

Unfortunately, George's joy at the single's worldwide success was interrupted by a lawsuit from Bright Tunes Music Publishers, claiming that George had copied The Chiffons' 1962 hit single, 'He's So Fine'. It took ten years but finally a judge ruled that George had subconsciously

HE WAS 58 AND LEFT THIS EARTH SURROUNDED BY HIS WIFE OLIVIA, THEIR SON DHANI AND TWO HARE KRISHNA DEVOTEES. HIS ASHES WERE LATER TAKEN TO INDIA AND SCATTERED IN THE GANGES RIVER

plagiarized the song and ordered him to pay the company one and half million dollars. George was not best pleased, eventually releasing a single 'This Song', which bitterly satirized the whole affair.

George's solo output followed the artistic path of his former Beatles companions: it was erratic – sometimes greatly inspirational, at others very mediocre. Interesting, too, how it could be argued that all four Beatles actually released their best solo work in the years just after the split.

George and Pattie divorced in 1975, Boyd famously taking up with George's close friend, Eric Clapton – and all with George's blessing. George went on to marry Olivia Arias, who worked as a secretary at A&M Records, where George held a recording contract.

In 1988 George helped form The Traveling Wilburys (Wilbury as in 'we will bury') with whom he enjoyed great success. The line up was star studded, full of myth and legend: George Harrison, Bob Dylan, Roy Orbison, Jeff Lynne and Tom Petty. The band came into being because they had been assembled to record a song for the B-side of George's solo single called 'This Is Love'. The musicians involved liked the session so much they continued as a band. Their debut album *The Traveling Wilburys Volume 1* sold very well and even won a Grammy Award. Roy Orbison died on 6 December 1988 but the band decided to continue and recorded a second album, *The Traveling Wilburys Volume 3* [sic], which again hit the charts.

In all the interviews he conducted, George was asked about The Beatles but it was the cinema that finally brought George back into the fold. In 1978 George had befriended the Monty Python performer, Eric Idle, of whom he was a huge fan. Idle's involvement in the spoof Beatles band,

The Rutles had also won George's favour, appealing to his dry laconic wit.

In 1979, when the original backers for the Monty Python film *The Life Of Brian* pulled out, George stepped in, forming a company called Handmade Films and financing the project single-handedly. The head of the company was George's old Apple friend, Denis O'Dell. *The Life Of Brian* proved to be enormously successful and financially allowed George to invest in two more Python-related projects, *Time Bandits* (1981) and *Monty Python Live At The Hollywood Bowl* (1982).

Handmade Films prospered, financing very successful films such as *The Long Good Friday* (1980), *A Private Function* (1984) and *Mona Lisa* (1986). Unfortunately, they also backed films that flopped badly, most notably *Shanghai Surprise* (1986) starring Madonna.

By the early 90s, George's finances had taken a huge battering thanks to the mismanagement of Handmade Films. In fact, there was talk of even having to sell his Friar Park home. Many people remained confused by George's ownership of this huge house set in lavish acres of countryside. Surely his belief that the spirit was all that truly mattered ran counter to his vast material acquisitions? It was a dichotomy that marked out George's life, as he swung between the spirit and material worlds, between hedonism and abstinence. When the idea of *The Beatles Anthology* was mooted, George's hand was forced. He agreed to participate. The question is, would he have done so had he been more financially secure?

In November 2001, George flew to Los Angeles and there at the house of Gavin de Becker, a security expert, George Harrison passed away. He was 58 and left this earth surrounded by his wife Olivia, their son Dhani and two Hare Krishna devotees. His ashes were later taken to India and scattered in the Ganges river.

Bob Dylan said of him, 'He was a giant, a great, great soul, with all of the humanity, all of the wit and humor, all the wisdom, the spirituality, the common sense of a man and compassion for people … The world is a profoundly emptier place without him.'

McCartney spoke of losing 'a baby brother'. Their relationship had not always been smooth but real love, plus understanding and acceptance, underpinned it all the way. An incident that occurred during the *Anthology* sessions illustrates this beautifully. During one recording session, Paul and George got into a massive argument. In fact, it got so heated that an onlooking engineer felt moved to intervene on McCartney's behalf. Before George could respond, Paul snapped at the man, 'Back off right now.' Then he pointed at George and he said, 'That man is still a Beatle.'

They truly are the gang that will never die.

Mourners in Liverpool observe a minute's silence for
George Harrison after he passed away from cancer aged 58.

DIARY

1940
07 July Ringo Starr is born
09 October John Lennon is born

1942
18 June Paul McCartney is born

1943
25 February George Harrison is born

1957
16 January The Cavern Club opens in Mathew Street, Liverpool
09 June The Quarrymen enter the TV Star Search competition
06 July John Lennon meets Paul McCartney at a village fete where The Quarrymen are playing
07 August The Quarrymen first play The Cavern Club
18 October Paul McCartney plays his first gig with The Quarrymen
07 November The Quarrymen embark on a tour of Liverpool clubs

1958
06 February George Harrison meets The Quarrymen
15 July Julia Lennon dies when hit by a car

1959
29 August The Quarrymen, including George Harrison, play the opening night of the Casbah Coffee Club, Liverpool
18 October The Quarrymen audition for *TV Star Search*

1960
10 May The Silver Beetles audition for Larry Parnes
20 May The Silver Beetles embark on a tour of Scotland
12 August Drummer Pete Best joins The Beatles
16 August The Beatles travel to Hamburg
17 August The Beatles begin their residency at the Indra Club
03 October The Beatles perform their last show at the Indra Club
04 October The Beatles begin their residency at the Kaiserkeller
15 October John, Paul, George and Ringo record together for the first time as the backing group for Lou Walters
21 November George Harrison is deported from Germany when the authorities discover he is under 18
29 November Paul McCartney and Pete Best are arrested in Hamburg after the Kaiserkeller owner accuses them of attempting to set fire to the cinema
30 November Paul McCartney and Pete Best are deported from Germany
10 December John Lennon returns to England
17 December The Beatles play a number of live gigs in Liverpool

1961
09 February The Beatles first play The Cavern Club
01 April The Beatles begin their residency at the Top Ten Club, Hamburg
22 June The Beatles record 'My Bonnie' in Hamburg
28 October Raymond Jones orders 'My Bonnie' from Brian Epstein
09 November Brian Epstein meets The Beatles at The Cavern Club
17 December The Beatles' first professional photo session

1962
01 January The Beatles audition for Decca Records and are told by A&R man, Dick Rowe, that 'guitar groups are on the way out'
05 February Ringo stands in for Pete Best with The Beatles
07 March The Beatles' first radio session
10 April Stuart Sutcliffe dies due to cerebral paralysis
13 April The Beatles commence their first residency at the Star-Club, Hamburg
02 June The Beatles return to Liverpool
06 June The Beatles have their first recording session with George Martin at Abbey Road
16 August Pete Best is sacked from The Beatles
18 August Ringo Starr joins The Beatles
23 August John Lennon marries Cynthia Powell
04 September The Beatles record 'How Do You Do It' and 'Love Me Do'
11 September The Beatles record 'P.S. I Love you' and 'Love Me Do' again
05 October The Beatles' debut single 'Love Me Do' is released in the UK
27 October The Beatles give their first radio interview for Hospital Radio Clatterbridge
01 November The Beatles commence their second residency at the Star-Club, Hamburg
26 November The Beatles record 'Please Please Me'

1963
01 January The Beatles return to the UK
03 January The Beatles commence a UK tour
11 January 'Please Please Me' single is released in the UK

05 April The Beatles receive their first silver disc for 'Please Please Me'

08 April Julian Lennon is born

11 April 'From Me To You' single is released in the UK

13 April The Beatles' first national TV appearance on *The 625 Show*

18 April Paul McCartney meets Jane Asher following a concert at The Royal Albert Hall

21 April The Beatles play the NME Poll-Winners' All-Star Concert

18 May The Beatles' third UK tour begins

20 June The Beatles Ltd is formed

12 July 'Twist And Shout' EP is released in the UK

03 August The Beatles' final performance at The Cavern Club

23 August 'She Loves You' single is released in the UK

26 August Paul McCartney receives a one-year driving ban for speeding

06 September 'The Beatles' Hits' EP is released in the UK

10 September Lennon and McCartney given Variety Club award for Top Vocal Group of the Year

04 October The Beatles' debut appearance on *Ready, Steady, Go!*

13 October The term 'Beatlemania' is coined by the media in connection with the screaming fans at a performance at The London Palladium

23 October The Beatles fly to Stockholm at the start of their first Scandinavian tour

01 November 'The Beatles No. 1' EP is released in the UK

04 November The Beatles play The Royal Variety Performance with Lennon delivering his famous 'the rest of you, if you'll just rattle your jewellery' quip

22 November *With The Beatles* LP is released in the UK

29 November 'I Want To Hold Your Hand' single is released in the UK

26 December 'I Want To Hold Your Hand' is the first Beatles single to be released in the US

1964

10 January *Introducing The Beatles* LP released in the US

20 January *Meet The Beatles* LP released in the US

01 February The Beatles reach number one in the US with 'I Want To Hold Your Hand'

07 February 'All My Loving' EP is released in the UK

07 February The Beatles' American invasion begins when they board a Boeing 707 bound for New York

09 February The Beatles' first *Ed Sullivan Show* performance

22 February The Beatles return to London greeted by crowds of screaming fans

25 February The Beatles start recording 'A Hard Day's Night'

02 March The Beatles begin filming *A Hard Day's Night*

19 March The Beatles are named Show Business Personalities of 1963 by The Variety Club of Great Britain

19 March The Beatles' first *Top Of The Pops* appearance

20 March 'Can't Buy Me Love' single is released in the UK

23 March John Lennon's first book *In His Own Write* is published

01 April John Lennon is reunited with his father Alf

04 April The Beatles occupy the top five Billboard Top 100 slots

10 April The Beatles' *Second Album* LP is released in USA

26 April The Beatles top the bill at the NME Poll-Winners' All-Star Concert

03 June Ringo Starr is taken ill before The Beatles' world tour

04 June The Beatles' world tour begins in Copenhagen with Jimmy Nicol on drums

11 June The Beatles arrive in Australia

19 June 'Long Tall Sally' EP is released in the UK

1 July The Beatles return to England

06 July The Beatles attend the world premiere of *A Hard Day's Night*

10 July 'A Hard Day's Night' single and LP are released in the UK

11 August The Beatles start recording *Beatles For Sale*

19 August The Beatles start their first 25-date American tour

28 August Bob Dylan introduces The Beatles to cannabis

21 September The Beatles return to England from America

09 October The Beatles start their 1964 British tour

06 November 'Extracts From The Album A Hard Day's Night' EP is released in the UK

27 November 'I Feel Fine' single released in the UK

02 December Ringo Starr's tonsils are removed

04 December *Beatles For Sale* LP is released in the UK

1965

11 February Ringo Starr marries Maureen Cox

15 February The Beatles start recording *Help!*

23 February The Beatles start filming *Help!* in the Bahamas

06 April 'Beatles For Sale' EP is released in the UK

09 April 'Ticket To Ride' single is released in the UK

26 May The Beatles' final BBC radio session is recorded

04 June 'Beatles For Sale No. 2' EP is released in the UK

11 June It is announced that The Beatles are to be awarded MBEs

14 June *Beatles VI* LP is released in the US

20 June The Beatles' final European tour begins at Palais des Sports, Paris

13 July Lennon and McCartney receive five Ivor Novello awards

23 July 'Help!' single is released in the UK

29 July The Beatles attend the world premiere of *Help!*

06 August *Help!* LP is released in the UK

13 August *Help!* LP is released in the US

14 August The Beatles record their fourth and final *Ed Sullivan Show*

15 August The Beatles' second full American concert tour starts with a record-breaking performance at Shea Stadium, New York

27 August The Beatles meet Elvis Presley

01 September The Beatles return to London

13 September Zak Starkey is born

12 October The Beatles start recording *Rubber Soul*

26 October The Beatles collect their MBEs from the Queen at Buckingham Palace

03 December 'We Can Work It Out'/'Day Tripper' single released in the UK

03 December *Rubber Soul* LP released in the UK

03 December The Beatles' final UK tour begins in Glasgow

06 December 'The Beatles' Million Sellers' EP released in the UK; *Rubber Soul* LP released in the US

1966

21 January George Harrison marries Pattie Boyd

04 March 'Yesterday' EP released in the UK

04 March John Lennon makes his infamous 'We're more popular than Jesus' statement in an interview

06 April The Beatles start recording *Revolver*

01 May The Beatles' final scheduled UK concert is at the NME Poll-Winners' concert

10 June 'Paperback Writer' single is released in the UK

15 June *Yesterday... And Today* LP is released in the US

24 June The Beatles' tour of Germany, Japan and the Philippines begins

05 July The Beatles hastily leave the Philippines after scenes associated with their supposed snubbing of First Lady, Imelda Marcos

05 July The Beatles' first trip to India

08 July The Beatles return to the UK

08 July 'Nowhere Man' EP released in the UK

05 August 'Eleanor Rigby'/ 'Yellow Submarine' single released in the UK

05 August *Revolver* LP released in the UK

08 August *Revolver* LP released in US

12 August The Beatles' final US tour begins amid the 'bigger than Jesus' controversy

13 August KLUE radio in Texas organizes a public Beatles bonfire

29 August The Beatles play their last-ever show, at Candlestick Park

30 August The Beatles return to London

14 September George and Pattie Harrison travel to India

26 September Brian Epstein hospitalized after overdose

09 November John Lennon meets Yoko Ono at an art gallery in Mayfair

24 November The Beatles start recording 'Strawberry Fields Forever'

09 December *A Collection Of Beatles' Oldies* LP is released in the UK

1967

04 January The Beatles start recording 'Penny Lane'

01 February The Beatles start recording *Sgt. Pepper's Lonely Hearts Club Band*

17 February 'Penny Lane'/ 'Strawberry Fields Forever' single is released in the UK

30 March The cover shoot for *Sgt. Pepper* takes place at Michael Cooper's London studio

19 April The Beatles & Co. is formed

15 May Paul meets Linda Eastman in The Bag O'Nails nightclub, Soho

20 May The BBC bans broadcast of 'A Day In The Life' as it promoted a permissive attitude to drug taking

01 June *Sgt. Pepper's Lonely Hearts Club Band* LP is released in the UK

02 June *Sgt. Pepper's Lonely Hearts Club Band* LP is released in the US

14 June The Beatles start recording 'All You Need Is Love'

19 June Paul McCartney admits taking LSD in a *Life* magazine interview

25 June The Beatles appear on *Our World*, 'All You Need Is Love' is broadcast to 400 million viewers

07 July 'All You Need Is Love' single is released in the UK

19 August Jason Starkey born

22 August The Beatles start recording the *Magical Mystery Tour* soundtrack

24 August The Beatles meet Maharishi Mahesh Yogi in London

27 August Brian Epstein dies from a drug overdose

11 September The Beatles begin filming the *Magical Mystery Tour*

17 October The Beatles attend a memorial service for Brian Epstein

24 November 'Hello, Goodbye' single is released in the UK

27 November *Magical Mystery Tour* LP released in the US

07 December The Apple Boutique opens

08 December *Magical Mystery Tour* LP released in the UK

25 December McCartney and Jane Asher announce their engagement

26 December *Magical Mystery Tour* is premiered on BBC 1

1968

22 January Apple opens offices at 95 Wigmore Street, London

25 January The Beatles record the end sequence for *Yellow Submarine*

03 February The Beatles start recording 'Lady Madonna' and 'Across The Universe'

15 February John Lennon and George Harrison fly to India

19 February Paul McCartney and Ringo Starr fly to India

15 March 'Lady Madonna' single released in the UK

30 May The Beatles begin recording *The White Album*

15 June John and Yoko plant acorns at Coventry Cathedral

22 June The Beatles purchase Apple headquarters at 3 Savile Row

17 July The Beatles attend the world premiere of *Yellow Submarine*

29 July The Beatles start recording 'Hey Jude'

22 August Cynthia Lennon sues John for divorce citing adultery with Yoko Ono

22 August Ringo Starr quits The Beatles during an argument

30 August 'Hey Jude' single is released in the UK

03 September Ringo Starr rejoins The Beatles

30 September Hunter Davies' biography of The Beatles is published

18 October John and Yoko are arrested for possession of drugs

08 November John and Cynthia Lennon are divorced

22 November *The Beatles* (*The White Album*) LP is released in the UK

25 November *The Beatles* (*The White Album*) LP is released in the US

08 November John Lennon is fined for cannabis possession

1969

02 January The Beatles commence the *Get Back/ Let It Be* sessions

10 January George Harrison quits The Beatles

13 January *Yellow Submarine* LP is released in the US

15 January George Harrison rejoins The Beatles

17 January *Yellow Submarine* LP is released in the UK

30 January The Beatles perform their last live concert on the roof of the Apple building

03 February Allen Klein is appointed The Beatles' manager

22 February The Beatles start recording *Abbey Road*

12 March Paul marries Linda

20 March John marries Yoko

25 March John and Yoko's first bed-in for peace is held in an Amsterdam hotel bedroom

11 April 'Get Back' single is released in the UK

14 April The Beatles record 'The Ballad Of John And Yoko'

30 May 'The Ballad Of John And Yoko' single is released in the UK

22 August The Beatles' final photo session takes place at John and Yoko's home, Tittenhurst Park

28 August Mary McCartney is born

20 September John Lennon tells the other Beatles he is leaving

26 September *Abbey Road* LP is released in the UK

01 October *Abbey Road* LP is released in the US

31 October 'Something'/ 'Come Together' single released in the UK

25 November John Lennon returns his MBE to the Queen

1970

04 January The Beatles' last recording session as a group

26 February *Hey Jude* LP is released in the US

06 March 'Let It Be' single released in the UK

10 April Paul McCartney announces The Beatles' split

10 April The Beatles' final press release

08 May *Let It Be* LP released in UK

18 May *Let It Be* LP released in the US

31 December Paul McCartney files a lawsuit to dissolve The Beatles' partnership

BIBLIOGRAPHY

The Beatles Anthology by The Beatles (Cassell 2000)

Liddypool: Birthplace Of The Beatles by David Bedford (Dalton Watson 2011)

Wonderful Today by Pattie Boyd (Headline 2007)

Magical Mystery Tours by Tony Bramwell (Thomas Dunne 2005)

Love Me Do by Michael Braun (Penguin 1964)

The Love You Make: An Insider's Story of The Beatles by Peter Brown (NAL 1984)

At The Movies: The Beatles by Roy Carr (UFO Music 1996)

The Quiet One: A Life Of George Harrison by Alan Clayson (Sanctuary 1991)

Ringo Starr by Alan Clayson (Paragon House 1992)

John Lennon by Ray Coleman (Futura 1984)

Brian Epstein by Ray Coleman (Viking 1989)

The Beatles: The Authorized Biography by Hunter Davies (Cassell 1968)

The Art And Music Of John Lennon by Peter Doggett (Omnibus 2005)

The Lives Of John Lennon by Albert Goldman (Bantam 1988)

The Cavern by Spencer Leigh (SAF 2008)

The Beatles In Hamburg by Spencer Leigh (Omnibus 2011)

John by Cynthia Lennon (Hodder and Stoughton 2005)

In His Own Write by John Lennon (Jonathan Cape 1964)

A Spaniard In The Works by John Lennon (Jonathan Cape 1965)

The Complete Beatles Chronicle by Mark Lewisohn (Hamlyn 1992)

Apple To The Core by Peter McCabe and Robert D. Schonfield (Sphere 1972)

The Macs: Mike McCartney's Family Album by Mike McCartney (Arthur Barker 1981)

Paul McCartney: Many Years From Now by Barry Miles (Vintage 1997)

The True Story Of The Beatles by Billy Shepherd (Beat Publications 1964)

In My Life by Pete Shotton (Coronet 1984)

A Hard Day's Write by Steve Turner (Carlton 1994)

The Gospel According To The Beatles by Steve Turner (Westminster John Knox Press 2006)

An Affectionate Punch by Justin de Villeneuve (Sidgwick and Jackson 1986)

The Beatles 365 Days by Simon Wells (Harry N. Abrams 2005)

The Man Who Gave The Beatles Away by Allan Williams (Elm Tree Books 1975)

INDEX

ACKNOWLEDGEMENTS

Thanks to Richard Green, this book's editor and top Swindon FC man who therefore truly knows the value of a Paolo, to David Luxton, my agent at Lords, to Kim Davies and Ame Verso for their editing skills, to Mr Wells and Mr Lewisohn for their brilliant support, to Dirty Den for his tactics, to Tracy for her cakes, to Sahika just for her presence, to Johnny Chandler for his love and Beatle library, and, above all, to Dean Johnson for his care and great hospitality.

I dedicate this book to the soul of Emmet Fox and especially to my daughter, Sarah Jane, because in writing it that is when the light came.

Quercus Editions Ltd
55 Baker Street
7th Floor, South Block
London
W1U 8EW

First published in 2012

Copyright © 2012 Paolo Hewitt

Produced by Therefore Publishing Limited

The moral right of Paolo Hewitt to be identified as the author of this work has been asserted in accordance with the Copyright, Design and Patents Act, 1988.

A catalogue record of this book is available from the British Library

UK and associated territories: ISBN 978 1 78087 329 9
Canada: ISBN 978 1 84866 205 6

Printed and bound in China

10 9 8 7 6 5 4 3 2 1

2–3 John Dominis/Getty Images; 8 Keystone Pictures USA/Alamy; 12 Mark and Colleen Hayward/Getty Images; 16 K & K Ulf Kruger OHG/Getty Images; 23 John Rodgers/Getty Images; 24 Juergen Vollmer/Getty Images; 28 Michael Ochs Archives/Getty Images; 32–3 Everett Collection/Rex Features; 34 Juergen Vollmer/Getty Images; 40 Keystone/Getty Images; 44 Keystone/Getty Images; 47 Michael Ochs Archives/Getty Images; 48 Bob Thomas/Getty Images; 52–3 Hulton Archive/Getty Images; 54 Popperfoto/Getty Images; 56 Star Press/Rex Features; 58 David Farrell/Getty Images; 62 Keystone/Getty Images; 65 Terry O'Neill/Getty Images; 66 Sharok Hatami/Rex Features; 70–1 Robert Whitaker/Getty Images; 72 Popperfoto/Getty Images; 76 Popperfoto/Getty Images; 78 Bettmann/Corbis; 82–3 Michael Ochs Archives/Getty Images; 84 Michael Ochs Archives/Getty Images; 86 Harry Myers/Rex Features; 90–1 United Artists/Getty Images; 92 Douglas R. Gilbert/Getty Images; 96 Val Wilmer/Getty Images; 100 New York Daily News Archive/Getty Images; 104 Michael Ochs Archives/Getty Images; 108 Keystone/Getty Images; 112 ITV/Rex Features; 116 Harry Benson/Getty Images; 120 Keystone/Getty Images; 122 Ron Howard/Getty Images; 127 Michael Ochs Archives/Getty Images; 128 Robert Whitaker/Getty Images; 132 Ed Freeman/Getty Images; 136 Bob Thomas/Getty Images; 139 E Wilkins/Rex Features; 142 Everett Collection/Rex Features; 146 GAB Archive/Getty Images; 150 John Pratt/Getty Images; 152–3 Keystone Pictures USA/Alamy; 154 Ivan Keeman/Getty Images; 156 Michael Ochs Archives/Getty Images; 158 Wallace/Daily Mail/Rex Features; 162 Cummings Archives/Getty Images; 166–7 Associated Newspapers /Rex Features; 168 Trinity Mirror/Mirrorpix/Alamy; 172 Keystone/Getty Images; 176 Keystone USA/Rex Features; 182–3 Keystone–France/Getty Images; 184 Mike Barnes/Getty Images; 188 Keystone–France/Getty Images; 192 Popperfoto/Getty Images; 196 Stefano Archetti/Rex Features; 200 Bettmann/Corbis; 204 Evening News/Rex Features; 210–11 Express/Getty Images; 212 Rex Features; 216 Cummings Archives/Getty Images; 222–3 Bentley Archive/Popperfoto/Getty Images; 224 Tom Hanley/Getty Images; 228 Associated Newspapers/Rex Features; 232–3 Pictorial Press Ltd/Alamy; 234 Trinity Mirror/Mirrorpix/Alamy; 238 Michael Ochs Archives/Getty Images; 240 Hulton Archive/Getty Images; 244 Pacific Press Service/Rex Features; 246 Everett Collection/Rex Features; 250 Terry O'Neill/Getty Images; 254 Tom Hanley/Getty Images; 258 Sion Touhig/Getty Images; 263 BWP Media/Getty Images

Title page: Ringo Starr, George Harrison, Paul McCartney and John Lennon, 1 August 1964.